国际市场营销双语教程

（第二版）

主　　编　江永洪　祁蔚茹
副主编　赵　锴　邸　勍　杨　蕾

扫码获取配套资源

南京大学出版社

图书在版编目(CIP)数据

国际市场营销双语教程 / 江永洪，祁蔚茹主编. —2 版. —南京：南京大学出版社，2022.7(2024.1 重印)
ISBN 978 - 7 - 305 - 25110 - 8

Ⅰ. ①国… Ⅱ. ①江… ②祁… Ⅲ. ①国际营销—双语教学—高等学校—教材 Ⅳ. ①F740.2

中国版本图书馆 CIP 数据核字(2021)第 228983 号

出版发行 南京大学出版社
社　　址 南京市汉口路 22 号　　邮　　编 210093

书　　名 国际市场营销双语教程
主　　编 江永洪　祁蔚茹
责任编辑 武　坦　　编辑热线 025 - 83592315

照　　排 南京开卷文化传媒有限公司
印　　刷 丹阳兴华印务有限公司
开　　本 787×1092 1/16 印张 18.75 字数 456 千
版　　次 2022 年 7 月第 2 版 2024 年 1 月第 2 次印刷
ISBN 978 - 7 - 305 - 25110 - 8
定　　价 49.80 元

网　　址：http://www.njupco.com
官方微博：http://weibo.com/njupco
微信服务号：njuyuexue
销售咨询热线：025 - 83594756

Foreword
前　言

结合十多年来从事《国际市场营销》课程的教学经验，编者一直在思考出版一部定位于应用型本科，中西融合，兼顾经济、管理与贸易三个相关专业的中英文结合的双语教材。

2017年本书第一版出版以来，受到了多所高校的关注，在教学过程中第一版教材也充分体现了它的使用价值。目前来看，国内引进菲利普·科特勒等多次再版的《国际市场营销》教材还以讲外国老品牌、老故事为主，几乎没有体现中国元素和新世纪时代特征，而且一般来说这些国外教材都比较厚重，老师和学生很难在一学期之内高效完成教与学。而国内汉语版《国际市场营销》教材更多以《市场营销》教材知识框架为主，偏理论性。营销本身是管理类专业课程，也适合经贸类专业学生学习经济、贸易类题材。能平衡这些需求和属性的优质双语教材确实很稀缺，国内定位于应用型本科的《国际市场营销》双语教材确实还比较少。本版力求在这些方面进一步精进，培养从中国出发，具备国际格局、全球视野，坚定四个自信的社会主义建设人才。

应该看到，现在的国际环境和国际局势变化太快了，国内环境变化也很大，很多传统思维不能很好地解释和理解这些现象，比如说逆全球化思潮暗流涌动、独角兽企业快速增长。中国经济社会进入新常态后，很多国家也在重新审视"三驾马车"的平衡结构，都在积极探索通过扩大需求特别是内需这个战略支点和创新驱动来实现高质量发展。新常态催生新理念，新理念催生新业态和新的商业模式。在新时代新常态下，中国经济在高质量发展背景下也努力为中国企业创造良好的内外部环境，如一带一路倡议、实施供给侧结构性改革、内部外部双循环等一系列举措。当然了，国际环境和国际局势变化以及跨境电商、中国的BATJ等独角兽孕育平台的催生、"双11""618"产生的短期爆发式业绩增长等颠覆了企业的传统营销手段和渠道模式。现在的企业，特别是中小企业，日益重视国际市场营销，利用互联网正成为中小企业从事国际营销、获取利润的必然途径。

今天，中国市场逐渐丧失"劳动力"成本低的要素禀赋。这就要求企业走出去，走出去就必须懂得国际环境、掌握国际营销知识、及时更新观念。因为，今天的跨国企业比过去任何时候都需要承担更多的社会责任，也比过去任何时候都受到更多的国际组织和贸易伙伴国相关规则的约束。

随着我国经济深度融入国际经济和对外开放规模的不断扩大，对国际经济与贸易类人才追加需求成为我国经济建设和社会发展的必然选择。为促进经济与贸易类专业的人才培养,使学生能尽快适应快速变化的国际经贸环境,及时更新数据、案例和知识体系,再版编纂成为应有之举。此外,使用本书的经验和改善本书的章节安排、内容更新要求和各位专家学者的意见也使新版的编纂成为必然选择。

本书编写感谢下列同志[①](排名不分先后):蔡华(易西商务集团),王宏婕(威时沛运集团),王皓白(浙江大学),张玺宝(青岛大学),赵文平(西安电子科技大学),尚娟(西安电子科技大学),高健(上海剑桥学院),王瑞(宁波财经学院),黄秋波(浙江树人大学),张文科(西安交通大学),王增涛(西安交通大学),傅钢善(陕西师范大学),田锋社(陕西工业职业技术学院),苏剑(北京大学),蒋军仙(上海杉达学院),黄卫平(中国人民大学),彭刚(中国人民大学),孙久文(中国人民大学),黄天柱(陕西科技大学),王雨晨(西安新丝路电商产业园),赵金凯(山东科技大学),李军(陕西省食品药品检验所),毛海涛(中南财经政法大学),武坦(南京大学出版社),沈剑(西安科技大学),郗峥(西安培华学院),王全意(重庆理工大学),任长江(河南理工大学),高连奎(北京大学),保罗·詹森(美国西北理工大学)。

上面列出的所有同志在本书第一版至今都以会议发言或书信往来的方式对本书的编写提供了宝贵素材和建议,其中大部分已为本书所采纳。因此,本书可以说是多所高等院校和业内人士协作的结果。对上述全体同志,本书编写组致以谢意。此外,许多用书的高校同仁包括学生都向本书的撰写提出了反馈意见,我们也在此致谢。

本书第二版参编人员变动幅度较大,编写组进行了调整。第二版参编人员构成和分工如下:陕西国际商贸学院江永洪副教授拟定大纲,并编写第二、十、十四、十五章;西安交通大学城市学院祁蔚茹副教授编写第一、三、九、十七章,并统稿;西安交通大学赵锴副教授编写第六、八章;西安交通大学邸勍博士编写第五、十一章;西安思源学院杨蕾副教授编写第十二、十三章;山西财经大学药朝诚教授编写第四章;西北政法大学李丹丹副教授编写第七章;宁波财经学院周巧萍副教授编写十六章;北京外交学院何敏副教授和西安翻译学院黄春丽副教授共同编写第十八章;全书的英文校对由西安电子科技大学董勇英教授完成。

限于编写人员的知识水平和教学经验,本书的缺点和疏漏之处在所难免。因此,希望使用本书的同志继续向编写人员提出宝贵意见,让我们能够不断完善。

江永洪

2022 年 3 月

---

① 本书所列人员的工作单位是在一起参会时,所提供意见和素材被本书采用及该同志向本书提交意见时的工作单位,特此说明。

Contents
目　录

Part 4 International Marketing Strategy Analysis

国际市场营销战略分析

Part 5 International Marketing Mix Strategy(4PS)

国际市场营销 4P 组合策略

Part 1

Overview of International Marketing

国际市场营销概述

There are two chapters in this part. We need to learn the concepts related to international marketing, understand organizations related to international marketing activities, learn marketing philosophy based on two perspectives, understand the driving forces and resistance of international enterprises to carry out marketing, and clarify the tasks of international marketing.

这一部分有两章的内容，我们要学习国际市场营销相关概念，了解与国际营销活动相关的组织，学习基于两个视角的营销哲学，明白国际企业开展营销的驱动力与阻力、明确国际营销的任务。

Chapter 1

Theoretical Basis of International Marketing 国际市场营销的理论基础

Learning Objectives 本章学习目标

(1) The concept and idea of marketing.
市场营销概念及其理念。
(2) Definition of international marketing.
国际市场营销的定义。
(3) International organizations related to international marketing.
与国际市场营销相关的国际组织。

Key Words 关键词

Marketing; International Marketing; Marketing Philosophy; Definition; Global Marketing; IMF; WBG; WTO; G20; APEC; SCO; AIIB

1.1 Basic Categories of Marketing 市场营销的基本范畴

Case Studies 1.1

Marketing is an applied subject based on economic science, behavioral science, and modern management theory. It is an economic management subject with comprehensive, marginal, practical which is closely integrated with economics, behavioral science, psychology, sociology, management, and public relations when it refers to a subject, it is used to translate as "marketing science". In addition, some people have translated it as "market operation", "marketing"(市场行销学) and "sales"(销售学).

1.1.1 The Origin of Marketing 市场营销的由来

At the beginning of the 20th century, marketing was first created in the United States. It differentiated from economics, and was widely used in various fields then. In the 1950s, marketing was adopted by other western countries. Japan began to introduce the definition of marketing in the early 1950s.

In 1960, Jerome McCarthy proposed the famous 4PS theory.

In the 1980s, Theodore Levitte proposed the idea of "global marketing", and at the same time, Schultz proposed the concept of "integrated marketing".

Philip Kotler is a master of modern marketing, known as "the father of modern marketing". The book "Marketing Management"(first edition in 1967) is regarded as the bible of marketing.

1.1.2 Marketing Courses 市场营销课程

In the early 20th century, the United States Pioneered courses in marketing. After years of development, a marketing course in the modern sense was formed in the 1950s. This course was introduced in our country after 1978(it was introduced in the 1930s and cancelled after the 1950s). In 1979, Jinan University and Harbin Institute of Technology took the lead in setting up marketing courses. The marketing profession was formally established in 1992. Today, almost all universities in our country have already established "marketing" as both a professional and foundational subject. Its influence and benefit are becoming increasingly extensive.

China started introducing marketing since the reform and opening-up.

In January 1984, the Chinese University Marketing Society was established, and then the provinces established the Marketing Society. These academic groups of marketing have played a huge role in promoting the theoretical research of marketing and its application in the business field.

1.1.3 Definition of Marketing 市场营销的定义

The American Marketing Association proposed in July 2013 that marketing is a series of activities, processes, and systems that bring value to customers, clients, partners, and the entire society in the creation, communication, dissemination, and exchange of products.

Philip Kotler gave "marketing" the shortest definition: "Meet customers' needs more profitably than competitors." Therefore, marketers need to find the needs of the consumers

and satisfy them.

Kotler believes: "The most important content of marketing is not sales, sales is just the marketing iceberg... If marketers do a good job in understanding various needs of consumers, developing appropriate products, pricing, distribution, and promotion, etc.These products will be easily sold."

1.1.4 Marketing Philosophy 市场营销理念

The marketing concept, also known as marketing philosophy, which is the attitude, thoughts and ideas held by the enterprise in dealing with the interests of the enterprise, customers and society in the development of marketing activities. We can divide marketing concepts into production-orientation, product-orientation, selling-orientation, market-orientation and social-orientation, according to the order in which they appear. The first three are traditional concepts based on enterprises, and the latter two are new concepts centered on markets and society. It has very important practical significance to understand the evolution of the business philosophy of the enterprise, update the concept of the enterprise, consciously adapt to the new and fast changing market situation and strengthen marketing management.

(1) **Production Orientation 生产观念**

The concept of production prevailed in the late 19th and early 20th century under the seller's market conditions of which level of productivity was relatively low, and the production was in short supply. Obviously, consumers buy what the enterprise has produced in this circumstance. In this case, business activities of the enterprise focuson reducing costs, improving production and maxmizing profits. The typical example was the Ford company in the 1920s and 1930s, and chinese enterprises before and after the reform and opening-up. Ford's Model T car, which was firstly produced in 1914, was a miracle created under the "production-oriented" management philosophy.

(2) **Product Orientation 产品观念**

With the development of productire forces, the market had begun to shift from a seller's market to a buyer's market, and consumers' living standards had been greatly improved. They were no longer satisfied with the basic function of products, and had begun to pursue products in terms of quality, performance, characteristics, and other differences. It is believed that consumers prefer high-quality, multi-functional, and distinctive products. Therefore, enterprises should focus on producing high-end products and continuously improve them. Under the guidance of this concept, The managment team are often so confident of their products that they might overlook that their products may not cater to fashion, and even the market may be developing in a

different direction. They relied too much on the engineering and technical department when designing products and rarely take preference of consumers into consideration.

(3) Selling Orientation 推销观念

In the 1930s and 1940s, the seller's market has completely changed to the buyer's market, and the supply of product exceeded demand of it. There has been fierce competition in the market. The sales concept was the result of market competition. The concept of marketing assumes that consumers usually have a mentality of buying inertia or resistance. Consumers would not consciously purchase the company's products in bulk. Therefore, the central task of enterprise management was to actively and vigorously promote sales to induce consumers to purchase their products. They were committed to launch promotions and organize advertising campaigns to persuade and even force consumers to buy. They hired a large number of sales experts, made many advertisements, and "bombed" consumers with pervasive promotional information.

(4) Marketing Orientation 营销观念

The market-oriented marketing concept emerged after World War Ⅱ, many companies no longer relied on their own sales representatives, and the modern market-centric marketing concept had been proposed. This new marketing concept demonstrated that the production value of an enterprise depended on whether consumers buy their products or not. Enterprises must take consumer needs as the initial point for all activities. The focus of marketing activities of enterprise was to produce products that meet consumer needs. "Customer First" had become the slogan of sales personnel in enterprises.

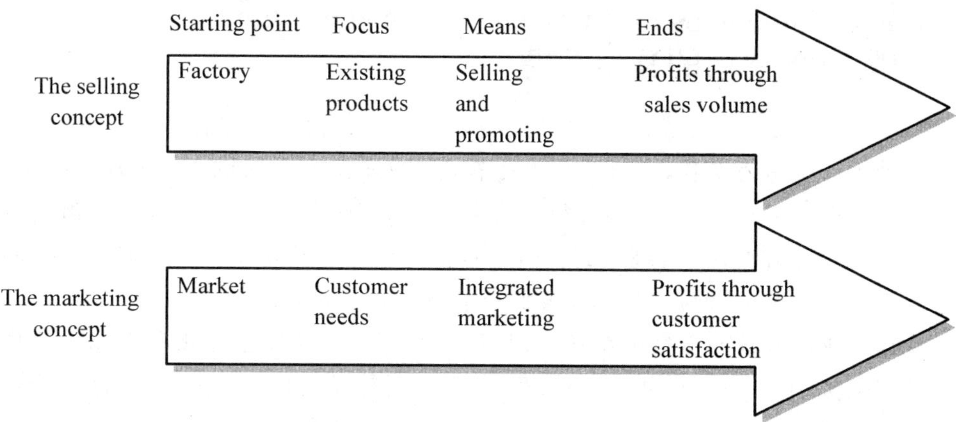

Figure 1.1 The Selling and Marketing Concepts Constrasted

(5) Societal Marketing Orientation 社会营销观念

Since the 1970s, people had come to realize that consumer needs are not always consistent with interests of consumers or the society. For example, cigarettes can meet the needs of smokers, but do harm to their health meanwhile, any encouragement of smoking and promotion of tobacco were harmful to society. In addition, some products, like disposable chopsticks(一次性筷子), wasted a lot of natural and social resources while satisfying consumers. With the destitution of the global environment, the scarcity of resources, the explosion of population and neglect of social interests are becoming increasingly serious, production department of enterprises must consider not only the needs of consumers, but also the long-term interests of the whole society. Such concepts were collectively referred to as the concept of social marketing centered on the long-term interests of society, supplemented and revised later. To obtain economic benefit, some misdeeds, such as indiscriminate discharge of sewage into rivers, killing protected animals, smuggling and selling drugs violate the concept of social marketing.

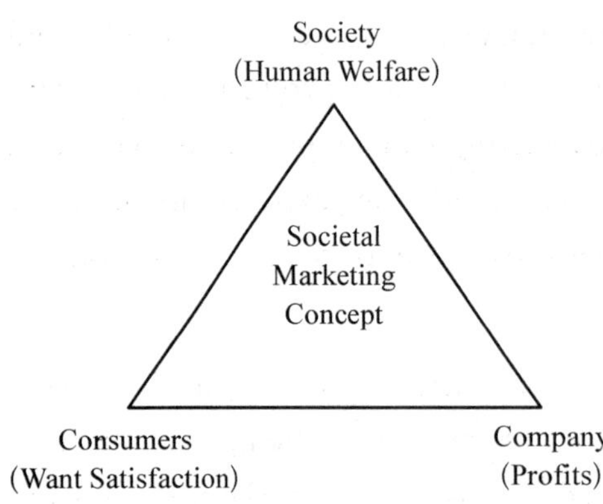

Figure 1.2 The Considerations Underlying the Societal Marketing Concept

With the development of society, many new concepts are also constantly proposed. We still classify them as social marketing concepts and understand them as updating social marketing concepts, such as ecological compulsion concept, wise consumption concept, humanity concept, family marketing concept, integrated marketing concept, green markcting concept, etc.

1.2 Basic Categories of International Marketing 国际市场营销的基本范畴

随着国际贸易的发展,市场营销活动不能仅仅局限在本国境内。全球化趋势下,经济扩张和开放成为必然,企业的行为越来越需要全球格局和国际考虑。国际市场营销是市场营销理念加上国际化视野,它将企业市场营销活动延伸到其他国家和地区。市场营销人员成功的关键在于理解和掌握国际市场营销知识。

对国际市场营销的研究主要基于以下背景:第一,经济全球化和全球一体化已经是必然趋势,只关注国内显然不够;第二,国际贸易动态发展,企业面对的竞争对手已经不能局限于国内;第三,全球连线在加强,企业不能忽视外部影响。

在国际国内错综复杂的环境和挑战下,很多不可控因素还在发生变化,国际交往日益密切,对国际市场和国际市场营销不了解的企业将陷入困境,因而国际市场营销的学习也越来越重要。

1.2.1 Definition of International Marketing 国际市场营销的定义

What is International Marketing is the study of international enterprise mangement and sales management, it is a science to formulate customers demard as the center and engage in international marketing activities in enterprises. International marketing is also the process of planning and conducting transactions across national borders to create exchanges that achieve the objectives of both individuals and organizations.

The definition of International Marketing is the performance of business activities designed to plan, price, promote and direct the flow of a company's goods and services to consumers or users in more than one nation for a profit.

1.2.2 International Marketing and Domestic Marketing, International Trade 国际市场营销与国内市场营销、国际贸易

Both international marketing and international trade are categorized into international business, which sharing a common theoretical basis, international environment and exchange objects. The main differences lie in the following five aspects: business scope, transaction subject, ways beyond borders, implementation process, source of income information.

The only difference in the definitions of domestic and international marketing is **in more than one nation**. Different environments, with the complexity and diversity of international marketing such as: competition, legal restraints, government controls, weather condition, fickle consumers, etc. In fact, the key to grasping international marketing on the basis of domestic marketing is to have an international perspective.

1.2.3 International Marketing and Global Marketing 国际市场营销与全球营销

Global marketing is the extension and development of international marketing. Global marketing focuses on the world, rather than a limited number of international or multiple target markets. It produces products in a planned manner and sells them all over the world, and has a certain degree of overall control over price strategies and promotional methods. Products may slightly very in different markets around the world. Global marketing companies tend to follow a local-centric or regional-orientation, which will be discussed in Chapter 2.

Some scholars tend to equate international marketing with global marketing and international markets with global markets. This book undertakes research on global marketing and global markets as an extension, high-end form of international marketing and international markets.

1.2.4 International Marketing Development Stage 国际营销的发展阶段

Marketing activities of enterprises often start with domestic marketing, and then may go through export marketing, international marketing, and global marketing, so corporate marketing activities may go through four levels. But when it comes to the international marketing stage of an enterprise, it is often explained in three stages. The first stage is export marketing, the second stage is international marketing, and the third stage is global marketing.

1.3 Related International and Regional Economic Organizations 国际市场营销相关的国际、区域经济组织

Although each country has some organizations to guide and regulate the marketing activities of enterprises, the role of many regional economic organizations in international marketing can not be ignored. The WTO (World Trade Organization), together with the WB(World Bank) and IMF(International Monetary Fund), are called the "three pillars" of today's world economic system. The G20(Group of Twenty) is the main forum for international economic cooperation, and APEC (Asia-Pacific Economic Cooperation), SCO (Shanghai Cooperation Organization), and AIIB(Asian Infrastructure Investment Bank)have a special impact on the development of China and other Asian countries. To understand these very important international and regional organizations, please scan the QR code in this paragraph to further study.

Conclusion 结语

Traditionally speaking, international marketing means that enterprises should be based on and satisfied domestic market in the first place, and then gradually move towards the international market. Encouraging Chinese companies to enter the international market and shaping more internationally renowned brands is clearly stated by the Chinese government in the government work report. This requires Chinese companies to establish correct marketing concepts, abide by international rules, and pay attention to the international environment. As a participant in international market, one should work hard to learn international marketing knowledge, improve international marketing skills, and contribute to the

internationalization of Chinese companies.

The Chapter's Referential Questions　本章参考题

(1) Define international marketing. How it is different from domestic marketing?
请谈谈国际市场营销的定义。国际市场营销与国内市场营销有何不同?

(2) Why is the international marketer's task more difficult than that of the domestic marketer?
为什么说,与国内市场营销相比国际市场营销的任务会更艰巨?

(3) How do you understand the internal factors of the evolution of marketing concepts?
如何理解市场营销理念演变的内部原因?

(4) 有 4 家企业,它们的经营决策的指导思想分别是:

(A) 公司生产手表,认为只要集中精力生产计时准确、造型优美、价格适中的名牌产品,就能使经营获得成功。

(B) 公司生产汽车,致力于扩大生产规模,追求规模效益,加强企业管理,力图降低成本、扩大销售。

(C) 公司生产电子仪器,认为产品不会主动变成现金,于是从社会上网罗了一大批能说会道的推销员。

(D) 公司生产面包,其宗旨是:顾客就是上帝,要尽最大努力使顾客的每一元钱都能买到十足价值和质量满意的面包。

请问:这 4 家企业的营销理念分别是什么?

Further Reading
拓展阅读

Chapter 2
The Scope and Challenges of International Marketing
国际市场营销的范围和挑战

Learning Objectives
本章学习目标

(1) The importance of international marketing.
国际市场营销的重要性。
(2) Motivation for enterprises entering the international market.
企业进入国际市场的动因。
(3) Obstacles for enterprises entering the international market.
企业进入国际市场的障碍。
(4) Different value orientations for enterprises entering the international market.
企业进入国际市场不同的价值取向。
(5) The task of international marketing.
国际市场营销的任务。

Key Words
关键词

Motivation; Obstacles; Self-Reference Criterion; Barriers; Ethnocentric Orientation; Polycentric Orientation; Regiocentric Orientation; Geocentric Orientation

Case Studies 2.1

2.1 The Importance of International Marketing 国际市场营销的重要性

企业活动国际化,进行国际市场营销,乃是当今世界经济、市场和企业发展的必然要求。企业(特别是大企业)只有进入国际市场,进行国际市场营销,才能不断降低产品成本,保证企业利润;才能保持企业竞争优势;才能保持并扩大企业的市场,企业也才能生存和发展。

The United States constitutes one of the most important target markets in the world, with a high proportion of global products and services consumed. Over time, however, even as the U. S. foreign investment in the United States continues to increase (2019 U.S. foreign capital absorption of 251 billion U.S. dollars, remaining the world's largest inflow of foreign capital, the 2019 inflow of foreign capital to China still increased to 141 billion U.S. dollars, ranking second. In fact, the gap between China and the United States in attracting foreign investment is getting smaller gradually), but it has become evident that this target market is losing its dominant position: the consumer market is gradually being overtaken by China (China's total retail sales of consumer goods in 2019 is $5.97 trillion, while the United States is 6.24 trillion US dollars, China's consumption scale is equivalent to 95.67% of the United States.). For American companies to fully reach their potential and compete effectively with foreign companies in the same alliance, it is essential that they must integrate into the international market rather than disengage from it to take advantage of global market opportunities and keep pace with the times, maximizing the potential of its product portfolio and multinationals.

In the long run, China's consumer market will become the world's largest domestic one. In addition to the large market size, The company has strong supporting ability, which provides a good foundation for foreign investment in China. China's innovation capability is also improving, and the potential of the Internet, information technology, artificial intelligence and other fields are also being released steadily.

The latest report from the German newspaper *Le Monde*(《世界报》) claimed that the 1920s were called the "Golden 1920s". Whether the second decade of this century will become the new "Golden Decade" is still unknown. But one thing is certain, China's economic scale will continue to expand, and is supposed to surpass the United States. According to the forecast of HSBC in the UK, China's GDP will reach approximately US$26 trillion in late 2020s and early 2030s, while GDP of US will be US$25.2 trillion then.

Predictably, with the spread of protectionism, the slowdown in international trade, and the continued decline in global transnational investment, China's attraction of foreign investment bucked the trend. Provide a growth opportunity that must not be missed for foreign investors will also inject stable and positive energy into the world economy at a crossroads.

Despite of the fact there is rapid development of China's economy and the huge improvement of its international status, there is no doubt that the United States is still the most influential economy in the world.

Table 2.1 Selected U.S. Companies and their International Sales

Company	Global Revenues (billions $)	Percentage of Revenues from Outside the u.s.(%)
Walmart	401.20	24.60
Ford Motor	146.3	51.9
General Electric	182.5	53.7
Citigroup	52.8	74.8
Hewlet-Packard	118.4	68.2
Boeing	60.9	38.9
Intel	37.6	85.4
Coca-Cola	31,9	77
Apple	36.5	46
Starbucks	10.4	20.8

Source: Annual Reports of Listed Firms, 2012.

Case Studies 2.2

International companies such as General Motors, Mitsubishi, Microsoft, and Exxon earn profits greater than the GDP of many low-income countries, and their total market value is several times the size of their profits. Even successful small business can be attributed to their survival and success to international markets. Additionally, companies may find that, with products in the late stage of their life cycle of business, emerging markets can bring them a new life, such as the case of Avon.

2.2 Motivation for Enterprises Entering the International Market 企业进入国际市场的动因

在经济全球化的背景下,极少有企业会只在封闭的市场内从事经营活动,而不受到国际市场的影响。企业所处的环境中会有很多力量驱动企业不得不走向国际化。放弃国际市场,意味着将市场份额向竞争者拱手相让。

Few companies operate in an isolated, country-specific environment, and even fewer effectively avoid international involvement. Local firms manufacturing for local consumers are dependent on equipment, components and raw materials from abroad. Their clients and final consumers are exposed to international trade pratices and international products. A complete isolation from international influence is only possible in a closed environment like North Korea, for varions reasons; consumers are shielded from international influence.

Increasingly, companies can't afford to avoid involvement in international

marketing. Avoiding international expansion could mean ceding market share to competitors and missing out on numerous opportunities created by changes in the international environment. Among reactive motivations to go international is the desire to remain competitiveness and maintain global market share. In addition, domestic business barriers and other disadvantaged government policies can provide incentives for companies to go global.

Firms, however, should be proactive in their approach to internationalization. A proactive rationale for internationalization can be, among others, the search for new markets, new customers, increased market share and profits, tax incentives, or cost reductions, as described in the sections.

2.2.1 Driving Forces in the Business Environment 商务环境与驱动力

(1) Competition 竞争驱动

Competition pressure is often a driver of internationalization. Over time, service providers and client companies develop closed relationships that will last as long as the firms enter new international markets. However, the relationship is in jeopardy when the service provider does not follow the client into the new market. McCann Erickson has for many years been the primary advertising agency for Coca-Cola and has followed the company into new markets, as illustrated in the following example.

(2) Regional Ecomomy and Political Integration 区域经济和政治一体化

In addition to cultural similarities-language and religion, for example, economic and political integration play an important part in facilitating international trade. Regional agreements such as NAFTA (North American Free Trade Aggrement), and the politically and economically integrated European Union are examples of successful attempts at reducing or eliminating barriers among member countries and promoting trade within the perimeter of each common market. The benefits of integration extend to companies from nonmember states as well. It permits subsidiaries incorporated in the respective markets to benefit from free trade within the region, allows firms outside the integrated regions to conduct business within the common market without the impediments typically posed by crossing national borders-customs paperwork, separate tariffs for each country, and so on.

Case Studies 2.3

A company exporting products from the United States to multiple counties in the European Union, for example, will cross borders once the company will do the customs paperwork and pay the required customs duties only once, instead of applying for an import license and paying customs duties in every country where it exports. A subsidiary of a company from the United States incorporated in any country of the European Union is a corporate citizen of the EU. Consequently, the subsidiary does not have to pay duties or foreign exchange charges when it crosses borders of EU member states because all transactions are settled in Euros.

(3) Technology 科技驱动

Technology has created opportunities for firms involved in international business. In terms of media development, consumers around the world are exposed to programming originating in other countries. The United States specially designated international broadcasting plan as follows: Law-Order is followed by audiences worldwide, CNN is popular with businesspeople around the world, and NBC eagerly exports its mix of late-night comedy and news magazines to the rest of the world. Advertising also crosses borders, exposing consumers to brands from other countries. The Web and the Internet have revolutionized the way many companies conduct business, offering businesses instant and unlimited international exposure-something that brick-and-mortar stores and traditional manufacturers years to achieve. Such exposure offers tremendous opportunities to small businesses which do not regularly have the advertising budget to communicate with the international market.

(4) Improvements in the Infrastructure 基础设施更新

Closely linked to technology are the leaps in the area of transportation particularly regarding technology infrastructure. In the not-so-remote past, a Mercedes-Benz service station in Bujumbura, Burundi (Sub-Saharan east Africa), trying to contact the company factory in Stuttgart, Germany, to order a part, would tie up an English or German-speaking employee for most of the day for this purpose. The employee would book calls with operators early in the morning and typically be answered in the afternoon. The call would be facilitated by an operator in Brussels, Belgium (all calls to Burundi went via cable from Belgium to its former colonies in East Africa), who would link the factory to the service station. The quality of the connection would often be problematic, necessitating a second request for a telephone connection. An alternative would have been placing the request via telex (fax was not an option, nor was the use of E-mail).

Today, many customer services are outsourced to developing countries, such as India and China, largely due to improvements in telecommunication.

Transportation has also greatly improved since the 1980s. The introduction of containers into international inter-modal (ship, truck, train) shipping greatly facilitates the transportation of physical goods. On the passenger side, efficient and rapid air travel has become more affordable, allowing for frequent interactions between expatriate or local employees and those from the company headquarters. Alternatively, high-speed train travel on inter-city routes allows for rapid transportation in developed countries, such as Japan, and many countries in the EU.

(5) Economic Growth 经济增长

Table 2.2 Comparison of the World's Top 5 Economic Powers in 2019

Country	2019 GDP (USD)	2018 GDP (USD)	Increased Amount (USD)	Nominal Growth Rate(%)	Actual Growth Rate(%)	Population (10,000)	GDP Per Capita (10,000 USD)
United States	214,289	205,802	8,487	4.12	2.3	32,676	6.56
China	143,635	138,918	4,717	3.4	6.1	140,005	1.03
Japan	50,873	49,559	1,314	2.65	0.7	12,718	4.00
Germany	38,459	39,500	-1,041	-2.64	0.6	8,229	4.67
United Kingdom	28,271	28,631	-360	-1.26	1.4	6,657	4.25
France	27,073	27,792	-719	-2.59	1.3	6,523	4.15

Economic growth constitutes an important driver of internationalization. Economic development in general and increased buying power-attributed to the emergence of a strong middle class in large markets, such as those of Brazil and India, for example, they have created great potential for international brands. Economic growth has also opened markets which were previously closed or have limited international competition. A case in point is China, where consumers are no longer restricted to spending and exercising. China also welcomes foreign direct investment and supports large-scale privatization of state-owned enterprises. Emerging economies are generally more open to foreign trade and no longer severely restricting international firms operating in these markets.

(6) Transition to a Market Economy 经济体制转型

The transition of the former Eastern Bloc countries and previously closed economies, such as that of China and Vietnam, to a market economy has contributed rapid economic development and created important new markets for international brands. Another important outcome of the transition to a market economy was deregulation. There are opportunities for manufacturers, such as Philip Morris, Whirlpool. Unilever, Procter & Gamble, Colgate-Palmolive, and other companies, to purchase or partner with local companies operating at a loss producing service providers, from Accenture to Pizza Hut, entered these markets, engaging in the highest level of commitment.

(7) Foreign Direct Investment 外国直接投资

Currently, international companies, joint ventures between multinationals and local companies, private local businesses, as well as some remnants of the former system, for example, state-owned enterprises competing for local consumers in these transition economies. At the same time, satellite television and the Internet expose these consumers to programming, information, and advertising for international brands, shaping consumer demand and brand preferences. Companies that have, over time, neglected these markets due to the obstacles they posed (limiting operations, limiting their access to hard currency and restricting repatriation of profits) are now embracing many opportunities open to international investors. Investing in transition economies is a brilliant strategy for company. Most rewards are acquired by those companies investing in large transition economies, such as China.

(8) Consumer Needs 消费需求

Exposure to global brands in one's home country and, to media advertising these brands while traveling abroad, has created demand for many global products. Consumers worldwide are fiercely loyal to international brands such as Nike sneakers, Levi's jeans, Coca-Cola, Heineken beer, and Ralph Lauren shirts. Unified consumer segments are emerging globally. Consumers in the United States and in Southeast Asia are loyal to the same soft-drink brands, wear the same branded apparel, listen to the same music, having the same

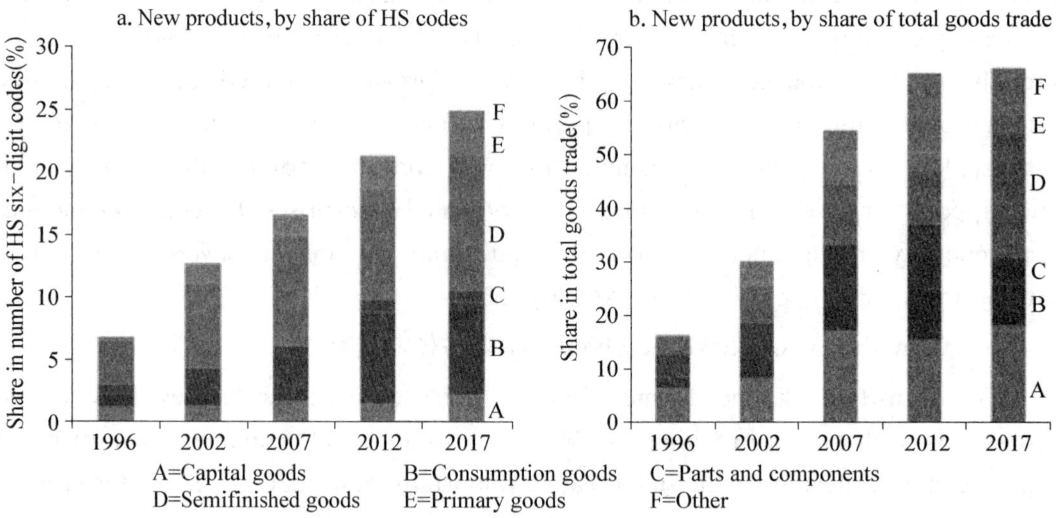

Source: UN Comtrade (International Trade Statistics, Import/Export Data).

Figure 2.1 Globally, the Number and Trade Share of New Products Increased From 1996 to 2017①

① Note: Products are classified by a Harmonized System (HS) six-digit code. New products are classified relative to the set of products in the first HS classification in 1988/1992. New codes are either genuinely new products, or old product codes that split into two new codes, or two old codes that merged into one new code. Products are further classified as final (consumption and capital), intermediate (parts and components and semifinished), or primary and other goods using the Broad Economic Categories revision 4 classification from the United Nations Conference on Trade and Development. The figure shows that over time trade in new products has grown dramatically.

idols, watching the same television shows, and watching MTV for entertainment. This would generate pull demand, whereby consumers request the product from the retailers, who subsequently convey the information up the distribution chain to wholesalers. The wholesalers Chamber then order the product.

Firms faced with similar consumers demands for uniform products have a relatively easy task in addressing the needs of these consumers, using a similar marketing strategy throughout the region. In this unified marked, access is facilitated by selling the same product regardless of market and by the use of the same advertising campaign to target the same generation in the United States, France, Malaysia, and Salvador.

2.2.2 Firm-specific Drivers Product Life-Cycle Considerations 基于产品周期的企业内部驱动

A main driver of international expansion is a firm's attempt to extend the life cycle of its products and thus create higher profits for the company from a larger customer base. Products those are in late maturity, or even in the decline stags, can change their position in the global product life-cycle stage by going into markets where the product is in high demand. To illustrate this point, the cigarette industry is in either the late maturity stage or in the decline stage in many industralized countries. By entering emerging markets where cigarettes are in the growth stage and consumers have increasing purchase power, such as India, China, and Central & Eastern Europe, the cigarette industry is in fact prolonging its products' life cycle.

(1) High New Product Development Costs 高昂的产品研发成本

The concept of high costs for new product development is related to the product life cycle. Companies often spend long periods and huge sum of money to develop new products. Nike, on the average, taking almost a year to develop, test, and manufacture new product designs that then displayed on the shelves in the United States for only 6 months. Despite the size and purchase power of the U.S. market, it is unlikely that Nike would fully recover its product development costs and make a profit as well if it limited its sales to this country. This is especially true for companies at the forefront of technology (manufacturers of high-tech equipment and electronics, pharmaceutical firms, and others), which need to develop large markets over long periods to recoup costs and also be profitable; as a result, for these companies, going international is not an option but a precondition necessary for survival.

(2) Standardization, Economies of Scale, and Cheap Labor 标准化、经济规模和廉价劳动力

During the maturity stage of the product life cycle the core product is likely to achieve a standard in a particular industry. Competitors typically an oligopoly-respond to consumer needs by offering products whose components are interchangeable and which converge toward the brand experiencing the greatest consumer demand. To offer a historical illustration, standards were established in the personal computer industry, which converged on the IBM standard. Also, In the maturity period, firms increasingly compete on pricing. Typically, they attempt to reduce the manufacturing costs through achieving economies of scale in production. In addition, firms with mature brands also move manufacturing operations and facilities abroad to developing countries in an attempt to take advantage of significantly lower labor costs.

The $4,995 Pedego Conveyor electric bike is produced in Vietnam with parts from all over the world (Figure 2.2).Gears, pedals, brakes, and other components are shipped from China, Europe, Indonesia, Japan and other economies to Vietnam for assembly before the bike itself is shipped to the United States for final sale. Roughly 60 percent of the bike's revenues is from outside Vietnam.

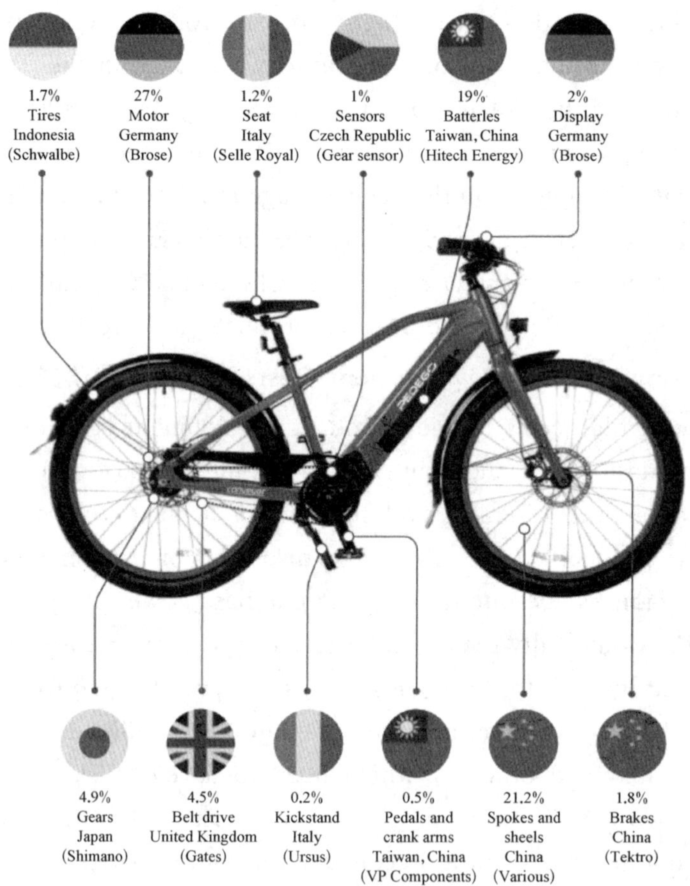

Source: Frothingham 2018.

Figure 2.2 The Complexity of Producing the Pedego Conveyor Electric Commuter Bike in Vietnam with Parts from all over the World①

① Note: Diagram shows the percentage of total value added by each component.

(3) Experience Transfers 经验转让

International companies benefit from lessons they learn in the different parts of the world. Colgate-Palmolive, for example developed its successful Axion dishwashing paste for its Latin American market when noting that women washed dishes by hand, dunking their hands in a small tub with a few slivers of soap. The same product was then provided to consumers in Central and Eastern Europe after noting that they washed dishes using a similar method and the product was a hit. Service providers such as Pizza Hut found that they were more successful with consumers in general, but especially with younger generations of consumers in Central and Eastern Europe if they played pop music on the rather loud side in their restaurants. As a result they started entering new markets by partnering with Radio Stations and Discos.

Such experience transfer cases are particularly helpful to retailers in the process of internationalization. The Tesco Extra hypermarket (Superstore) in the city of Newcastle, United Kingdom, and busy Tesco hypermarket in the southern Czech Republic, are based on a Tesco hypermarket first introduced by the same U. K. retailer in Hungary. Taking advantage of experience transfers, the company is capable to go to different international markets and thus reduce its reliance on any single market.

2.3 Obstacles for Enterprises Entering the International Market 企业进入国际市场的障碍

企业在国际化进程中绝不会一帆风顺，一定会遇到很多困难和障碍。这些问题和障碍来自企业的内部和外部。企业家需要懂得如何将这些问题和障碍转化为资本。其实，对企业家而言，最大的障碍莫过于对国际市场的恐惧。

Companies attempting to establish and maintain an international presence are likely to encounter obstacles to internationalization both from within the company and outside. Such obstacles can be financial in nature. The company might not have the finances to expand beyond national frontiers. Others are psychological. Fear of an unknown international environment or of local business practices may steer the company away from international engagement. These two types of barriers, however, could equally affect the company's local expansion efforts. Companies may not have the funds to expand beyond a small regional market, or they fear going into new markets where consumers may not be familiar with their products and hence may not respond to their marketing strategy.

Some obstacles are encountered only by firms in their process of internationalization that they are unlikely to be encountered in other expansion efforts. They are self-reference criterion, government barriers and international competition.

2.3.1 Self-Reference Criterion 自我参照标准

Of crucial importance to international operations is the ability of the firm, and especially its marketing program, to adapt to the local business environment to satisfy the needs of local consumers and to address the requirements of local government, industry and distribution channels. An impediment to adaptation is the self-reference criterion, defined as individual conscious and unconscious reference to their own national culture and to home-country norms and values, as well as to their knowledge and experience, in the process of making decisions in the host country. At the company level, self-reference may resuit in a failure to understand local consumers and their needs, to understand the local business culture, and to deal effectively with local nationals.

Self-reference may contribute to a breakdown in communication between parties from different cultures. For example, an employee from a large multinational company in the United States has been trained by career counselors that looking one's counterpart in the eyes conveys directness and honesty. When this individual conducts business in Japan using direct eye contact, he is likely to be perceived as abrasive and challenging. Similarly, if an employee proceeds directly to transacting the business deal in Latin America or southern Europe instead of first interacting in a social setting to establish rapport, he would be perceived as arrogant, interested only in the bottom line, rather than a long-term working relationship.

The first step to minimizing the effect of the self-reference criterion is selecting the appropriate personnel for international assignments. Such employees are sensitive to others and experienced in working in different environments. Second, it is important to train expatriates to focus on and be sensitive to the local culture, rather than limiting their personal interactions to own-country nationals or to expatriate from countries with cultures that are similar to their own. In fact, it is advisable that firms institute an organization-wide general orientation that instills and demonstrates sensitivity to international environment and to openly spurns value judgments and national stereotyping.

2.3.2 Government Barriers 政府限制

National governments, especially in developing countries, keep a tight control over foreign investment. They scrutinize international market entrants, permitting or denying access to international firms based on criteria that are deemed important for national industry and/or security considerations. Among formal methods used by national governments to restrict or impede entrance of international firms in the local market are tariffs and barriers such as import quotas. Barriers may be imposed by restrictions in import license awards, foreign exchange restrictions, local content requirements, etc. Governments may decide to devalue the currency, amend commercial laws, or radically change commercial regulations.

Member countries of the WTO or members of regional economic and political integration agreements such as NAFTA and the European Union, find it difficult to utilize tariffs as a means of restricting international expansion of companies in the countries' territories. Increasingly, they are using non-tariff barriers such as cumbersome procedures for import paperwork processing, delays in granting licenses, or preference given to local service providers and product manufactures in all contracted work.

2.3.3 International Competition 国际竞争

Although competition can be a driver of internationalization, competitors can also impose barriers to new entrants in a market. Competitors' arsenals of barriers include the following: blocking channels of distribution, tying retailers to exclusive agreements, slashing prices temporarily to prevent product adoption, or engaging in an advertising blitz that could hurt a company's initial sales in a market and cause it to retrench. With fierce competition from new and lesser-known brands in Asia, Central and Eastern Europe, and North Africa and the Middle East, Marlboro created a strong defensive strategy for its cigarettes: It slashed prices by as much as third and advertised heavily anywhere it was legal to do so, especially on billboards in the center of different capital cities and towns in the provinces.

As an example, sales of Marlboro in southeastern Europe were hurt by various local competitors and, in particular, by a successful regional brand, Assos, from Greece. Assos was rapidly gaining a leading position in a number of markets in the region when Marlboro went on the offensive, limiting Asses's market share to a point where the company was forced to abandon many of its markets. Marlboro effectively put in question the international expansion of many new European and Asian brands, as well as new brands from the United States. It decimated, for instance, sales of new brands of U.S. cigarettes created specifically for the Russian market by small enterprises.

2.4 Different Value Orientations for Enterprises Entering the International Market 企业进入国际市场不同的价值取向

All companies are affected by elements of the international marketing environment. In terms of international marketing involvement, however, companies have different degrees of commitment. A company engaged in domestic marketing has the least Commitment to international marketing. This company focuses solely on domestic consumers and home-country environment. Home-country environment, however, is affected by developments in the international environment. Furthermore, local companies are directly affected in competition brought by international firms.

At the next level, export marketing, a company could be involved in exporting indirectly—the company takes orders from international clients—or directly the company actively seeks international clients. For both export marketers and domestic marketers, the international market constitutes an extension of the domestic market and is not given special consideration. Such firms have an ethnocentric(民族中心主义的) philosophy to internationalization.

International marketing activities require a substantial focus on international consumers in a particular economy, and when inrowing more countries, international marketing is often called multinational marketing. International companies have presences in different countries with sales offices and subsidiaries or is an active partner in strategic alliances with local companies. It is noteworthy that in this case, international activities are not coordinated in different countries or regions. An international company, according to this definition, has a polycentric(跨区域—多中心), or regiocentric(以单一区域为中心) philosophy internationalization.

Global marketing involves marketing activities in different countries, rather than focusing primarily on national or regional segmentation. Global marketing is possible due to the emergence of global consumer segments the efficient allocation of company talents and resources worldwide. A company engaging in global marketing has a geocentric philosophy to internationalization.

It should be noted, however, that the terms defined in the preceding paragraphs are often used interchangeably by non-business and operational personnel, even by international managers. International, global, and multinational are used to refer to any company crossing borders, without particular reference to the global strategy used. The descriptions of the levels of international marketing involvement should primarily guide one to understand when to make distinctions. A better approach to distinguish between companies' international orientation and philosophy is the ethnocentric, polycentric, regiocentric, and geocentric(EPRG) framework.

Management's orientation toward the internationalization of the firm's operations affects each of the functional areas of the firm and, as such, has a direct effect on the marketing functions within the firm. Management's philosophy on international involvement affects decisions such as the firm's response to global threats, opportunities and related resource allocation. Companies' philosophies on international involvement can be described, on the basis of the EPRG framework, as ethnocentric,

polycentric, regiocentric, and geocentric.

2.4.1 Ethnocentric Orientation 民族中心主义理念为导向

Eli Lilly is an ethnocentric firm. Top management at Eli Lilly places most of the emphasis on product research and development in an effort to bring to the marketplace high-performance pharmaceutical products. Firms with an ethnocentric orientation are guided by the concept of domestic market expansion. In general, the top managers of firms with an ethnocentric orientation consider that domestic strategies, techniques, and personnel are superior to those of foreign and therefore provide the most effective framework for the company's overseas involvement; consequently, international operations and customers are considered secondary to domestic operations and customers. Ethnocentric firms are likely to be highly centralized and consider that the purpose of their international operations is to identity markets that could absorb surplus domestic production; alternatively, international operations could represent a cash cow that generates revenue and necessitates only minimal attention and investment. As a result, plans for international markets are developed primarily in-house by an international division and are similar to those for the domestic market. Firms in the tobacco industry, as well as firms at the forefront of technology, tend to have an ethnocentric marketing orientation.

It should be mentioned that, often, ethnocentric firms approach globalization by internationalizing at the level of the function, not at the corporate level. For example, a marketing department may have a geocentric strategy even if top management has an ethnocentric orientation.

In many cases, U.S. firms sell American brands along with their related U.S. life styles and traditions—for example, cigarettes, blue jeans, and entertainment. Hollywood movies is an example of entertainment category. Another example is Disney, where an ethnocentric marketing approach worked well in some markets, but not in others.

2.4.2 Polycentric Orientation 跨区域—多中心理念为导向

Case Studies 2.4

Firms with a polycentric orientation are guided by a multi-domestic market concept. Managers of polycentric firms are well aware of the importance of individual international markets to their business success and are likely to establish individual businesses, typically wholly owned or marketing subsidiaries, in each countries where they operate. The company's assumption is that each market is unique and supposed to be addressed individually. Consequently, the company is fully decentralized and engages in minimal coordination with headquarters.

Each subsidiary has its own marketing plans and objectives and operates autonomously as an independent profit center in individual country to achieve its goals; all marketing activities are performed in each country independent of the headquarters of business. To address local consumer needs, marketing research is conducted independently in each overseas market, and products are fully adapted to meet these needs. Alternatively, separated product lines are developed to meet the needs of the individual market.

In the process of developing individual strategy for each market, the company does not coordinate activities in the different countries and cannot benefit from economies of scale that such coordination would bring. Furthermore, numerous functions are duplicated, and ultimately, the cost of final products is higher than that of end consumer. For decades, Ford adopted a polycentric strategy in meeting the needs budget-conscious consumers by developing a Ford Escort automobile for the United Kingdom that looked different from the one sold in the United States or Southeast Asia. Currently, the automobile addressing the needs of the budget-conscious consumer, the Ford Focus, seems identical in each market: Ford has adopted a geocentric approach to product development.

2.4.3 Regiocentric Orientation 以单一区域为中心的理念导向

Firms with a regiocentric or a geocentric orientation are guided by local marketing concepts. Companies adopting a regiocentric orientation view world regions as distinct markets that share economic, political, and cultural traits such that they would be viable candidates for a region-wide marketing approach. A regiocentric orientation is now possible due to the success of regional economic and political integration that allows implementing a uniform marketing strategy in the entire region. Member countries of the European Union, for example, are candidates for Pan-European marketing strategies, whereas signatory countries of the North American Free Trade Agreement (NAFTA) lend themselves to a successful marketing strategy aimed at the North American market. PepsiCo appears to have a regiocentric orientation: Its divisions are organized on the basis of location, with regional offices coordinating all local marketing activities. For example, Pepsi's Eastern European operations are coordinated by its Vienna (Austria) Office, which devises the company's regional objectives and oversees the implementation of the company's marketing strategy in the region.

2.4.4 Geocentric Orientation 以地球为中心的理念导向

Firms in which top management adopts a geocentric orientation perceive the entire world—without national and regional distinctions—as a potential market with identifiable, homogeneous segments that need to be addressed with tailored marketing strategies, regardless of geography or nationality. Coordinated management policies are designed to reflect the full integration among worldwide operations.

The objective of a geocentric company is usually to achieve its position as a low-cost manufacturer and marketer of its product line, such a firm achieves a strategic competitive advantage by developing manufacturing processes that add more value per unit cost to the final product than its rivals. An example of a geocentric company is McDonald's.

2.5 The task of International Marketing 国际市场营销的任务

Case Studies 2.5

国际市场营销的基本任务是让企业的决策者在综合考虑分析国内外市场营销环境的基础上,捕捉营销机会,避免营销风险,制定进入国际市场的营销战略、策略,以实现企业的基本目标。

Specifically, the tasks of international marketing generally have to solve the following problems.

2.5.1 Assess the International Marketing Environment 评估国际营销环境

The international marketing environment includes political environment, economic environment, cultural environment, technological environment, etc. All changes in the environment may bring new challenges and of development opportunities to the company's international marketing. Therefore, companies must thoroughly evaluate and understand the international market before entering the international market.

2.5.2 Decide whether to Enter the International Market 决定是否进入国际市场

Not every enterprise is necessary to enter the international market, nor is it necessary for every enterprise to enter the international market. Enterprises should make the right decision based on environmental analysis and their own resource conditions as well as production capacity, marketing capabilities and product characteristics. Therefore, companies must conduct sufficient research and analysis to formulate their own international marketing goals and strategies.

2.5.3 Decide which Market to Enter 决定所进入的市场

After deciding to enter the international market, the further decision should be which one or which target markets to enter. In the selection, it is necessary to use some scientific analysis methods to evaluate and financially analyze the target market, estimate the current market potential and risks, forecast costs, profits, and future return on investment.

2.5.4 Decide how to Enter the International Market 决定如何进入国际市场

The enterprise has chosen the target market, and there are many options for how to enter, such as indirect export, direct export, trade permission, joint venture and direct investment. Enterprises must consider environmental factors and their own actual situation and make appropriate choices.

2.5.5 Decide on Marketing Mix 决定营销组合

Marketing is the optimal combination of various market instruments that enterprises can control in order to better achieve marketing goals. Since the international marketing environment is different from the domestic marketing environment, when making international marketing mix decisions, it is necessary to make some decisions that are different from domestic marketing in terms of products, prices, distribution, and promotions in accordance with specific circumstances.

2.5.6 Decide on the Marketing Organization Form, and Plan and Control 决定营销组织形式,并进行计划和控制

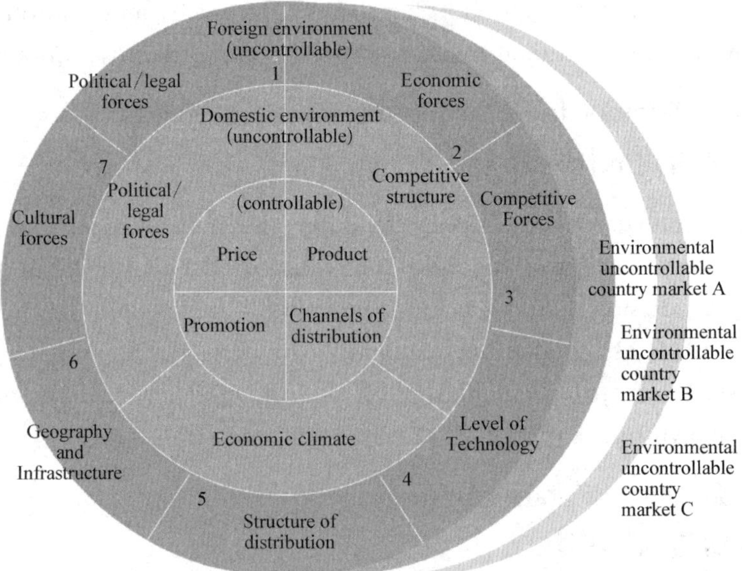

Figure 2.3 The International Marketing Task

The realization of marketing strategies requires organizational guarantees. Therefore, enterprises should set up reasonable organizations and carry out reasonable planning, coordination and control to achieve their international marketing goals.

Conclusion 结语

The output value of some large multinational companies can often be compared with the GDP of some countries, which must be achieved through internationalization. Entering the international market will inevitably face various obstacles and challenges. As multinational companies from all over the world, they all understand the importance of the international market. But different conceptual orientations will produce different effects. The task of international marketing is to overcome various obstacles based on comprehensive consideration and analysis of the domestic and foreign marketing environment, and finally achieve the company's marketing goals through the formulation and implementation of scientific and appropriate strategies.

The Chapter's Referential Questions 本章参考题

(1) What are the primary obstacles to access international market?
企业进入国际市场会遭遇哪些主要障碍?

(2) Discuss the conditions necessary for development in global market.
谈谈企业开发全球市场需要具备哪些条件。

(3) How do you understand the internal reasons for the evolution of international marketing concepts?
您如何理解国际市场营销理念演变的内在原因?

(4) Why could the regionalization be the driving force for companies go international?
为什么说区域一体化会成为企业国际化的驱动力?

(5) Why is it said that "Although competition can be a driver of internationalization, competitors can also erect barriers to new entrants in a market"?
为什么说"竞争既是企业国际化的推动力,又会成为企业进入国际市场的障碍"?

(6) How could government set barriers for foreign companies in international marketing?
在国际市场营销中,政府通常采用哪些手段为外国公司设置障碍?

Further Reading 拓展阅读

Part 2
International Marketing Environment
国际市场营销环境

This part focuses on the introduction and analysis of various elements in the international marketing environment. In addition to the new dynamic trade environment in this edition, it introduces and analyzes the impact of uncontrollable factors such as Social Culture, Economy, Politics, Law, Techndogy and Natural environment on the international marketing operation of enterprises according to the traditional logic.

本部分重点介绍和分析国际营销环境中的各要素。除了本版新增的动态贸易环境外，按照传统逻辑介绍和分析社会文化、经济、政治、法律、技术和自然环境这些不可控因素对企业国际营销运作的影响。

Chapter 3
The Dynamic Environment of International Trade
国际贸易的动态环境

Learning Objectives
本章学习目标

(1) The influence of protectionism on world trade.
保护主义对世界贸易的影响。
(2) Eight forms of trade barriers.
贸易壁垒的 8 种形式。
(3) The influence of trade friction between the United States and China.
美国与中国贸易摩擦的影响。

Key Words
关键词

GVCs; Trade Protection; Trade Barrier; Tariff; Quota; VER; Anti-dumping; Standard; Trade Friction; Anti-globalization

3.1 The Second Decade of the 21st Century and Prospect 21 世纪第二个十年及展望

Case Studies 3.1

几百年来,至少自 18 世纪初纺织业开始实现工业化以来,"机器正在争夺我们的工作机会"一直是备受人们关注的热点;工业化提高了生产率,也让人们担心成千上万的工人会因此流落街头。创新和技术进步造成了剧烈影响,但它们创造的繁荣甚于它们造成的破坏。然而今天,随着创新进程的不断加快,技术渗透到生活的方方面面,我们正在经历新一轮不确定性的困扰。

Binding rules for global trade in goods and services have facilitated dramatic growth in cross-border business activity. Since 1995, the dollar value of world trade has nearly quadrupled, while real world has expanded by 2.7 times. This far outstrips the two-fold increase in world GDP over that period.

Average tariffs have almost halved, from 10.5% to 6.4%. For the dozens of economies that joined the WTO after its creation, accession involved far-reaching reforms and market-opening commitments that research suggests have been associated with a lasting boost to national income.

Technology offers new paths for the poorest countries to catch up with the rest of the world, brings a risk that they might fall farther behind meanwhile. In Africa, where population growth could outpace job creation in the coming decades, the digital economy brings an exciting opportunity. Through innovations in digital infrastructure, digital identity and fintech, technology enables breakthroughs in a wide range of sectors, creating opportunities for people, governments and businesses.

Around the world, the process of delivering goods and services to consumers has become specialized to a degree no one could have ever imagined. Businesses focus on what they do best in their home markets and outsource the rest. Samsung makes its mobile phones with parts from 2,500 suppliers across the globe. One country—Vietnam—produces more than a third of those phones, and it has reaped the benefits. The provinces in which the phones are produced, Thai Nguyen and Bac Ninh, have become two of the richest in Vietnam, and poverty there has been reduced dramatically as a result.

Global value chains(GVCs) expanded rapidly. The expansion was revolutionary for many poorer countries, which boosted growth by joining a GVC, thereby eliminating the need to build whole industries from scratch. The experience of the last three decades has demonstrated that it costs to specialize. Yet GVCs are at a crossroads. Their growth has leveled off since 2008, when GVCs peaked at 52 percent of global trade. The reasons are complex. Slowing global growth and investment are one factor. And value chains have matured, making further specialization more challenging. Meanwhile, efforts to liberalise international trade has stalled. The growth of automation and other labor-saving technologies, such as 3D printing, may encourage countries to reduce production overseas. Unless trade liberalization is reinforced, value chains are unlikely to expand. Under the circumstances, do GVCs still offer developing countries a clear path to progress? And the answer is yes: developing countries can achieve better outcomes by undertaking market-oriented reforms, depending on their stage of development. This Report offers a detailed perspective on GVCs(Global Value Chains). It covers not only the degree to which they contribute to economic growth and poverty reduction, but also the extent to which they lead to inequality and environmental degradation. It discusses how new technologies are reshaping trade, demonstrating that automation will help rather than hurt trade. It also raises concerns about the inadequacies in the global trading system that have exacerbated divisions among nations. In particular, the Report highlights what can be done by countries that have been largely left out of the GVC revolution. Important steps such as speeding up customs procedures and reducing border delays can yield big benefits for countries making the transition from simply exporting commodities to basic manufacturing. Strengthening the rule of law reinforces trade as well. Also helpful are investments that improve connectivity by modernizing communications and roads, railways, and ports. Liberalizing road, sea, and air transport is also important, and it is often less costly. In the meantime, knowledge and services have become integral to global production, delivering important benefits to developing countries through the supply chain. In Colombia, a program led by a multinational firm induced suppliers to upgrade their coffee farms while planting trees and incorporating more efficient and sustainable practices. About 80,000 farmers and 1,000 villages benefited from the program: the quality of coffee improved, while farmers' profits increased by 15 percent. Overall, participation in global value chains can deliver a double dividend. First, firms are more likely to focus on their most productive job. Second, firms are able to gain from connections with foreign firms, which pass on the best managerial and technological practices. As a result, countries enjoy faster income growth and falling poverty. All countries stand to benefit from the increased trade and commerce spurred by the growth of GVCs.

In 1995, more than one-third of the world's population living around the world fell below the World Bank's $1.90 threshold for extreme poverty. Today, the extreme poverty rate is less than 10%, the lowest ever.

Economic growth has been a key engine for global poverty reduction. However, in many countries, especially resource-based economies, the benefits of growth weren't allowed to spread—growth helped increase average incomes, yet it did not increase median incomes or lift the poorest 40 percent of the population. As global growth slows, median income growth is sluggish in many parts of the world and declining in many poorer countries. In middle-income countries, slower growth erodes the living standards of the middle class, with many joining the ranks of the poor. This adds to the challenges facing the 2030 Sustainable Development Goals, and the key poverty reduction goal is at risk of not being met.

3.2 Trade Protection 贸易保护

The operators of international companies know that they will face many tariffs, quotas and non-tariff barriers. These barriers are designed to protect a country's market from invasion by foreign companies. There is nothing wrong with supporting the development of domestic infant industries. Although the World Trade Organization has effectively reduced tariffs, some countries still adopt some trade protectionism measures, such as legal barriers, exchange rate barriers and psychological barriers to prevent unnecessary goods from entering their own markets.

Trade protectionism refers to the idea and policy of restricting imports in foreign trade to protect domestic commodities from foreign competition in the domestic market, and to provide domestic commodities with various preferential policies to enhance their international competitiveness.

When it comes to trade protection, article 301 must be said to be a legislative power clause in the US trade law concerning unilateral actions against foreign legislative or administrative violations of agreements and damage to the interests of the United States.

3.2.1 The Right and Wrong of Protection 保护的是非曲直

为支持政府对贸易进行限制,保护主义者提出了无数条理由。但归纳起来无非是如下几条:① 保护幼稚工业;② 保护国内市场;③ 防止货币外流;④ 鼓励资本积累;⑤ 维持生活水平和实际工资;⑥ 保护自然资源;⑦ 实现欠发达国家工业化;⑧ 维持就业机会,减少实业;⑨ 国防;⑩ 扩大企业规模;⑪ 报复和讨价还价。这其中,经济学家一般仅认可保护幼稚工业、国防和实现欠发达国家工业化这三条理由。

Today, due to the improvement of people's awareness of environmental protection and the shortage of raw materials and agricultural products in the world, the reasons for resource protection are more and more accepted. When a country's production capacity or labor surplus, Congress will impose temporary market protection to facilitate the smooth transfer of these surplus resources. Unfortunately, this kind of temporary protection measures tend to become long-term behaviors, resulting in low industrial efficiency, which is not conducive to the adjustment of the country to adapt to the objective situation of the world.

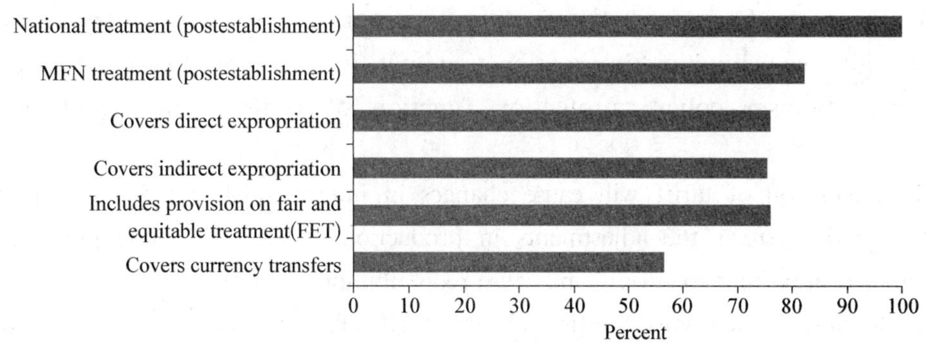

Source: Mattoo, Rocha, and Ruta, forthcoming.

Figure 3.1 A Majority of PTAs Protect Investors from Discrimination and Expropriation[①]

① Note: National treatment requires imported products to be treated no less favorably than "like domestic products". MFN = most-favored-nation; PTAs = preferential trade agreements.

3.2.2 Trade Barrier 贸易壁垒

In order to encourage the development of domestic industries and protect existing industries, governments of various countries may set up various trade barriers against imported goods and foreign companies, such as tariffs and non-tariff barriers including quotas, boycotts, currency barriers and market barriers. These barriers may be set up for economic or political purposes and are supported by the industry. Regardless of whether these barriers are economically reasonable or not, the fact is that they do exist.

(1) Tariff 关税

关税是指一国海关根据该国法律规定,对通过其关境的引进出口货物征收的一种税收。关税具有强制性和歧视性,往往被用作报复贸易伙伴的保护主义行为的手段。

Tariff is one of the ways for a government to increase its fiscal revenue. However, with the continuous development of world trade, the proportion of tariffs in national fiscal revenue is declining. Each country will levy a certain tax on the import and export of goods according to their types and value. Its function is to raise the price of imported goods through tax collection, reduce its market competitiveness, reduce the adverse impact on domestic products in the market. Tariff has the function of protecting domestic industries, but in the time of economic globalization, its adverse effects are gradually emerging, especially on the employment rate.

Generally speaking, when the economic strength is strong and it is in an advantage in the international competition, often pursue free trade policy, tariff mainly reflects the function of taxation; on the contrary, when a country's economic development lags behind and international competitiveness is not fierce, often pursues trade protectionism policy, protection function of tariff is important or even dominant.

The imposition of tariff will cause changes in international and domestic prices of imported goods, affects the adjustments in production, trade and consumption in both exporting and importing countries, and cause redistribution of income.

Worldwide, most-favored-nation (MFN) tariffs fell by about a third between 2001 and 2013. Of this liberalization, more than half was the result of countries cutting tariffs on their own initiative. This included unilateral cuts of between 10 and 20 percent in ad valorem tariffs by India, Morocco, Nigeria, Peru, and Tunisia, and between 5 and 10 percent by Bangladesh, Kenya, and Mexico. Although there is still scope for an international effort to lower tariffs—bilaterally, regionally, or in a multilateral round.The scope for countries to engage in unilateral liberalization remains substantial. Tariff schedules that place higher duties on processed goods than on unprocessed goods—a feature known as tariff escalation—have particularly negative effects on developing countries in GVCs. Escalation acts as a barrier preventing developing countries from upgrading to higher value-added segments of the value chain, potentially locking them into lower-value, limited-processing activities. Trade agreements have significantly reduced the extent of tariff escalation in high-income countries, but the process needs to go further, particularly for agricultural products.

High tariffs and tariff escalation can undermine the development of regional value chains. For example, in south Africa, despite the customs union of Botswana, Eswatini, Lesotho, Namibia and South Africa, as well as the expressed strategic interests in developing regional agriculture value chains, protection of domestic agricultural interests has resulted in multiple trade restrictions, including seasonal import bans and quotas, and tarrifs of up to 40 percent on grain, feed, dairy and poultry products. Moreover, in many parts of the world, tariffs and other forms of trade protectionism have seen a resurgence during the last two years, fueled by tensions between the United States to China to a certain extent.

(2) Quotas and Import Licensing 配额与进口许可

Quota is a certain amount or amount of import restrictions imposed on a specific kind of commodity. In order to control the flow of foreign exchange and the import volume of specific commodities, some countries often implement import licensing. Quota and import licensing are both means of import control. The fundamental difference between them is that import licensing is more flexible than quota. As long as the quota is not used up, imports can still be carried out; however, licensing can restrict imports on a case by case basis.

(3) Voluntary Export Restraint (VER)自愿出口限制

Voluntary export restriction is an agreement between importing and exporting countries to limit the amount of exports. It is commonly used in textile, clothing, steel, agricultural products and automobile industries. The reason why the voluntary export quota is called "automatic" is because the quota is set by the exporting country; however, the implementation of the voluntary export quota by the exporting country is due to the threat of the importing country: if the voluntary export quota system is not implemented, the importing country will impose more stringent quota and tariff measures.

(4) Boycotts and Embargoes 抵制和禁运

A total boycott of imports from other countries. An embargo is a ban on exports to specific countries. Public boycotts can be formal or informal, either initiated by the government or by an industry. The United States has imposed boycotts and embargoes on countries with which it has disputes. For example, the United States imposed sanctions on Cuba, Iran and Iraq. At the urging of the government or civil society, it is not uncommon for citizens of one country to boycott goods from other countries. A non-governmental organization that has launched a campaign against Nestle products believes that Nestle's approach to marketing infant milk powder can mislead mothers in less developed countries and harm their babies.

(5) Monetary Barrier 货币壁垒

A government can effectively manage a international trade situation of a country through various forms of exchange control facts. In order to safeguard the balance of payments situation or the interests of specific industries, a government may implement these restrictions. Currency blockade, differential exchange rates and the conditions for obtaining foreign exchange approved by the government.

(6) Standard 标准

Such non-tariff barriers include health standards, safety standards and product quality standards. Sometimes, for the purpose of restricting trade, the government will adopt too strict or discriminatory standards. The large number of such regulations has itself become a barrier to restrict trade.The United States and other countries require certain products (especially automobiles) to have a certain percentage of local content before they can enter the market. The North American Free Trade Agreement stipulates that cars from member states must have a North American content of at least 62.5% to prevent foreign car dealers from using one member state as a springboard for entering another member state.

(7) Anti-dumping Penalties 反倾销惩罚

That is, the anti-dumping law aimed at driving foreign products out of a certain market. The purpose of anti-dumping law is to prevent foreign manufacturers from using indicative pricing, that is, deliberately selling their products in the United States at a price lower than the production cost, so as to weaken the competitiveness of competitors and control the market. Anti-dumping law is called the antitrust law in international trade. If foreign producers sell their products at a price lower than the cost of production, they will be subject to anti-dumping or countervailing duties, so as to prevent other countries from using government subsidies to infringe American industries. Many countries have enacted similar laws, which are in line with WTO rules.

(8) Domestic Subsidies and Economic Incentives 国内补贴与经济激励

Since the economic crisis in 2008, some big economic countries have implemented new and huge domestic subsidies to their banks and automobile manufacturers. In response, developing countries complain that these subsidies to domestic industries give their enterprises an unfair advantage in global market competition. To this end, small economies have adopted various methods to protect themselves. For example, Malaysia imposed traffic restrictions on ports that can handle large quantities of goods, and Ecuador increased tariffs on 600 categories of products. Argentina and other countries have asked whether these subsidies are categorized into incentives or not. If so, the trading partner state has the right to retaliate in accordance with WTO rules.

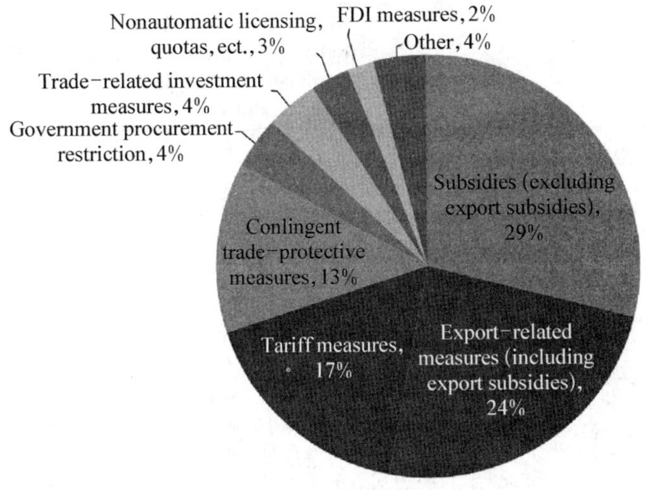

Source: WDR 2020 team using data from Global Trade Alert (https: //www.globaltradealert.org/).

Figure 3.2 Subsidies Account for more than half of Distortionary Trade Policy Instruments Worldwide①

Table 3.1 Policy Rationale, Externalities, and Cooperative Solution②

Policy area	National motive	International externality	Cooperative solution
Tariffs and other restrictions on trade and investment	Improve lerms of trade; protect special interests; gain revenue	Negative impact on trading partners and possible prisoner's dilemma	Mutualy agreed reduction in protection plus legal binding to reduce policy uncertainty
Subsidies	Support infant, senescent, or strategic industries or stages of production; address market failures (e.g., positive environmental externalities)	Negative impact on trading parthers' industries but positive impact on foreign consumers—at least in the short run	Disciplines on use of specific types of subsidies and other forms of assistance such as tax incentives
Regulatory requirements	Protect consumers, the environment, and intellectual property rights	Industries in trading partners face higher costs for compliance, but benefit from enhanced supply of public goods	Regulatory cooperation in the form of harmonization, mutual recognition, or exporter regulatory commitments

① Note: Data are from November 2018. FDI = foreign direct investment.

② Note: BEPS = base erosion and profit shifting; OECD = Organisation for Economic Co-operation and Development.

Continued

Policy area	National motive	International externality	Cooperative solution
Corporate taxes, investment incentives, FDI policies	Attract investment	Negative impacts on other investment locations and tax jurisdictions, potential tax competition, and a race to the bottom	Tax cooperation (e. g., the existing BEPS initiative at the OECD); destination-based taxes
Competition law, public ownership and control	Promote contestable markets; provide public goods	Abuse of market power; foreclosure of ability of firms to compete on a level playing field	To control firm behavior
Investment in trade-facilitating infrastructure	Reduce trade costs	Positive externality for trading partners; potential coordination failure and underinvestment	Investment coordination to exploit synergies across countries and forms of infrastructure

Source: WDR 2020 team.

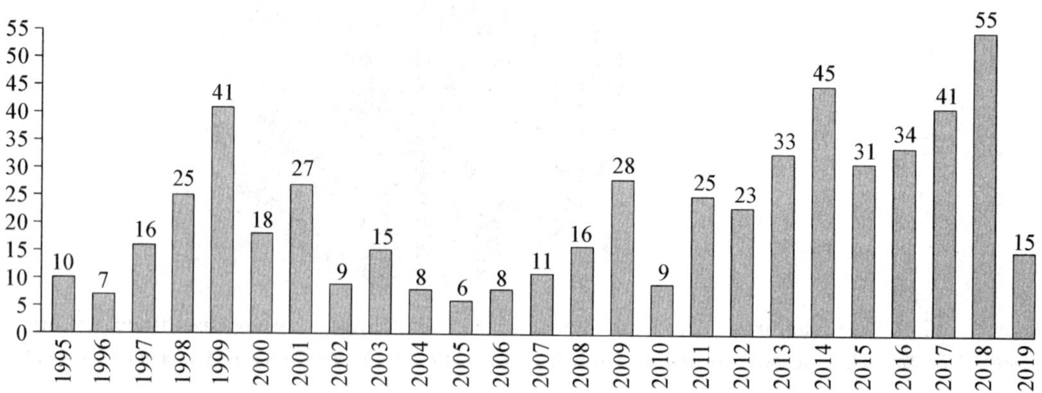

Source: World Trade Organization Annual Report 2020.

Figure 3.3 Countervailing Initiations by WTO Members, 1 January 1995 to end-June 2019①

3.3 Trade Restrictions 贸易限制

The 2019 reports showed that trade restrictions by WTO members continued at historically high levels. New trade restrictions and increasing trade tensions added to the uncertainty surrounding international trade and the world economy. Strong collective leadership from the membership would make an important contribution to increasing certainty, encouraging investment and bolstering trade and economic growth.

① Note: Figure 3.3 covers initiations up to the end of June 2019. Data for the latter half of 2019 are not yet available.

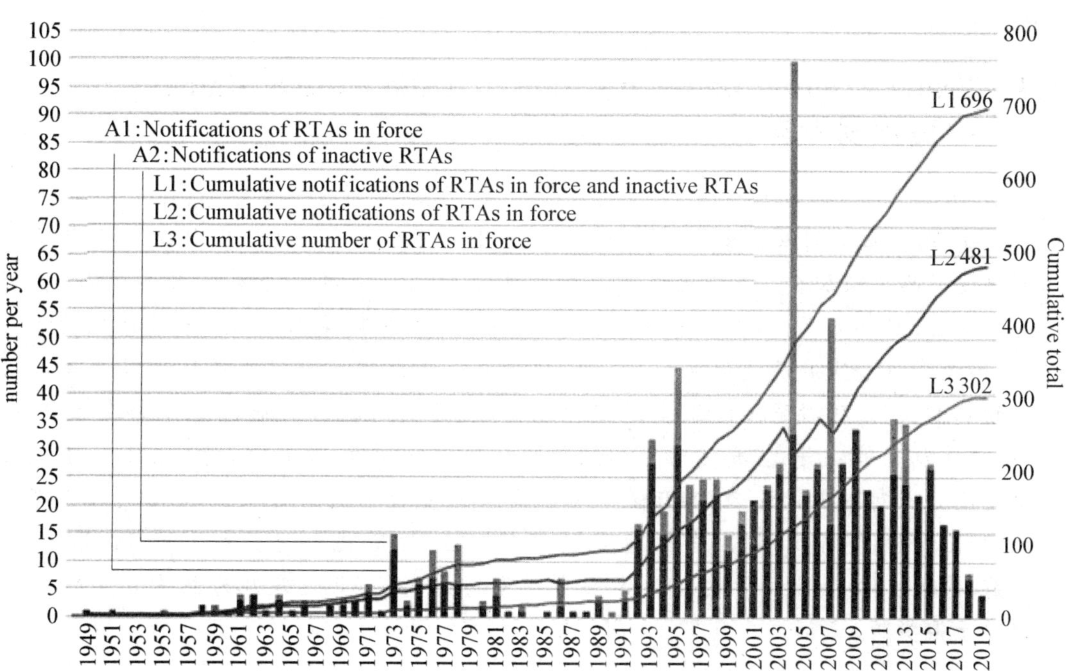

Figure 3.4 RTAs Notified to the GATT/WTO (1948 to 2019) by Year of Entry into Force①

Historically, high levels of trade-restrictive measures do harm to growth, job creation and purchasing power around the world. Strong collective leadership from the membership would make an important contribution to improving certainty, encouraging investment, bolstering trade and economic growth. Without such measures, however, the adverse trends is likely to get even worse.

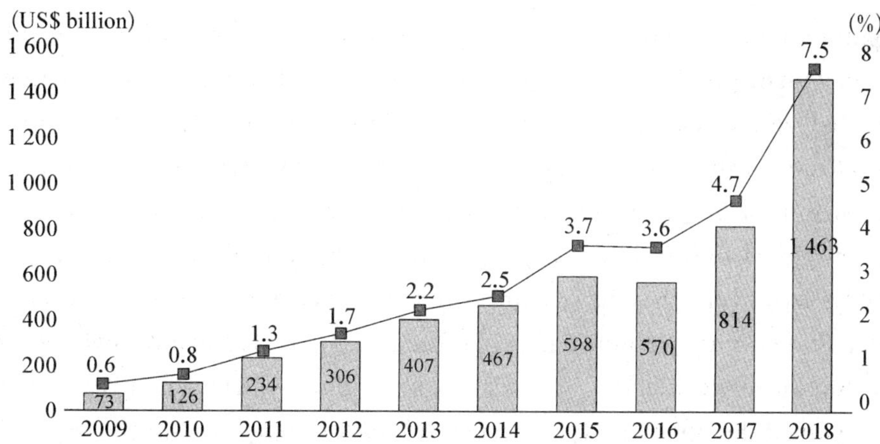

Figure 3.5 Cumulative Trade Coverage of Import-restrictive Measures in Force since 2009 (US $ Billion and Percentage of World Merchandise Imports)

① Note: Notifications of RTAs: goods, services and accessions to an RTA are counted separately. The cumulative lines show the number of RTAs/notifications that were in force for a given year. The notifications of RTAs in force are shown by year of entry into force and the notifications of inactive RTAs are shown by inactive year.

3.4 Trade Friction between China and the United States 中美贸易摩擦

众所周知，美国以国家安全为由对中国有非常严格的高科技产品出口限制，很多高科技产品是根本不卖给中国的。这也是美中贸易逆差的一个非常重要的原因。其实从2018年8月13日，美国总统签署《2019年国防授权法案》并同时生效了《外国投资风险审查现代化法案》和《出口管制改革法案》，就可见美国对华政策收紧的端倪。《外国投资风险审查现代化法案》主要针对的是外资对美投资的审查，《出口管制改革法案》主要是为了加强美国对外出口物项、技术的管控，虽然没有明确提及是针对中国投资者，实际上让中国企业赴美投资越发艰难。《出口管制改革法案》出台后，美国以"危害美国国家安全"的理由，不断把中国实体加入实体清单。目前，中国实体在《出口管制条例》实体清单中的数量已经迅速跃升为世界第二大国，仅次于俄罗斯。

A series of the latest regulations of the US government are mainly aimed at China's high-tech fields, such as electronics, communications, computers, information security, material processing, sensors and lasers, propulsion devices, military industry and civil-military integration domain. They continue the U.S. China policy since 2018. Its main purpose is to curb the development of China's high-tech field, so as to maintain the leading position of high-tech development of the United States in the world.

Trump represents a large part of the American mind. They often one sidedly see the unemployment problem caused by free trade in the United States, but they do not seriously analyze the real reasons affecting job opportunities. It is not free trade that causes job losses in the US, but the development of new technologies and innovations and the pursuit of more efficient productivity. In fact, all countries and regions involved in globalization have all experienced the initial pain and thus suffered respectively. However, they have gained greater benefits from the "big cake". Taking the United States as an example, although the transfer of labor-intensive industries has led some American workers lose their jobs, the manufacturing industry in the United States has gained the opportunity to accelerate its development into the high-end of the industrial chain, and has been at the top of the value chain, and has achieved a number of globally well-known brands including apple, Oracle, IBM, Google, Microsoft, Intel, Ford, Qualcomm, caterpillar, etc. In turn, these enterprises have created millions of new jobs for the United States, and promoted the rapid upgrading and transformation of the United States to an innovative society and an innovative economy. Therefore, blindly speaking of globalization will not solve the economic problems of the United States.

The transition toward a multipolar world order seen in 2019—with multiple challenges to multilateralism and free trade—is expected to be continued. Although the US and China have reached a "phase one" trade deal, it is unlikely to permanently resolve their dispute on trade. The two countries are likely to remain strategically opposed on issues such as protection of intellectual property and state support for certain industries. Indeed, the *World Economic Forum's Global Risks Report 2020* states: "Economic confrontations between major powers is the most concerning risk for 2020."

In addition, the trade war between China and the US will remain a drag on growth. Despite the optimism surrounding a "Phase-1" deal announced on 15 December 2019, the average tariff level on USD 250 billion worth of Chinese exports to the US remain at a record of 19% compared to that of 3% before the trade war.

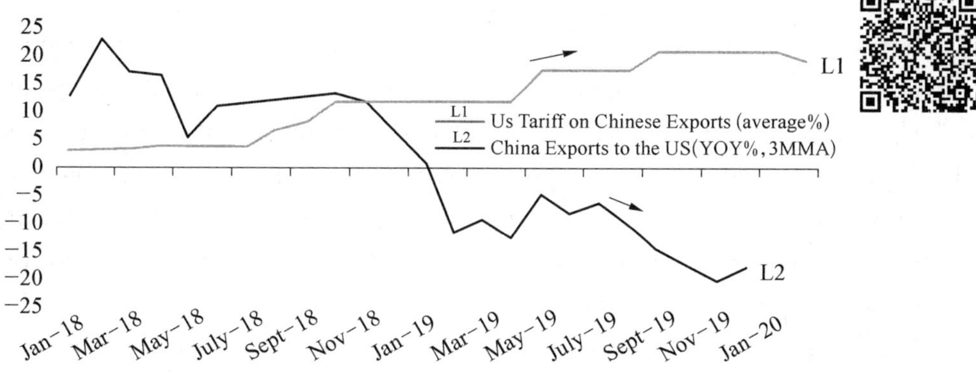

Source: China Customs, Peterson Institute for International Economics, Bloomberg and Coface.

Figure 3.6 Average Tariffs on Chinese Exports to the US and Exports YOY

3.5 China's Market Economy Status 中国市场经济地位问题

美国不承认中国的市场经济地位，并且限制其高技术产品对中国出口一直以来都是制约中国的有力武器。

According to the first chapter "Protocol on the accession of the people's Republic of China to the World Trade Organization", Article 15 of the protocol stipulates that "if the producer under investigation can not clearly prove that the industry producing the same kind of product has market economy conditions for manufacturing, producing and selling the product, the importing WTO member may use a method not based on strict comparison with China's domestic price or cost", which "shall be terminated within 15 years after the date of accession".

3.6 Challenges of Global Manufacturing Reflow to Globalization 全球制造业回流对全球化的挑战

Although the "manufacturing return strategy" of the United States has been in place for 10 years, it has produced little success, but this time it is different. The epidemic situation makes the manufacturing industry realize that there is an extreme situation of "closing down the city" or even "closing the country", which is a small Submission, but it is fatal. Rational entrepreneurs will be well prepared to hedge this risk by positioning themselves in manufacturing chains outside China. In the past, the return of manufacturing industry was still an option, but the epidemic situation made it increasingly more close to the necessary option, and there was a trend of acceleration.

Japan has also introduced policies to move enterprises away from China, providing $2.2 billion in support, which is also aimed at reducing dependence on Chinese manufacturing. Recently, the European Union has also launched a series of "European Industrial Renaissance" re-industrialization plans, the manufacturing sector will be restored to an important position. For a while, many media have published articles that the status of China's manufacturing factories is not guaranteed. In fact, it has also affected some of China's economy.

People in Europe and the United States still seek profits and freedom. They want to force enterprises to return. Unless they are nationalized, capital is for profit. It is not easy for them to give up cheaper and skilled labos to hire expensive European and American people instead.

According to the Ministry of Commerce of the people's Republic of China, "the formation of the global industrial supply chain pattern is not a one-day feat, and it can not be changed by the withdrawal of an enterprise". It can be seen that the global industrial chain is also difficult to reverse changes in the short term, and the global industrial chain will not and can not be decoupled from China in the short term.

Generally speaking, manufacturing will not return to other countries on a large scale in the short term. Multinational companies will not move out of China on a large scale for the sake of relocation costs or tax relief proposed by some countries. This is not a wise choice. A spokesman for China's Ministry of commerce also said that despite the impact of the epidemic on foreign-funded enterprises in China, there has been and will not be a large-scale withdrawal of foreign investment from China.

The last two administrations of the United States have continuously introduced tax, fiscal and financial policies that are conducive to the return of manufacturing industry. So far, the effect is not obvious, and the return of manufacturing industry is not good enough. The problem is that the U.S. government seems to ignore the objective factors that limit the effect of the policy, and still insists on accumulating various policy measures subjectively. In the case that the tariff on products exported to China to the United States has not been cancelled, a new policy has been launched with the help of the epidemic situation. Therefore, we can't rule out that the policy factors lasting for several years may have a certain impact.

Under the trend of "renationalization", the government's universal interference in the market. Whether it is from the stress instinct in the face of the epidemic, or from the political considerations of economic growth and employment protection after the epidemic, these governments will exert pressure on market players to force relevant enterprises to increase investment in their own country.

Judging from the existing industrial clusters and market scale, the competitive advantage of China's original manufacturing will not be lost, nor will the manufacturing industry scale will be maintained. However, we must not take it lightly and pay attention to the possible major adjustment of the global industrial chain pattern.

For multinational companies, the migration of production lines often needs to meet at least four requirements. Firstly, the immigrating area needs to provide a large number of skilled and well-trained industrial workers; secondly, the cost of labor, land and public utilities must be low; thirdly, the immigrating place must be able to provide perfect and efficient industrial supporting capacity; fourthly, the market scale (including potential market scale) and its predictable development prospect are better. As we all know, the characteristics of enterprises and capital are profit-seeking in nature. If the U.S. domestic market can not meet the four conditions above, then the large-scale return of American companies may only be Trump's wishful thinking and dream. According to the current position of the United States in the global industrial chain, compared with the above conditions, it is obvious that the United States does not have the capacity to absorb the manufacturing industry. Therefore, it is almost impossible to expect large-scale return of manufacturing industry to the United States. In the future, a small part of the manufacturing industry may move back to the United States for various reasons, but it should not and will never become the mainstream.

SWOT Analysis: Strengths (S), Weaknesses (W), Opportunities (O), and Threats (T)

The goal of SWOT analysis is to match the company's strengths to attractive opportunities in the environment, while eliminating or overcoming the weaknesses and minimizing the threats. SWOT analysis is a widely used tool for conducting a situation analysis. You will find yourself using it a lot in the future, especially when anayzing business cases.

	Postive	Negative
Internal	**Strength** Internal capabilities that may help a company reach its objectives	**Weaknesses** Internal limitations that may interfere With a company's ability to achieve its objectives
External	**Opportunities** External factors that the company may be able to exploit to its advantage	**Threats** Current and emerging external factors that may challenge the company's performance

Conclusion 结语

Economic globalization has become an irreversible world trend, and this view is universally recognized by most countries. However, in recent years, some countries have implemented the strategy of returning to the manufacturing industry, coupled with the increasing trade frictions, international public security incidents are also affecting the trading environment. These factors have a certain impact on companies from various countries entering the international market. Therefore, for companies engaged in international marketing, it is very necessary to grasp the dynamic trading environment in time to avoid unnecessary losses in international trade.

The Chapter's Referential Questions 本章参考题

(1) What is the purpose of imposing trade barriers and what are the forms?
设置贸易壁垒的目的是什么,形式有哪些?

(2) How do you understand the trade friction between China and the United States and analyze how its outcome will evolve?
你是如何理解中国与美国的贸易摩擦的,分析其结局如何演变?

(3) In your opinion, what challenges do you think global manufacturing will bring to

globalization, and how should the Chinese government and Chinese companies cope?
你觉得全球制造业回流对全球化带来哪些挑战,中国政府和中国企业又该如何应对?

Further Reading
拓展阅读

Chapter 4

The Cultural and Social Environment of International Marketing
国际市场营销的文化和社会环境

Learning Objectives
本章学习目标

(1) Definition of culture.
文化的定义。

(2) Management of cultural differences.
对文化差异的管理。

(3) The impact of major international public health security incidents.
重大国际公共卫生安全事件的影响。

(4) The impact of the epidemic on all walks of life.
疫情对各行各业的影响。

Key Words
关键词

Culture; Cultural Biases; Custom; Host Country; Home Country; Cross-culture; Public Health Event

4.1 Culture Environment——Definition of the Culture 文化环境——文化的定义

Case Studies 4.1

文化的元素包括,人们所共同享有的价值观、信仰、态度、期盼和行为准则。也有这样的解释,"文化是一个社会及其个体所拥有的知识、信仰、艺术、道德观、习俗以及其他任何能力和习惯的总成。"

A Latin proverb says: "Custom rules the law."

The most important factor in determining whether your marketing strategy is a right and proper one or not, is to have a comprehensive understanding of the culture in the specific market. Cultures can be painted with very broad strokes or minutely dissected. The more layers that are peeled away, the greater the market segmentation available. It is truly a case in which knowledge is power-marketing power. Because this book deals with multinational business, "culture" will be viewed as the overarching pattern of human behavior in multinational business situations.

Dutch writer, Geert Hofstede referred as: "Culture is Software of the Mind—the social programming that runs the way we think, act and perceive ourselves and others." Culture is not innate, but externally cultivated. A society's culture is far from stagnant; rather, it is forever evolving and reinventing itself.

Culture refers to common values, beliefs, attitudes, expectations, and norms found within countries, regions, social groups, industries, corporations and even departments and work groups within a business firm. As someone said that culture is a complex whole which includes knowledge, belief, art, morality, customs, and any other capabilities and habits acquired by one as a member of society. Culture is a group of people's unique way of life—is the complete design of their lives; it is "the behavioral norms that a group of people, at a certain time and place, have agreed upon to survive and co-exist. Culture is acquired. Rather than inheriting culture at birth, an individual learns a set or rules and behavior patterns. For every society, these norms and behavioral responses develop into different cultural patterns that are passed down through the generations, with continual embellishment and adaptation.

For many individuals, cultural conditioning works like a mirage—they are unaware of nine tenths of it. The subtle process of inculcating culture over time through example of rewards and punishments, is generally much more powerful than direct instruction, as individuals tend to unwittingly adopt cultural norms. This process of learning a cultural pattern, called acculturation, conditions individuals so that a large portion of their behavior fit the requirements of their culture and is determined below the level of conscious thought. The depth and width of the acculturation process explains in part why it is so difficult to break cultural patterns.

Many dimensions of culture can be identified. A manager's first experience of a new culture is often though exposure to less esoteric, more specific factors that form a culture. This is the explicit culture level. Explicit culture is the observable reality of language and communication styles, time and space orientation, work habits and practices, all forms of interpersonal and social relationships, food and eating habits, clothing and outward fashion, art, public buildings, housing, monuments, agriculture, shrines, and markets.

The Chinese culture provides another example. China's long tradition of family-based business draws in many ways on Confucian philosophy. The international impact of this tightly controlled family-based approach has been enormous. The Chinese have a long tradition of international trade, extending back thousands of years to its ancient "Silk Road" which served as a trading link westward to Europe. This cultural tradition encourages international exchanges and suggests that China is primed to greatly expand and eventually become a major force in international trade.Cultural differences can have a major impact on multinational management. Failing to recognize and effectively manage then accounts for many of blunders committed everyday by thousands of international executives around the word. Due to space constraints, please scan the QR code in this paragraph to continue learning.

4.2 International Social Environment 国际社会环境

4.2.1 International Community Organizations 国际社会组织

一般来说,社会组织往往会涉及亲属关系、相关群体、社会阶层等,而本书在这部分重点讲一个社会组组,那就是 IEP。IEP 提供了两个非常有用的指数:PPI(积极和平指数)和 GPI(全球和平指数),在分析后面各章节涉及的环境以及战略部分的竞争力时非常有用,下面我们一起来学习。

(1) About IEP 关于 IEP

The Institute for Economics & Peace (IEP) is an independent, non-partisan, non-profit think tank dedicated to shifting the world's focus to peace as a positive, achievable, and tangible measure of human wellbeing and progress. IEP achieves its goals by developing new conceptual frameworks to define peacefulness, providing metrics for measuring peace and uncovering the relationships between business, peace and prosperity, as well as promoting a better understanding of the cultural, economic and political factors that create peace. IEP is headquartered in Sydney, with offices in New York, The Hague, Mexico City, Brussels and Harare. It works with a wide range of partners internationally and collaborates with intergovernmental organisations on measuring and communicating the economic value of peace.

High levels of Positive Peace lead to: Stronger resilience, Better environmental outcomes, Higher measures of wellbeing, Better performance on development goals, Higher per capita income.

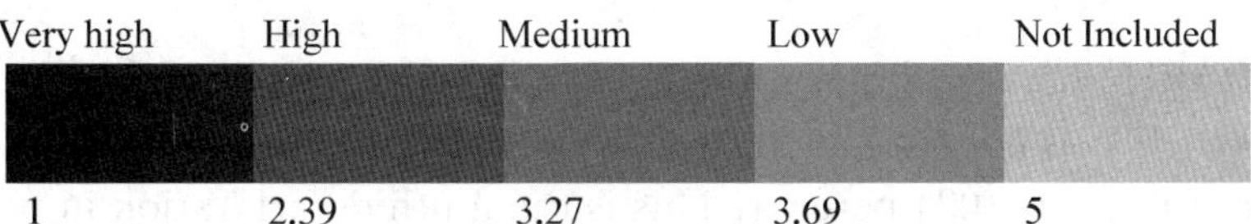

Figure 4.1 The State of Postive Peace

(2) PPI (Positive Peace Index)积极和平指数

Positive Peace is measured by the Positive Peace Index (PPI), which consists of eight Pillars, each containing three indicators. This provides a baseline measure of the effectiveness of a country's capabilities to build and maintain peace. It also provides a measure for policymakers, researchers and corporations to use for effective monitoring and evaluation. Positive peace can be used as the basis of empirically measuring a country's resilience—its ability to absorb, adapt and recover from shocks, such as climate change or economic transition. It can also be used to measure fragility and help predict the likelihood of conflict, violence and instability.

The PPI contains 8 pillars across 24 domains to show the strongest relationships with the absence of violence and the absence of fear of violence. You can scan the QR code nearby to view which reflects the correlation coefficient to the GPI(Global Peace Index). Meanwhile, PPI changes among countries, there lists some examples such as Georgia、Belarus、Cote d'Ivoire、Armenia、Arabia、Syria、Greece、Yemen、Venezuela、Brazil、European countries. You can also scan the QR code nearby to view.

(3) GPI (Global Peace Index)全球和平指数

The GPI, which ranks 163 independent states and territories according to their level of peacefulness, is produced by the Institute for Economics and Peace (IEP), the GPI is the world's leading measure of global peacefulness. The report presents the most comprehensive data-driven analysis to-date on trends in peace, its economic value, and how to develop peaceful societies.

The GPI covers 99.7 percent of the world's population, uses 23 qualitative and quantitative indicators from highly respected sources, and measures the state of peace across three domains: the level of Societal Safety and Security; the extent of Ongoing Domestic and International Conflict; and the degree of Militarization.

The results this year (2020) show that the level of global peacefulness deteriorated, with the average country score falling by 0.34 percent. This is the ninth deterioration in peacefulness in the last 12 years, with 81 countries improving, and 80 recording deteriorations over the past year. The 2020 GPI reveals a world in which the conflicts and crises that emerged in the past decade have begun to abate, only to be replaced with a new wave of tension and uncertainty as a result of the COVID-19 pandemic.

1) Global Overview

Last year, the level of global peacefulness deteriorated, with the countries' average scores falling by 0.34 percent. This is the ninth deterioration in peacefulness in the last twelve years, with 81 countries improving, and 80 recording deteriorations over the past year.

Only two of the nine regions in the world became more peaceful over the past year. The greatest improvement occurred in the Russia and Eurasia region, followed by North America. North America was the only region to improve in all three domains, while Russia and Eurasia improved in the area of ongoing conflict, but deteriorated in the area of Militarization and security.

South America and Central America and the Caribbean recorded the largest and second largest deterioration on the 2020 GPI. While South America's average deterioration in peacefulness was driven by deteriorations on Militarization and Safety and Security, the fall in peacefulness in Central America and the Caribbean was driven by changes in Ongoing Conflict.

Peace Levels have declined 2.5 percent since 2008 with 81 GPI countries recording a deterioration, and 79 improving.

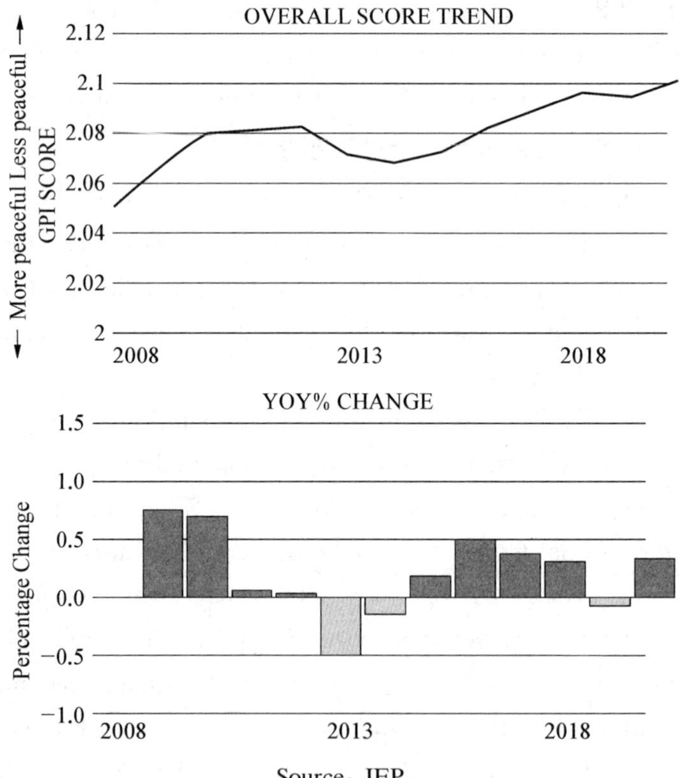

Source: IEP.

Figure 4.2　GPI Overall Trend and Year-on-Year Percentage Change, 2008—2020

Environmental pressures continue to have a negative impact on peace. The number of natural disasters has tripled in the past four decades, with the economic impact also increasing—rising from US $ 50 billion in the 1980s to US $ 200 billion per year in the last decade. From 2011 to 2019, the number of riots, general strikes and anti-government demonstrations around the world increased by 244 percent.

Trends in the global economic impact of violence, trillions PPP, 2007—2019 peacefulness has declined year-on-year for nine of the last 12 years.

2) Result of 2020 GPI

The Global Peace Index 2020 finds that the level of global peacefulness deteriorated, with the average country score falling by 0.34 percent. This is the ninth deterioration in peacefulness in the last 12 years, with 81 countries improving, and 80 recording deteriorations over the past year. The 2020 GPI reveals a world in which the conflicts and crises that emerged in the past decade have begun to abate, only to be replaced with a new wave of tension and uncertainty as a result of the COVID - 19 pandemic.

The average level of global peace declined by 0.34 percent in the 2020 GPI, making the ninth time in the last 12 years has deteriorated.

The gap between the least and most peaceful countries continues to widen. Since 2008, the 25 least peaceful countries have declined by an average of 12.9 percent, while the 25 most peaceful countries have improved by 2.1 percent.

The impact of violence on the global economy improved for the second year in a row, decreasing by 0.2 percent or $ 29 billion from 2018 to 2019. However, it is $ 1.25 trillion higher than what is was in 2012.

By 2050, climate change is estimated to create up to 86 million additional migrants in sub-Saharan Africa, 40 million in South Asia and 17 million in Latin America.

The economic impact of COVID - 19 will negatively affect political instability, international relations, conflict, civil rights and violence, undoing many years of socio-economic development.

Civil unrest has doubled since 2011—96 countries recorded a violent demonstration in 2019, with Europe recording the most. Political instability is likely to be exacerbated by the emerging economic crisis.

3) Index System of GPI GPI 指标体系

Table 4.1 Indicator Weights in the GPI, Internal Peace 60%/External Peace 40%

INTERNAL PEACE (Weight 1 to 5)		EXTERNAL PEACE (Weight 1 to 5)	
Perceptions of criminality	3	Military expenditure (% GDP)	2
Security officers and police rate	3	Armed services personnel rate	2

Continued

INTERNAL PEACE (Weight 1 to 5)		EXTERNAL PEACE (Weight 1 to 5)	
Homicide rate	4	UN peacekeeping funding	2
Incarceration rate	3	Nuclear and heavy weapons capabilities	3
Access to small arms	3	Weapons exports	3
Intensity of internal conflict	5	Refugees and IDPs	4
Violent demonstrations	3	Neighbouring countries relations	5
Violent crime	4	External conflicts fought	2.28
Political instability	4	Deaths from external conflict	5
Political terror	4		
Weapons imports	2		
Terrorism impact	2		
Deaths from internal conflict	5		
Internal conflicts fought	2.56		

Scan the QR code image next to it to see three tables: Ongoing Domestic and International Conflict domain, most peaceful to least, Societal Safety and Security domain, most to least peaceful, Militarisation domain, most peaceful to least. From these three areas, the overall performance of the Nordic countries is relatively prominent, the overall performance of African countries is relatively low, Singapore is the best in Asia, while in the military field, the United States, Russia, France, the United Kingdom and other large economies rank relatively low. From the perspective of GPI regional performance in 2019, there are nine tables in 4.2～4.10 Introducing Regional GPI results, such as Asia-Pacific、Central America & The Carribean、Europe (36 countries)、Middle East & North Africa、North America、Russia & Eurasia、South America、South Asia、Sub-Saharan Africa.

4.2.2 Social Responsibility and Ethics 社会责任与伦理

所谓企业社会责任,是指企业在创造利润、对股东负责的同时,还应承担起对劳动者、消费者、环境、社区等利益相关者的责任,实现企业与其相关区域的统筹、协调发展,企业与社会的和谐、可持续发展,企业利益和社会发展的双赢。

In international marketing, an enterprise that is really responsible for the society should not only pursue profits, but also attach importance to social responsibility and ethics. Corporate social responsibility and ethics are the foundation of an enterprise to establish itself in the international market. The first goal of an enterprise is to survive, and then to pursue profits.

Over the past few years, some multinational companies have focused on their public welfare undertakings in the Chinese market in three areas: children's education, environmental protection and sports.

High level of human capital and sound business environment tend to be correlated. Data from OECD countries illustrates this.

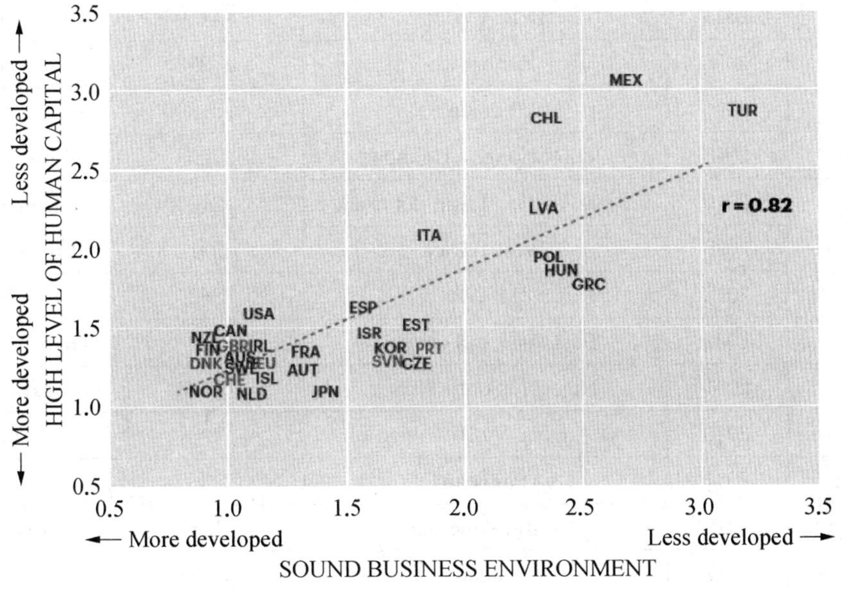

Source: IEP.

Figure 4.3 Business Environment and Human Capital in OECD Countries, 2020

4.2.3 Major Public Health Emergency 重大突发公共卫生事件

本部分我们重点分析一下国际疫情，这应该是一个综合性的社会问题，同时又与经济、政治、法律、自然等密切相关。认清某些国家甚至利用疫情搞政治污蔑、阻碍国际正常贸易往来和经济全球化等的根本目的。

(1) International Epidemic in the 21st Century 进入21世纪出现的国际疫情

Eleven out of the 18 most severe epidemics of the century took place exclusively in regions with low to medium socio-economic development. However, the new outbreak is the most serious one， with greatest impact. It may have a long-term influence on the world economic recovery.

Table 4.2 Large Epidemics of the 21_{st} Century

EPIDEMIC	START	REGIONS AFFECTED	NUMBER OF DEATHS	REGIONAL POSITIVE PEACE
COVID-19	2019	Worldwide	370,000	All
H1N1/09 (swine flu) Ebola	2009 2013	North America， part of Asia and Africa West Africa	18,036 ＞11,300	All Low to medium
Cholera	2010	Haiti	＞10,000	Low
Measles	2019	D.R. Congo	＞5,000	Low
Measles	2011	D.R. Congo	＞4,500	Low
Cholera	2008	Zimbabwe	4,293	Low
Cholera	2016	Yemen	＞3,800	Low
Ebola	2018	D.R. Congo， Uganda	2,253	Low， medium
Dengue	2019	Asia-Pacific， Latin America	＞2,000	Low to high
Meningitis	2009	West Africa	931	Low to medium
MERS-CoV	2012	MENA	862	Low to high
SARS	2002	East Asia and Canada	774	High to very high
Cholera	2001	Nigeria， South Africa	＞400	Low， high
Yellow Fever	2016	Angola， D.R. Congo	393	Low
Dengue	2011	Pakistan	＞350	Low
Chikungunya	2013	Latin America	183	Low to high
Yellow Fever	2012	Sudan	＞171	Low
Comparison Items				
HIV/AIDS	1980s	Worldwide	32 million	All
Spanish Flu	1918	Worldwide	50 million	All
Hunger	n.a.	Worldwide	9 million per year	Mostly low to medium
Cardiovascular diseases	n.a.	Worldwide	18 million per year	All
Suicide	n.a.	Worldwide	800,000 per year	All

Source： Sen Nag (2018)； Gholipour (2013)； World Health Organization Country Profiles， Situation Reports and Global Health Observatory； Worldometer； Pan-American Health Organization； Press Trust of India； Center for Disease Control and Prevention； BBC News； Mercycorps； IHME Global Burden of Disease； IEP.

(2) Impact of the Epidemic 疫情的影响

Countries with greater degrees of economic sovereignty will be less affected by a possible reduction in global trade, either as a result of the pandemic itself or of post-pandemic geopolitical tensions. Regarding the various effects of the epidemic, please scan the QR code to continue learning.

Conclusion 结语

The failure of international marketing resulting from ignoring cultural differences is very common. This warns that multinational companies entering the international market should attach great importance to the culture of countries and regions around the world. At the same time, social factors are also affecting companies' international marketing activities, especially international events. Therefore, in the international marketing activities, companies should pay special attention to the impact of these environments on themselves, strive to overcome difficulties and adapt to these environments then.

The Chapter's Referential Questions 本章参考题

(1) Discuss the definition and concept "culture" and the different ways it can impact on international marketing.
谈谈关于"文化"的定义和概念,以及文化对于国际市场营销活动所产生的影响。

(2) Describe some of the problems involved in balancing global and local approaches in international marketing.
举例说明在实施国际市场营销中平衡全球化思维和当地化运作过程中会面临的问题。

(3) What are common frameworks in managing the cultural differences?
在管理文化差异方面,有哪些可以应用的通用型方法?

(4) Identify some general guidelines for understanding and managing cultural differences.
简述在理解和管理文化差异方面的普遍原则。

(5) Discuss the role of personal relationships in different cultures and the ways in which these varying roles can affect business dealings in different countries cultures. Give specific examples.

举例说明人际关系在不同文化中的作用,人际关系在不同文化背景下商业运作所起的作用。

(6) How to synergistically manage cultural differences in international marketing?
谈谈在国际市场营销实践中,如何将差异转化为合力?

(7) Why is that the English is the generally accepted language of business, but most managers of international business shall have to use a second language, not their native one?
为什么英语是通用的第一语言,但作为跨国企业的领导人除了母语之外还应掌握第二语言?

(8) Being a student majoring International Marketing, do you have your own Cultural Biases and Mental Sets and how to manage them?
作为一名学习国际市场营销专业的学生,你有自己的文化偏见和思维定式吗?如何管理你的文化偏见和思维定式?

(9) From the global spread of COVID-19 and the countermeasures of various countries, how do you evaluate the Chinese government's countermeasures? What impact will these measures have on China's economic recovery?
从COVID-19全球蔓延和各个国家的应对措施的角度,你是如何评价中国政府的应对措施,这些举措会对中国经济复苏产生哪些影响?

Further Reading 拓展阅读

Chapter 5
The Economic Environment of International Marketing
国际市场营销的经济环境

Learning Objectives
本章学习目标

(1) General perception of the world economic environment.
对世界经济环境的总体认知。
(2) Rostow's theory of economic development stages.
罗斯托的经济发展阶段论。
(3) The world bank's standards for income classification.
世界银行关于收入的划分标准。
(4) International financial risks.
国际金融风险。

Key Words
关键词

World Economy; GDP; Globalization; GVC; Rostow; Financial Environment; Urbanization

5.1 The World Economy 世界经济

Case Studies 5.1

It is common today to hear that, when the United States sneezes, Europe and Japan catch a cold. This is an understatement. When the United States experiences a downturn in the economy, reverberations echo throughout the world: central and south countries need to be rescued by the International Monetary Fund; all the Asian economies suffer; banks in developing countries default on the debt. The United States is equally affected by the world economy.

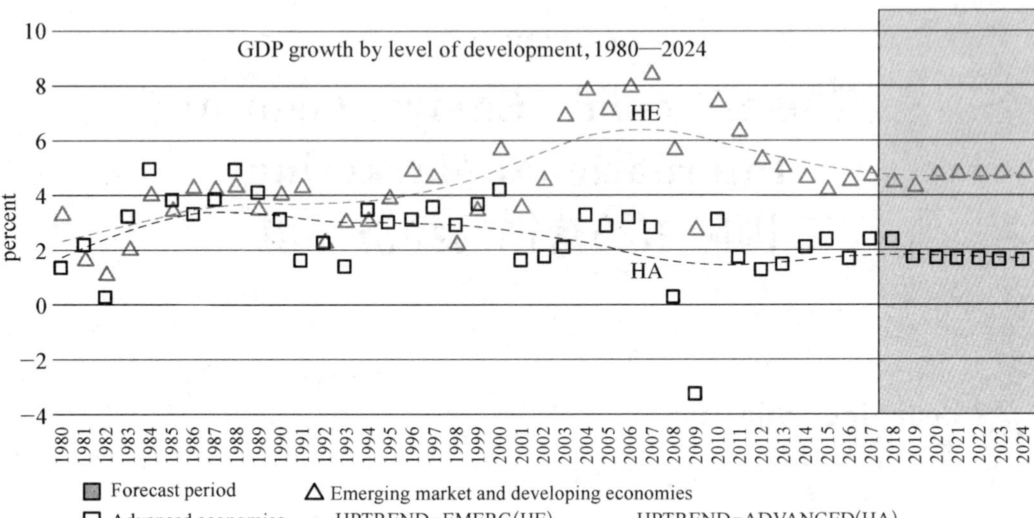

Source: IMF World Economic Outlook and WTO Secretariat Calculations.

Figure 5.1 Countries' GDP is Predicted to Converge①

The Asian crisis of the 1990s sent stock markets tumbling in the United States and the rest of the world. In the Internet era, countries are becoming more and more connected by trade, capital markets, the flow of technology and ideas across national borders, and psychology: Rather than rising and falling separately, national economies increasingly respond to the same forces. Interdependence has become the leading principle of globalization.

Table 5.1 Economic Growth of the World's Major Economies from 2011 to 2021

Real GDP Growth (Annual Percent Change)	2011	2012	2013	2014	2015	2016	2017	2018	2019	2020	2021
Argentina	6	−1	2.4	−2.5	2.7	−2.1	2.7	−2.5	−2.2	−5.7	4.4
Brazil	4	1.9	3	0.5	−3.6	−3.3	1.3	1.3	1.1	−5.3	2.9
China	9.5	7.9	7.8	7.3	6.9	6.8	6.9	6.7	6.1	1.2	9.2
France	2.2	0.3	0.6	1	1.1	1.1	2.3	1.7	1.3	−7.2	4.5
Germany	3.9	0.4	0.4	2.2	1.7	2.2	2.5	1.5	0.6	−7	5.2
India	6.6	5.5	6.4	7.4	8	8.3	7	6.1	4.2	1.9	7.4
Italy	0.7	−3	−1.8	0	0.8	1.3	1.7	0.8	0.3	−9.1	4.8
Australia	2.8	3.8	2.1	2.6	2.3	2.8	2.5	2.7	1.8	−6.7	6.1

① Notes: Smoothed trends are estimated by applying the Hoderick-Prescott (HP) filter to annual growth rates at constant prices (percentage change). We denoted these trends as HPTREND in the figure, for advanced economies (in blue) and emerging economies (in orange).

Continued

Real GDP Growth (Annual Percent Change)	2011	2012	2013	2014	2015	2016	2017	2018	2019	2020	2021
Japan	−0.1	1.5	2	0.4	1.2	0.5	2.2	0.3	0.7	−5.2	3
Korea, Republic of	3.7	2.4	3.2	3.2	2.8	2.9	3.2	2.7	2	−1.2	3.4
Russian Federation	5.1	3.7	1.8	0.7	−2	0.3	1.8	2.5	1.3	−5.5	3.5
South Africa	3.3	2.2	2.5	1.8	1.2	0.4	1.4	0.8	0.2	−5.8	4
United Kingdom	1.5	1.5	2.1	2.6	2.4	1.9	1.9	1.3	1.4	−6.5	4
United States	1.6	2.2	1.8	2.5	2.9	1.6	2.4	2.9	2.3	−5.9	4.7
Africa (Region)	2.9	6.8	3.7	4	3.3	2.1	3.6	3.5	3.2	−1.7	4.6
Asia and Pacific	6.4	5.7	5.9	5.6	5.6	5.5	5.8	5.3	4.5	−0.2	7.4
East Asia	6.7	5.8	6	5.5	5.3	5.2	5.7	5.3	4.8	−0.1	7.7
Middle East (Region)	6.4	2.6	3	3	1.9	6.3	0.7	−0.1	−0.8	−4	3.7
North America	1.9	2.3	1.8	2.6	2.8	1.7	2.4	2.7	2	−6	4.5
Western Europe	1.6	−0.5	0.2	1.7	2.3	1.9	2.4	1.8	1.3	−7.3	4.5
European Union	1.9	−0.7	0	1.7	2.5	2.2	2.9	2.3	1.7	−7.1	4.8
Latin America and the Caribbean	4.6	2.9	2.9	1.3	0.3	−0.6	1.3	1.1	0.1	−5.2	3.4
Advanced economies	1.7	1.2	1.4	2.1	2.3	1.7	2.5	2.2	1.7	−6.1	4.5
Emerging market and developing economies	6.4	5.3	5.1	4.7	4.3	4.6	4.8	4.5	3.7	−1	6.6
World	**4.3**	**3.5**	**3.5**	**3.6**	**3.5**	**3.4**	**3.9**	**3.6**	**2.9**	**−3**	**5.8**

Source: IMF, 2020.

Table 5.2 Projected Cumulative Growth Rates of Population, GDP, Labor Force and Number of Skilled and Unskilled Workers, 2018—2040①

	Population	GDP per capita	GDP	Labor force	Unskilled labor	Skilled labor
Asian LDCs	17	161	204	20	13	109
Australia	32	27	67	28	10	64

① Notes: The table displays cumulative growth rates from 2018 to 2040. The number of skilled and unskilled workers is calculated as employment times the share of tertiary educated workers in all workers. Global averages are calculated based on shares in 2018.

Source: Population numbers reproduced with permission from the UN (Medium Scenario), GDP per capita reproduced with permission from IMF (up until 2023) and OECD (shared socio-economic pathways (SSP) 2, a middle-of-the-road scenario for the future). Employment reproduced with permission from IMF (until 2023) and UN (Medium Scenario). Skilled and unskilled workers based on UN employment data, and shares of tertiary educated workers from KG and Lutz (2018).

Continued

	Population	GDP per capita	GDP	Labor force	Unskilled labor	Skilled labor
Brazil	11	41	56	9	-1	53
Canada	20	25	51	13	-7	31
China	-1	144	141	-14	-22	65
European Union(28)	4	40	45	-4	-16	37
European Free Trade Association (EFTA)	18	21	43	8	-8	44
India	23	166	226	23	14	106
Japan	-8	30	19	-14	-36	14
Republic of Korea	0	65	65	-17	-51	26
Latin America	16	58	83	16	3	71
Mexico	17	57	83	15	5	82
Middle East and North Africa	31	59	108	35	19	121
Russian Federation	-3	65	61	-8	-13	14
Sourtheast Asia	17	118	154	16	3	93
Sub-Saharan African LDCs	56	111	229	78	75	214
United States	15	28	47	10	0	35
Other Asian economies	31	52	99	31	26	73
Other sub-Saharan Africa	50	72	158	66	48	186
Rest of world	4	94	101	5	-3	35
Average	**19**	**51**	**30**	**17**	**8**	**71**

We can find in the table 5.3 value share of services output in total value of output in 2018 and 2040 in the baseline and in 2040 under the digitalization scenarios.

The international economy has indeed become one single unit. Major companies simply cannot afford to focus on a local, home-country. The market share of the tour is played on a world scale. The commercial future of a world is becoming a reality of multinational domination. Multinational companies are the main actors of today's international economic activities. They control 40% of global production, 50%~60%

of international merchandise trade, 60%～70% of international technology trade, 80%～90% of scientific research and development, and 90% of international investment. Multinational companies account for two-thirds of word trade, and many have economic weight, more than half of the 100 biggest economies in the world are now corporations, not nations. Mitsubishi is bigger than Indonesia, Ford is bigger than Turkey and Wal-Mart is bigger than Israel. As a result, multinationals are able to break down barriers that have withstood armies, missionaries, crusader, and politicians.

Table 5.3 The Share of Services Output in Total Output is Projected to Rise①

Region	2018 baseline	2040 baseline	2040 digitalization
Asian LDCs	64%	83%	86%
Australia	80%	85%	86%
Brazil	76%	84%	84%
Canada	80%	86%	88%
China	62%	75%	79%
European Union(28)	81%	87%	89%
EFTA	75%	82%	84%
India	71%	83%	86%
Japan	81%	86%	88%
Republic of Korea	69%	79%	81%
Latin America	69%	79%	80%
Mexico	72%	80%	82%
Middle East and North Africa	54%	64%	69%
Russian Feberation	64%	71%	74%
Unite States	83%	88%	90%
Southeast Asia	61%	73%	76%
Other Asian economies	73%	80%	82%
Sub-Saharan African LDCs	55%	64%	70%
Sub-Saharan Afica other	49%	63%	65%
Rest of world	68%	78%	81%
Global average	**74%**	**82%**	**84%**

Source: Simulations with WTO Global Trade Model.

In the current economic environment, companies from high income,

① Notes: The table displays the share of services (net) output in total value (net) output.

industrialized countries and their representative governments dominate the world economy, allocating resources worldwide based on market potential, rather than on local population needs, creating a growing gap between the rich countries and those are not. Low income countries, on the other hand, control resources (raw materials, labor) that multinationals need and access to local consumers, and they frequently pose barriers to international business operations in an attempt to narrow the development gap. It is important, under this environment, to understand the existing dynamic between countries at different levels of economic and market development and the philosophies underlying those dynamics.

Wave of Globalization

This wave of globalization has some new features. For example, by integrating in GVCs developing countries can take advantage of richer states' industrial bases rather than having to build entire industries for scratch. In this way, they accelerate their industrialization and development. Moreover, trade within GVCs intensifies the effects of standard trade integration. Fragmented production makes it possible for firms in developing countries to enter foreign markets at lower costs, benefit from specialization in niche tasks, and gain access to larger markets for their output. Companies can also access cheaper and better inputs, productivity-enhancing technologies, and improved management practices developed elsewhere, and thus grow at a faster rate, contributing to the creation of better, higher-paid jobs. Because of these features, GVCs are becoming more attractive to policymakers in developing countries. Trade growth is lower because output growth is lower in the major trading economies, including Europe—which accounts for one-fourth of global output and one-third of world trade—and China. The slowdown is also structural. Trade growth has become less responsive to income growth over the last decade, particularly in China and the United States, both major actors in GVCs. Part of this development reflects changes in the two economies as China moves up in the value chain and the U.S. energy sector expands.

Second, the intensification of GVC trade is concentrated in a handful of regions, sectors and firms. GVC linkages have expanded fastest in three trade hubs—East Asia, Europe, and North America—in part because these regions account for a large share of production in the sectors whose production processes have become the most fragmented across countries, particularly electronics, machinery, and transport equipment. In each country, GVCs tend to be concentrated among 15 percent of large firms that both import and export and together account for 80 percent of total trade flows. Related-party trade, such as that through multinational corporations, is particularly important.

Third, more-complex value chains tend to have especially strong regional linkages, although the expansion of GVCs is global and regional. Europe is the most integrated region, with four times as many regional linkages. In contrast, GVCs in North America depend somewhat more on global partners than regional ones, and integration has been increasing on both fronts. Elsewhere, GVC integration has been mostly global and has been increasing primarily with global partners. Importantly, in recent decades, the differences in GVC participation across regions have been far greater than the changes within regions.

5.2 Rostow's Theory of Economic Development Stages 罗斯托的经济发展阶段理论

本部分主要介绍罗斯托经济发展阶段论，该理论是在考察了世界经济发展的历史后提出的，它正确地强调了国际贸易对一国经济发展的重要性，对落后国家追赶先进国家具有重要的指导意义，是一种重要的现代化理论。一些国家在现代化进程中曾经自觉地实践了罗斯托的理论，并取得了巨大的成功。

In 1960, American economist Walt Whitman Rostow put forward his "Economic Growth Stage Theory" in the article "Stages of Economic Growth", which divided the economic development process of a country into five stages. In 1971, he added the sixth stage to the article "Politics and Growth Stages". The six stages of economic development are, in sequence, the stage of traditional society, preparation for take-off, take-off, maturity, mass consumption and the stage of consumption beyond the masses.

According to Rostow modernization model, each stage is a function of productivity, economic exchange, technological improvements, and income. Economic growth requires advancing from one stage to another.

5.2.1 Traditional Society 传统社会阶段

The traditional society has developed under the limited production functions. It is a survival-centered economy, usually closed or isolated. The technology used in production activities is the technology before the Newtonian era, and the way of looking at the material world. It is also the way before the Newtonian era, and society seems to have no interest in modernization. Some countries in the sub-Saharan Africa are still at this stage of development.

5.2.2 Ready to Take Off 准备起飞阶段

This stage is the preparatory stage to get rid of poverty and backwardness and move towards prosperity and strength. Its characteristic is that society begins to consider economic reforms, hoping to enhance national strength and improve people's living standard through modernization. An important task at this stage is economic system reform, and to create conditions for development. The dominant industry in this stage is usually the primary industry or labor-intensive manufacturing. The key problem to be solved at this stage is to obtain the funds needed for development.

5.2.3 Take-off 起飞阶段

This is the transitional period from the backward stage to the advanced stage. Rostow believes that four conditions must be met for economic take-off: ① Increase the rate of productive investment and increase the proportion of national income to more than 10%; ② There will be one or more leading department with a high growth rate in the economy; ③ Invention and innovation are very active, and the production process has absorbed the power of science and technology; ④ A suitable political, social and cultural environment.

In the take-off stage, With the improvement of agricultural labor productivity, a large number of labor is transferred from the primary industry to the manufacturing industry, and foreign investment has increased significantly. Based on some fast-growing industries, the country has seen several regional growth poles. The sign of completion is that the country's comparative advantage in international trade has shifted from agricultural exports to the export of labor-intensive products, and it has begun to export a large number of clothing, shoes, toys, small handicrafts and standardized home appliances. Some major capitalist countries have experienced a take-off stage. The period is as follows: Britain (1783—1802), France (1830—1860), the United States (1843—1860), Germany (1850—1873), Japan (1878—1900). China took off in 1977—1987.

5.2.4 To Mature 走向成熟阶段

This refers to the period in which a society has effectively applied modern technology to most of its industries. At this stage, the country's industries and exported products have begun to diversify, and high value-added export industries have continued to increase, manufacturers and consumers are keen on new technologies and products, and the focus of investment has shifted from labor-intensive industries to capital-intensive industries. National welfare, transportation and communication facilities have improved significantly, economic growth has benefited the entire society, companies have begun to invest abroad, and some economic growth poles has begun to transform into technological innovation pole. Some major capitalist countries entered into the maturity stage are: 1850 of the United Kingdom, 1900 of the United States, 1910 of Germany, and 1940 of Japan. China has also entered this stage.

5.2.5 Mass Consumption 大众消费阶段

At this stage, the main economic sector shifted from manufacturing to the service industry, consumption of luxury goods rose upward, and both producers and consumers began to use high-tech achievements in large quantities. People are involved in leisure, education, health care, national security and social security projects. Expenses on the market have increased, and foreign products have begun to welcome the entry. At present, major developed countries have entered this stage of development.

5.2.6 Beyond Mass Consumption 超越大众消费阶段

Rostow does not have a clear concept of society after the mass consumption stage, but he believes that the main goal of this stage is to improve quality of life. With the arrival of this stage, some old and difficult problems that have plagued society for a long time are expected to be gradually solved.

In Rostow's theory of stages of economic growth, the third stage, the take-off stage, is linked to the rapid changes in the mode of production, which means the beginning of industrialization and economic development. It is the most critical stage of all stages, and the economy gets rid of underdevelopment. Rostow's analysis of this stage is also the most thorough, so Rostow's theory is also called the take-off theory.

5.3 Levels of Economic Development 经济发展水平

本部分中将从历史上的所谓“三个世界”的划分，以世界银行 2010 年对不同国家收入水平的分组标准，逐一介绍关于不同国家的经济发展水平定义的发展历程。

In the course of economic development, there are many countries competing with each other. Historically, the informal and frequently used classification in the west has referred to highly industrialized, developed countries as the First World, to socialist countries as the Second World, and to developing countries as the Third World. Of this classification, only the term "Third World" has been used widely. A United Nations classification contrasts LLDCS (Least-Developed and the Lowest Income Countries) and LDCs (Less-Developed Countries and Lower-Income Countries) to developed countries. Yet other classifications exist. For example, the term NIC (newly industrialized country) is used to describe the economies of Taiwan China, Singapore, South Korea, and Hong Kong China (known in the 1980s and 1990s as the Asian Tigers), whereas countries such as Brazil, Argentina, Chile, Peru, and the transitional economies of central and eastern europe are described as emerging markets. For the purpose of this textbook, we will refer to three categories of countries, based on the classification used by the World Bank.

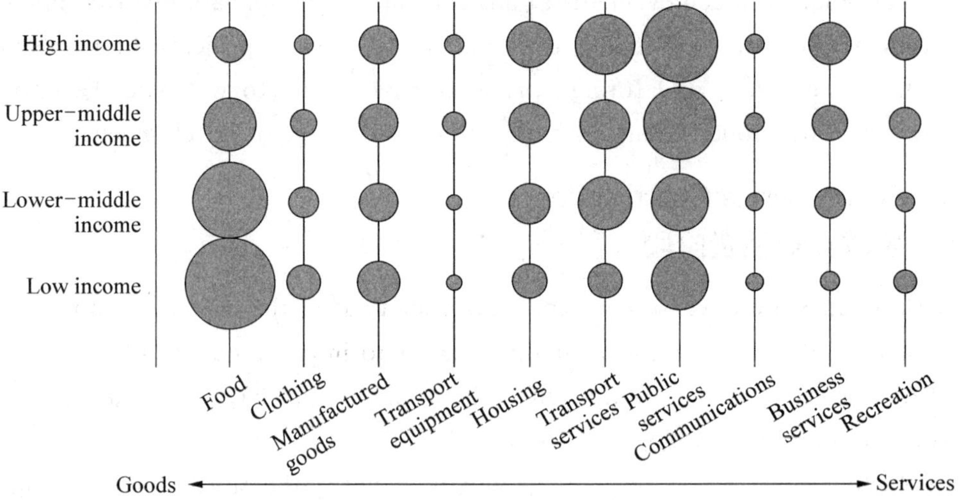

Source: calculation based on GTAP data for 2014.

Figure 5.2 The Composition of Expenditure Changes According to Income①

Looking specifically at services consumption by household income level, Figure 5.3 clearly shows that the share of spending on hotels and restaurants, health and social, recreational, financial and professional services increases as the level of income increases. Conversely, the share of spending on construction services remains constant across income groups, while the share of real estate services, represented by expenditures on rent, dramastically declines with income. Overall, as income grows, countries increasingly consume services, especially skills-intensive services. Not only do services industries have a higher income elasticity than goods, but services that have higher income elasticity are also the most skills-intensive. There exists positive relationship between income elasticity and skill intensity.

---

① Notes: Income categories are based on World Bank country classifications in 2017.

5.3.1 High-Income Countries
高收入国家

These are highly industrialized countries with advanced industrial and service sectors. This category includes newly industrialized countries, as well as countries that have had a developed status for many years. Although these countries present great potential because they have consumers with the highest per capita income, they also present challenges to international firms because their markets are in the maturity stage, consumers have established preferences, and competition is fierce. The World Bank refers to the countries in this category as high-income countries, with a GNI per capita of US ＄12,276 or more.

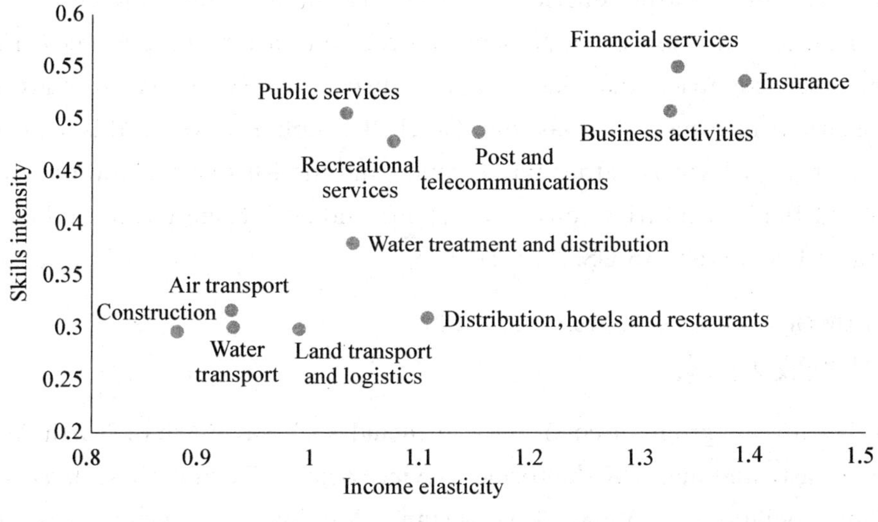

Source: Caron et al. (2014).

Figure 5.3 As Income Grows, Countries Increasingly Consume Skills-intensive Services①

5.3.2 Middle-Income Countries
中等收入国家

Countries with emerging markets are both developing rapidly and have great potential. They are Latin America countries, such as Argentina, Brazil, Uruguay, Paraguay, Chile, Peru, and Bolivia, to name a few; countries in Asia, such as China, with its immense market, and India, with its substantial middle class; and the

① Notes: Skills intensity is measured by the ratio of skilled labor to total labor input. It is computed including the factor usage embedded in the intermediate sectors used in each sector's production. "Distribution, hotels and restaurants" includes wholesale, retail and repair services. "Recreational activities" include cultural and sporting activities. "Public services" include public administration, education, health and social work, and sanitation activities.

transition economies of central and eastern europe, which are rapidly privatizing state-owned industries and adopting market reforms. Important in this category are big emerging markets (BEAMS), which present the greatest potential for international trade and expansion. The World Bank refers to the countries in this category as middle-income countries, with a GNI per capita of US \$1,006 to US \$12, 275. The middle-income country category is further divided into two income groups, such as the elderly.

5.3.3 Upper Middle Income Countries 中高收入国家

These countries have rapidly developing economics, and especially in urban areas, they have an infrastructure that is on par with that of developed countries. Among them are countries in Latin America, such as Argentina, Chile, and Mexico. In this category are the transition economies of central and eastern europe, new European Union member countries that have rapidly privatized state-owned industries and adopted market reforms, such as the Czech Republic; also in this category are Estonia, Hungary, Latvia, Lithuania, Poland, and the Russian Federation. According to the World Bank, countries considered upper middle income countries have a GNI per capita of US \$3,976 to US \$12,275.

5.3.4 Lower Middle Income Countries 中低收入国家

This is a diverse group of countries that includes China, much of North Africa and the Middle East, and many of the former Soviet Socialist Republics, such as Armenia, Azerbaijan, Belarus, Georgia, Kazakhstan, Moldova, Turkmenistan, and the Ukraine. According to the World Bank, countries in this category have a GNI per capita of US \$1006 to US \$3,975.

Table 5.4 Percentage of Income Share Held by the Lowest 20%①

Countries	2000	2010	2017
Argentina	3.2	4.1	5.1
Brazil	2.5[1]	3.2	3.2
China	5.6	5.1	6.5
Germany	8.8	8.4	7.6[2]
Spain	7.1	6.3	6.2

① Note: 1 is from the year of 2001,2、3、4 are all from the year of 2016

Continued

Countries	2000	2010	2017
Finland	9.6	9.2	9.4
France	8.2	7.7	8.1
United Kingdom	/	7.3	7.1[3]
Luxembourg	8.4	8.2	6.5
Norway	9.7	9.5	8.9
The Russian Federation	6.4	6.4	7.1
Sweden	9.3	8.6	8.3
United States	5.4	5.1	5.1[4]

Source: The World Bank.

5.3.5 Low Income Countries 低收入国家

Countries in this category are predomirantly agricultural countries with low per capita income levels, spread across different regions of Asia and sub-Saharan Africa. Low-income countries are often neglected or underserved by large multinationals and consequently present great potential as niche markets. Even the countries with the lowest per capita income have a stratum of society that can afford global products. Furthermore, because they are primary recipients of international development aid, they present important opportunities for firms operating in the areas of infrastructure development and industrial sector development and for related consultancies. The World Bank refers to the countries in this category as low income countries, with a GNI per capita of less than US $1,005. It is important to note that these markets are gross underserved by the international community and that consumer needs-even the most base ones-in these markets are barely met by local administration.

5.4 Total Economy 经济的总量

As of 2019, the world economy totaled 87.7 trillion U.S. dollars, of which the United States, China, and the European Union accounted for approximately 60% of the world economy. Therefore, the stable and healthy development of these economies is conducive to the steady and orderly development of the world economy.

Table 5.5 Comparison of China and the U.S. Economy

Year	China			American		
	GDP (Trillion USD)	Annual Growth Rate	% of the World	GDP (Trillion USD)	Annual Growth Rate	% of the World
2019	14.36	6.11%	16.60%	21.43	2.33%	24.80%
2018	13.61	6.75%	15.84%	20.54	3.18%	23.91%
2017	12.14	6.95%	15.00%	19.49	2.22%	24.07%
2016	11.14	6.85%	14.62%	18.71	1.57%	24.56%
2015	11.02	7.04%	14.68%	18.22	2.88%	24.28%
2014	10.44	7.42%	13.16%	17.52	2.45%	22.09%
2013	9.57	7.77%	12.39%	16.78	1.84%	21.73%
2012	8.53	7.86%	11.36%	16.2	2.25%	21.57%
2011	7.55	9.55%	10.29%	15.54	1.55%	21.18%
2010	6.09	10.64%	9.22%	14.99	2.56%	22.70%
2009	5.1	9.40%	8.46%	14.45	−2.54%	23.95%
2008	4.59	9.65%	7.22%	14.71	−0.14%	23.13%
2007	3.55	14.23%	6.12%	14.45	1.88%	24.93%
2006	2.75	12.72%	5.35%	13.81	2.85%	26.85%
2005	2.29	11.40%	4.82%	13.04	3.51%	27.47%
2004	1.96	10.11%	4.46%	12.21	3.80%	27.87%
2003	1.66	10.04%	4.27%	11.46	2.86%	29.45%
2002	1.47	9.13%	4.24%	10.94	1.74%	31.54%
2001	1.34	8.34%	4.01%	10.58	1.00%	31.69%

A survey on R & D investment in 18 economies found that from 2000 to 2018, the proportion of R & D investment in GDP has basically increased significantly, while several countries such as China, South Korea, and Sweden have performed more prominently, entering technology-driven In the economic era, various countries are paying more and more attention to the investment in technological research and development, and technological innovation has become increasingly obvious in promoting the upgrading of industrial structure.

Table 5.6 R & D Expenditure as a Percentage of GDP

Countries	2000	2010	2018
China	0.89	1.71	2.19
United States	2.63	2.74	2.84
Australia	1.58	2.38	1.81[1]
Germany	2.40	2.71	3.09
Spain	0.88	1.35	1.24
Finland	3.25	3.73	2.77
France	2.09	2.18	2.20
United Kingdom	1.63	1.66	1.72
Indonesia	0.07	0.08[2]	0.23
India	0.76	0.79	0.65
Italy	1.01	1.22	1.40
Japan	2.91	3.14	3.26
Republic of Korea	2.18	3.47	4.81
Singapore	1.82	1.93	1.94[3]
Netherlands	1.79	1.70	2.16
Poland	0.64	0.72	1.21
The Russian Federation	1.05	1.13	0.99
Sweden	1.99[4]	3.21	3.34

Note: 1—from 2017, 2—from 2009, 3—from 2017, 4—from 1999.

With the global spread of the COVID-19 epidemic, the IMF has updated its global economic trend forecast in its June 2020 Global Outlook. China will undoubtedly drive the global economy out of its predicament.

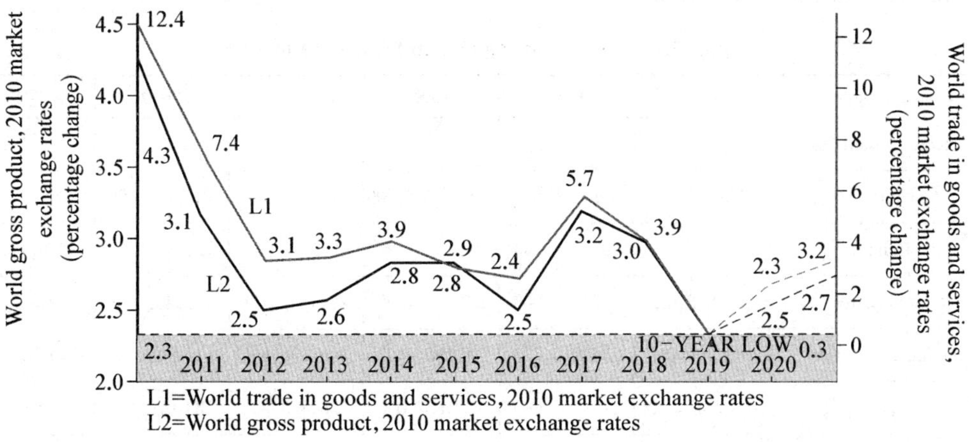

Source: UN DESA, including estimates and forecasts for 2019—2021.

Figure 5.4 The Trend of World Gross Product Growth and World Trade Growth in a Decade

Rising tariffs and months of shifting between the escalation and de-escalation of global trade tensions have fuelled policy uncertainty, significantly curtailed investment, and pushed global trade growth down to 0.3 percent in 2019—its lowest level in a decade.

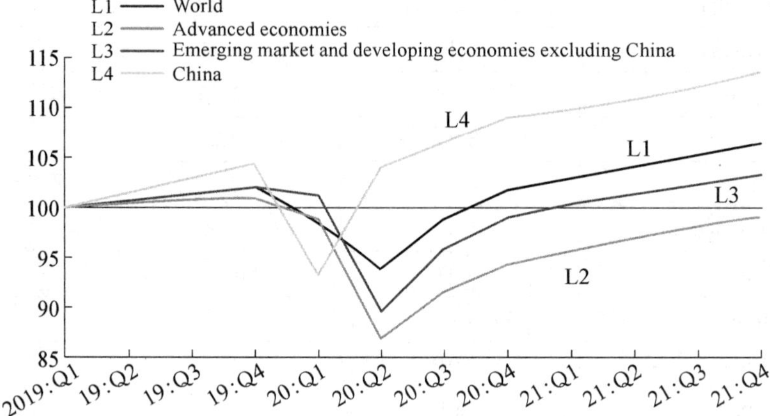

Source: World Economic Outlook, June 2020 Update.

Figure 5.5 Quarterly World GDP (2019: Q1=100)

5.5 Population and Distribution 人口数量及分布

Population growth determines the types of markets that multinational companies, as well as small and medium enterprises. In the high-income countries, marketers have a more mature market to contend with-markets with a substantial population aged 65 and older. Population growth also has implications with regard to access to goods and services and to the environment.

Table 5.7 The World Population from 1970 to 2019

Country Name	1970	1980	1990	2000	2010	2019
Selected Countries						
China	818,315,000	981,235,000	1,135,185,000	1,262,645,000	1,337,705,000	1,397,715,000
India	555,189,792	698,952,844	873,277,798	1,056,575,549	1,234,281,170	1,366,417,754
United States	205,052,000	227,225,000	249,623,000	282,162,411	309,321,666	328,239,523
Russian Federation	130,404,000	139,010,000	14,796,9407	146,596,869	142,849,468	144,373,535
Japan	104,345,000	116,782,000	123,537,000	126,843,000	128,070,000	126,264,931
Income Range						

Continued

Country Name	1970	1980	1990	2000	2010	2019
Low income	182,760,628	234,993,767	303,390,406	401,768,207	531,260,028	668,454,965
Lower middle income	1,099,849,866	1,390,765,927	1,765,242,835	2,155,781,287	2,548,154,994	2,913,363,391
Low & middle income	2,808,816,765	3,475,736,527	4,251,636,963	5,012,852,779	5,742,542,551	6,437,681,145
Middle income	2,626,056,137	3,240,742,760	3,948,246,557	4,611,084,572	5,211,282,523	5,769,226,180
Upper middle income	1,526,206,271	1,849,976,833	2,183,003,722	2,455,303,285	2,663,127,529	2,855,862,789
High income	874,094,274	957,189,063	1,028,439,321	1,101,479,757	1,179,329,063	1,235,852,827
Main Area						
South Asia	713,711,349	900,620,572	1,133,495,196	1,390,946,064	1,638,792,934	1,835,776,742
South Asia (IDA & IBRD)	713,711,349	900,620,572	1,133,495,196	1,390,946,064	1,638,792,934	1,835,776,742
East Asia & Pacific	1,290,384,064	1,559,194,619	1,822,193,192	2,047,640,119	2,206,884,624	2,340,628,292
East Asia & Pacific (IDA & IBRD countries)	1,102,743,566	1,342,952,245	1,584,871,832	1,793,498,351	1,941,377,349	2,067,984,156
Europe & Central Asia	737,524,802	793,299,477	841,520,445	861,278,548	887,926,820	921,140,092
Europe & Central Asia (IDA & IBRD countries)	351,017,856	389,610,122	427,265,655	434,313,570	440,420,861	460,799,505
European Union	386,322,908	407,875,852	420,477,979	429,328,624	441,532,412	447,512,041
North America	226,431,000	251,795,337	277,373,464	312,909,974	343,391,679	365,892,703
Middle East & North Africa	138,473,064	184,628,605	254,215,138	315,326,801	385,917,886	456,707,404
Middle East & North Africa (IDA & IBRD countries)	127,335,091	166,616,401	224,280,789	276,357,481	328,991,663	384,771,780
Sub-Saharan Africa	290,526,189	383,188,232	509,451,851	665,327,581	869,025,106	1,106,957,898
Sub-Saharan Africa (IDA & IBRD countries)	290,526,189	383,188,232	509,451,851	665,327,581	869,025,106	1,106,957,898
Latin America & the Caribbean (IDA & IBRD countries)	273,723,955	346,328,182	426,777,908	504,921,261	573,800,641	630,644,770
Arab World	121,785,650	164,420,785	222,653,373	282,344,154	354,890,042	427,870,270
OECD members	917,065,338	1,016,539,124	1,104,136,517	1,196,874,050	1,287,527,866	1,359,963,500
World	3,682,911,039	4,432,925,590	5,280,076,284	6,114,332,536	6,921,871,614	7,673,533,972

Source: The World Bank.

5.5.1 Age Distribution of the Population 人口的年龄分布

According to the survey data of the World Bank, among the population distribution proportions of all ages, the global average proportion of 0～14 years old is 25.65%, while developed economies and large economies are far below this average. Low-income countries are much higher than this figure, reaching 41.81% (Table 5.8), which reflects the risk of labor shortages in advanced economies and high-income countries in the future.

Table 5.8 Percentage of Population Aged 0 to 14 in Total Population

Countries	1970	1980	1990	2000	2010	2019
China	40.41	35.94	28.59	24.79	18.66	17.80
United States	28.10	22.67	21.67	21.70	20.20	18.55
Australia	29.16	25.30	22.10	20.88	19.03	19.26
Germany	23.32	18.57	15.95	15.67	13.57	13.80
Spain	28.11	25.95	19.99	14.74	14.79	14.58
Finland	24.62	20.30	19.31	18.14	16.52	16.02
France	24.82	22.42	20.08	18.91	18.48	17.80
United Kingdom	24.17	21.02	18.97	19.03	17.50	17.70
Indonesia	43.24	41.09	36.45	30.69	28.83	26.22
India	40.91	39.25	37.97	34.73	30.81	26.62
Italy	24.65	21.98	16.47	14.32	14.08	13.17
Japan	24.11	23.58	18.48	14.78	13.35	12.57
Republic of Korea	41.87	33.87	25.44	20.61	16.10	12.75
Luxembourg	22.20	18.76	17.36	18.94	17.64	15.71
Netherlands	27.43	22.33	18.21	18.47	17.52	15.88
Poland	27.23	24.03	25.12	19.56	15.22	15.19
The Russian Federation	26.22	21.56	22.90	18.24	14.93	18.15
Sweden	20.84	19.59	17.92	18.42	16.51	17.63
Low-income	44.17	44.80	45.09	44.85	43.94	41.81
Middle and low income	40.76	38.51	35.70	32.55	29.00	27.42
Middle-income	40.52	38.05	34.98	31.48	27.48	25.75
Upper middle income	39.75	36.22	31.35	27.13	22.22	21.03
High-income	27.20	23.80	21.11	19.27	17.35	16.44
World	37.54	35.33	32.86	30.16	27.02	25.65

Source: The World Bank.

According to The 2019 Revision of World Population Prospects issued by the United Nations, it is estimated that by 2030, the global population will be 8.5 billion, and the global population is expected to reach 9.7 billion by 2050. India is expected to replace China as the world's most populous country around 2027; at the same time, from a global perspective, population growth will generally slow in the coming decades.

From 1990 to 2019, the life expectancy of the global population increased from 64.2 years to 72.6 years old, and the average life expectancy of the global population is expected to increase to 77.1 years by 2050; in addition, the global fertility rate has dropped from 3.2% in 1990 to 2.5% in 2019, which is expected to decrease to 2.2% by 2050.

It will be illustrated the global differences in urban population distribution about urbanization later in this chapter.

Along with changes in demographics, generational preferences will also play a significant role in shaping services consumption. Millennials (born between 1980 and 1996), Generation Z (born between 1997 and 2012) and the New Generation (born after 2012), having lived in a mostly digital world, are likely to increase the demand for online and on-demand services. By 2030, Generation Z and the New Generation will constitute more than 50 percent of global population (Figure 5.6) and their consumption of social media and on-demand services will increase services trade through digital platforms.

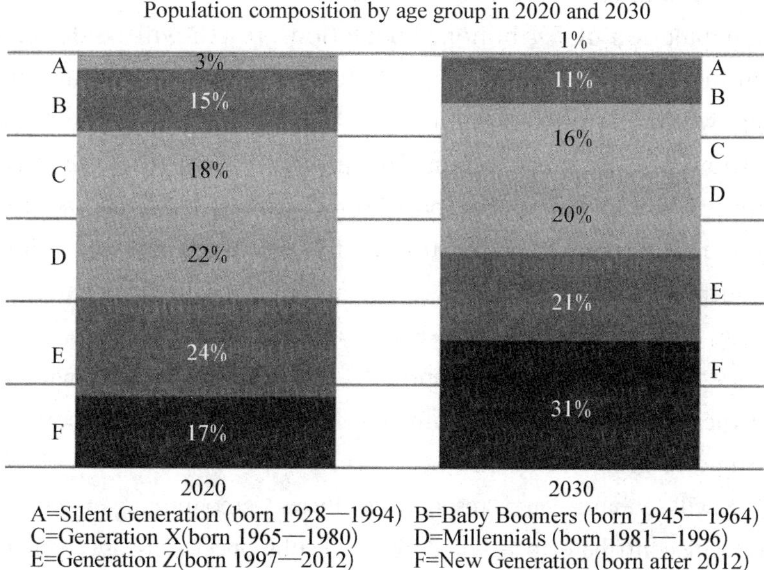

Source: WTO calculations based on data from UNDESA.

Figure 5.6 By 2030, Generation Z and the New Generation will Constitute more than 50 Percent of the Global Population

Past consumption trends show that Millennials and Generation Z tend to be the greatest consumers of digital services, in particular sharing applications, social media and on-demand services. According to a global survey by Nielsen (2014), 42 percent of Millennial and Generation Z respondents are likely to rent products in shared communities compared to 17 percent of global Generation X respondents (those born between 1965 and 1980) and 7 percent of global Baby Boomers (i.e. those born between 1945 and 1964).

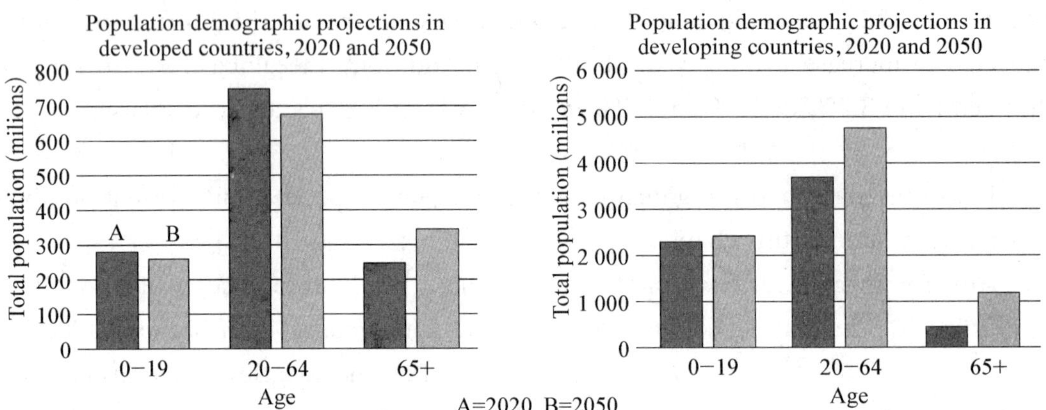

Source: WTO calculations based on United Nations Department of Economic and Social Affairs (UNDESA), Population Division data.

Figure 5.7 The Population in Developed Countries is Ageing, The Young Population in Developing Countries is Growing

The global population will reach 9.5 billion by 2045①—a 28% increase over the current world population of 7.4 billion. Population growth will be driven by a decline in deaths from infectious diseases, rising birth rates and declining infant mortality in the developing world, improved sanitation, and enhanced access to medical care. Developing nations are likely to account for around 97% of this growth, with Africa alone accounting for 49% of global population growth by 2050. As the population grows, it is also aging—over the next 30 years the median global age will increase from 29.6 to 36.1, with 1.4 billion people over the age of 65. Climate change, civil unrest, and the shifting global economic landscape will also drive an increase in migration. While migratory flows from the developing to the developed world will continue, It is supposed that increased migration within the developing world as economies in Africa and Asia continue to grow toward mid-century.

Technology will enhance and respond to these demographic changes. Advances in medical science will contribute to a reduction in deaths due to disease, genetic conditions, and lifestyle-related illness. Medical advances will also reduce infant and mother mortality

① United Nations (2015). World Population Prospects. Available from http: //esa.un.org/unpd/wpp/.

lates, especially in the developing world. Life extension technologies will also increase the number of senior citizens who remain productive well into their 70's and 80's. At the same time, an overall increase in the population will drive greater demand for health care analytics and robots designed to assist the elderly. Migration will create additional demand for communications technology as immigrants seek to maintain ties to friends and family in other parts of the world. In addition to mobile communications, technologies like virtual and augmented reality could allow immigrants to "visit" their homes and maintain contact with their own cultures. Migration could also encourage governments to develop new applications for analytics to track migratory flows—which could have unintended consequences if used for racial or ethnic profiling.

5.5.2 Aging Problem 老龄化问题

It is estimated that by 2050, the proportion of the elderly over the age of 65 years in the world will rise to 16%; regionally, the elderly population in west Asia and north Africa, central and south Asia, east Asia and southeast Asia, and Latin America and the Caribbean are expected to be doubled by 2050. The report warns that the aging of population in these areas will bring a series of social problems, increasing the pressure on social security system of these countries particularly.

Figure 5.8 shows the positive correlation between the old age dependency ratio and the share of aggregate expenditure on health services for 40 economies between 2000 and 2014. As the old age dependency ratio increases, the share for aggregate health expenditure also increases.

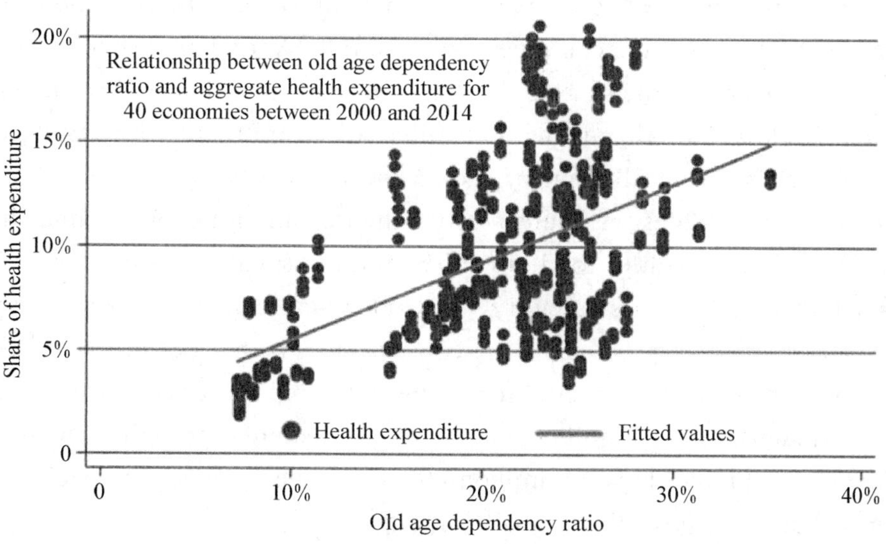

Source: World Trade Report 2019.

Figure 5.8 The Correlation between the Old Age Dependency Ratio and Aggregate Health Expenditure is Positive

In 2019, China's population over 60 years old has reached 254 million, accounting for 18.1% of the total population, and the population over 65 years old will reach 176 million, accounting for 12.57% of the total population. In the decades to come, the situation of providing for the aged in our country will be increasingly serious.

5.6 World Food Security and Nutrition 世界粮食安全和营养状况

The "State of Food Security and Nutrition in the World"① released by the United Nations in 2020 shows that nearly 690 million people suffered from hunger in 2019, an increase of 10 million compared with 2018, and an increase of nearly 60 million compared with five years ago. High cost and low economic affordability mean that billions of people cannot eat healthy and nutritious food. Asia has the largest number of hungry people, but Africa has the fastest growing number of hungry people.

The annual report concludes that after decades of steady decline in the number of chronically hungry people, they have slowly increased since 2014 and continue to maintain this trend.

Asia still has the highest number of undernourished people (381 million), Africa ranks second (250 million), followed by Latin America and the Caribbean (48 million). The global incidence of undernourishment, that is, the proportion of hungry people, has basically remained at 8.9%, but the absolute number has been increasing since 2014. This means that in the past five years, the number of hungry people has increased in tandem with the global population.

The huge difference between regions is: In terms of percentages, the situation in Africa is the most serious and continues to deteriorate. A total of 19.1% of the African population is undernourished. This is Asia (8.3%) and Latin America and the Caribbean (7.4%). More than twice. According to current trends, by 2030, more than half of the world's chronically hungry people will be in Africa.

According to the latest estimates, More than 3 billion people around the world can not affard to eat healthy food. In sub-Saharan Africa and South Asia, 57% of the population falls into this category, and no other regions are spared, including North America and Europe. One of the consequences is that our efforts to eliminate malnutrition seem to be frustrated. According to the report, one-quarter to one-third of children under five (191 million) in 2019 faced stunted growth or wasting, that is, underweight. In addition, 38 million children under five are overweight. At the same time, obesity is spreading globally among adults.

---

① Source: http://www.fao.org/3/ca9692en/CA9692EN.pdf

5.7 Per Capita Income 人均收入

5.7.1 GDP per Capita 人均 GDP

Per capita income is a very useful indicator of the consumer market and spending power of a country or region. Due to the small population of Nordic countries, per capita GDP has always been relatively high. In recent years, China's economy has been developing steadily, and the per capita GDP has been increasing. In terms of per capita GDP, China has reached US $10,986 in 2019, and will soon become a high-income country according to the world bank's criteria.

Table 5.9 World Ranking Forecast of GDP per Capita in 2020

Ranking	Countries/Regions	GDP Per Capita(USD)	Ranking	Countries/Regions	GDP Per Capita(USD)
1	Luxembourg	$120,511.56	25	United Kingdom	$41,624.11
2	Macao, China	$98,464.19	27	Italy	$35,577.31
3	Iceland	$92,041.99	29	Korea	$33,367.91
4	Switzerland	$85,996.71	30	Spain	$33,241.82
5	Ireland	$80,918.09	38	Taiwan China	$26,346.38
6	Norway	$77,759.69	66	Russia	$11,565.76
7	Qatar	$72,563.37	69	China	$10,986.47
8	United States	$65,895.68	137	India	$2,354.68
9	Denmark	$64,615.10	176	Liberia	$522.88
10	Australia	$62,903.40	177	Gambia	$518.34
17	Germany	$50,837.46	178	Burundi	$499.70
20	Hong Kong China	$48,778.76	179	Niger	$489.73
22	France	$45,214.04	180	Madagascar	$463.92
24	Japan	$42,049.62	181	Malawi	$366.12

Source: World Economic Information Network.

5.7.2 Rise of Global Middle Class 全球中产阶级的崛起[①]

Membership in the global middle class is expected to more than double in 2016—2030,

① Souece: ODASA(R & T) | Emerging S & T Trends: 2016—2045

from 1.8 billion to almost 5 billion. By 2030, 60% of the world's population could be categorized to the middle class, with the majority of middle class growth occurring in Asia.①

The growth of the global middle class will be accompanied by significant growth in levels of education and technology access worldwide—by 2030, around 90% of the world's population will know how to read, and 50% will have Internet access. However, the quality and availability of education and technology will remain uneven, with developed nations holding significant advantages over the developing world well into the 2040s.

As incomes rise, people around the world will have more disposable income to spend on electronics and other goods and services. This could fuel significant innovation across a wide range of technologies. Mobile and cloud computing could receive a significant boost in investment as more people are able to afford smartphones with connections to high speed wireless Internet service. Social technologies would likely grow in parallel as Internet access becomes more widespread. Demand for human augmentation technologies could also grow, especially for less expensive augmentations such as wearables and pharmaceutical enhancements. Blended reality technologies may become more ubiquitous as delivery vehicles for immersive, interactive entertainment and distributed education. Investments in the Internet of things may grow as the emerging middle class invests in smartphones products and governments make investments in digitally-enhanced infrastructure. While the rate of growth in these and other technology sectors will depend on how much global incomes rise, it is likely that the rise of the global middle class will fuel broad-based innovation in science and technology.

5.8 Financial Environment 金融环境

目前，国际货币体系并不稳定，企业面临的国际金融风险增加。因此，了解当地国际金融环境的特征，选择合理手段规避风险是企业国际营销活动中必不可少的内容。

International financial market refers to the sum of places and relationships for international financial business activities between residents and non-residents, or between non-residents and non-residents. In the international field, the international financial market is very important. The international economic exchanges such as the international transfer of goods and services, the international transfer of capital, the

① European Strategy and Policy Analysis System (2015). Global trends to 2030: Can the EU meet the challenges ahead? Available from http://europa.eu/espas/pdf/espas-report-2015.pdf.

export and import of gold, the trading of foreign exchange and even the operation of the international monetary system are inseparable from the international financial market. In the international financial market, new financing means, investment opportunities and investment methods emerge in endlessly.

As an important part of international economic relations, international finance has a very important impact on international marketing. International marketing is different from domestic marketing. It is a cross-border economic activity. This kind of activity involves the turnover and circulation of international monetary capital. The turnover and circulation of international currency mainly come through foreign exchange. Therefore, international marketing participants must understand and pay attention to foreign exchange, exchange rate, foreign exchange transaction and other matters. The fluctuation of exchange rate has a great influence on import and export, foreign direct investment, production decision and financial management of multinational companies. For example, if the exchange rate of the home currency of an international marketing enterprise rises, the price of the export products of the enterprise will rise, which will reduce the international competitiveness of the product and the exports will be reduced. when domestic exchange rate is strong, the enterprise can earn more by converting the currency of the host country into the domestic currency. Therefore, enterprises must understand the operation law of international financial market and analyze the financial environment of the host country market.

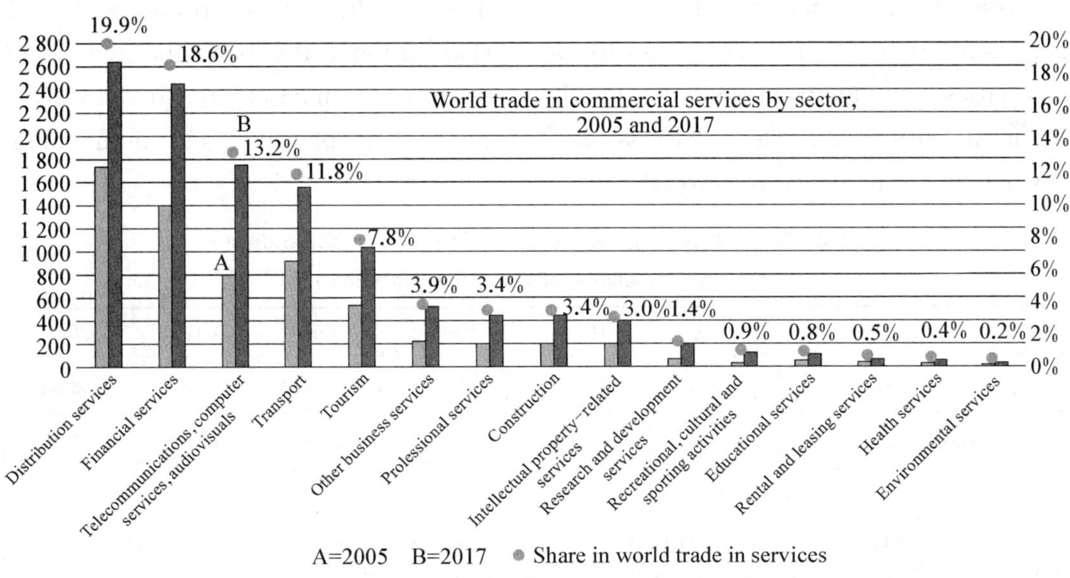

Source: World Trade Report 2019.

Figure 5.9 Distribution and Financial Services are the most Traded Services①

① Note: World trade is calculated as the average of world exports and world imports.

According to estimates, world trade in financial services and in distribution services takes place predominantly by means of the establishment of a commercial presence in other countries. In 2017, around 77 percent of financial services, or some US $ 1, 941 billion, and over 70 percent of distribution services, some US $ 1, 852 billion, were traded worldwide through foreign affiliates.

Although banks and other financial services institutions operate overseas, they are adapting to changeing consumers' preferences by offering an increasing number of services online, from credit card transactions to finaneial management. Insurance companies are making it possible to underwrite and submit claims online. These are only a fraction of the online crossborder services that digitalization is expected to bring to the industry in the foreseeable future.

Information on international financial payments and transactions will be explained in the chapter on pricing and distribution channels.

5.9 Urbanization 城市化

By 2045, approximately 70% of the world's population will live in urban areas.[①] The majority of this growth is likely to occur in the developing countries, particularly in Asia, as economic growth in China and India draw more residents to job opportunities near cities. The trend towards urbanization will expand the number of megacities—cities with more than 10 million residents—from 28 in 2015 to 41 by 2030.[②] If urbanization is managed successfully, millions of people could be raised out of poverty by strong economic growth.[③]

Table 5.10 Percentage of Population in Urban Agglomerations with a Population of more than 1 Million

Countries	1970	1980	1990	2000	2010	2019
China	7.88	8.20	10.33	17.13	23.27	28.54
United States	41.59	41.13	42.15	43.79	44.50	46.49

① OECD (2012). Environmental Outlook to 2050. Available from http://www.oecd.org/env/indicators-modelling-outlooks/oecdenvironmentaloutlookto2050theconsequencesofinaction.htm

② United Nations (2014). World Urbanization Prospects: Highlights. Available from http://esa.un.org/unpd/wup/Publications/Files/WUP2014-Highlights.pdf.

③ McKinsey Global Institute (2012). Urban World: Cities and the Rise of the Consuming Class. Available from http://www.mckinsey.com/global-themes/urbanization/urban-world-cities-and-the-rise-of-the-consuming-class.

Continued

Countries	1970	1980	1990	2000	2010	2019
Australia	62.64	62.07	61.20	58.90	59.24	60.90
Germany	9.14	8.91	9.10	8.83	9.28	9.60
Spain	20.71	21.58	21.91	23.10	23.02	25.70
Finland	11.01	14.10	17.47	19.69	20.99	23.41
France	21.96	22.25	22.49	22.43	22.49	22.85
United Kingdom	28.27	26.06	25.55	25.70	26.12	26.96
Indonesia	8.82	10.55	11.77	12.09	12.74	13.50
India	8.64	9.87	11.03	12.42	13.69	15.67
Italy	18.42	18.79	18.97	18.65	18.50	18.83
Japan	51.84	55.25	58.22	59.30	62.75	64.72
Republic of Korea	31.89	42.89	52.29	51.18	50.25	50.21
Singapore	99.89	99.91	98.88	97.17	99.95	100.00
Netherlands	14.53	13.09	12.62	12.53	12.44	12.40
Poland	3.98	4.40	4.27	4.36	4.48	4.68
The Russian Federation	17.40	19.08	19.43	19.94	21.77	23.32
Sweden	13.63	11.93	12.13	13.59	14.50	15.63
Low-income	6.17	8.30	10.44	11.24	11.86	12.38
Middle and low income	11.21	12.75	14.30	17.00	19.41	21.56
Middle-income	11.54	13.06	14.58	17.48	20.14	22.57
Upper middle income	13.25	14.87	16.80	21.21	25.36	28.76
World	15.71	16.86	18.11	20.28	22.30	24.22

On the other hand, mismanaged growth could lead to cities which can not provide enough fresh water, food, electricity, transportation access, and sanitation to sustain a healthy, productive population. Rapid migration to cities and increasing urban population densities could also exacerbate ethnic or religious tensions, particularly in cities which can not provide sufficient resources to keep people safe and employed.

From a technology perspective, urbanization will encourage innovation on multiple fronts. Successful cities will develop innovative transportation systems that move people and goods efficiently without increasing smog and other forms of pollution. Technological developments will include autonomous vehicles and mass transit systems that can be retrofitted to existing urban footprints. The need to provide food and fresh water to millions of urban residents will drive innovations such as vertical farming and water harvesting (e.g., graywater recycling). Cities will also drive innovation in information and communications technology. Urban centers will become central hubs for the Internet of Things, as millions of sensors form an information network the monitors traffic, air and water quality, power distribution, public safety, and numerous other facets of urban life. Many cities in the developing world will leap-frog traditional landline telecommunications and drive innovation in wireless and mobile communication. Robots might take over many roles currently held by human workers, such as sanitation.

Conclusion 结语

With the acceleration of globalization, the integration of the Chinese economy with the international economy is becoming increasingly obvious. With the improvment of per capita income, China's economy will definitely overcome the middle-income trap. However, from a global perspective, the economic gap between developed and developing countries is pretty obvious. Therefore, the economic development of developing countries' markets is crucial to the health and stability of the global economy. We should research more on population, per capita income, aging, regional economic cooperation, etc.

Engel Coefficient and Gini Coefficient

恩格尔系数和基尼系数

1. Engel Coefficient

Engel's Coefficient is the ratio of total food expenditure to total personal consumption expenditure. In the 19_{th} century, German statistician Engel drew a rule for changes in consumption structure based on statistical data: the lower a family's income, the greater the proportion of household income (or total expenditure) spent on food. As household income increases, the proportion of household income (or total expenditure) spent on food purchases will decrease. By extension, the poorer a country is, the larger the average income (or average expenditure) of each citizen, the greater the proportion of expenditure on food purchases. As the country becomes richer, this proportion tends to decrease.

The United Nations uses the Engel coefficient to evaluate a country's wealth. The specific criteria are as follows:

(1) Absolute poverty (绝对贫穷)＞60%.

(2) Intensity-free days (勉强度日)50%～60%.

(3) Well-off level (小康水平)40%～50%.

(4) Wealth level (富裕水平)30%～40%.

(5) The richest level (最富裕水平)＜30%.

The proportion of China's three industries in 2019 is 7.1∶39∶53.9, the contribution rate of final consumption expenditure to GDP growth is 57.8%, and the national residents' Engel coefficient is 28.2%.

2. Gini Coefficient

The Gini Index(or Coefficient) was first proposed by Corrado Gini, an Italian statistician and sociologist in 1912. A common indicator used to measure the income gap of residents in a country or region.

The specific division of Gini coefficient is based on the regulations of relevant organizations such as the United Nations Development Program:

(1) Gini coefficient is lower than 0.2, income is highly average;(高度平均)

(2) Gini coefficient 0.2～0.29, income is relatively average;(比较平均)

(3) Gini coefficient is 0.3～0.39, income is relatively reasonable;(相对合理)

(4) The Gini coefficient is 0.4～0.59, and the income gap is large;(差距较大)

(5) The Gini coefficient is above 0.6, and the income gap is huge.(差距悬殊)

According to statistics from the United Nations Development Program, China's Gini coefficient is around 0.45 in 2019. Due to the existence of hidden benefits for some groups, the actual income gap in China is even higher. This should arouse a high degree of vigilance, otherwise it will cause a series of social problems, which will cause social unrest and endanger social stability.

If the Engel coefficient and Gini coefficient are used alone, these indicators often can not truly reflect the actual standard of living and the gap between the rich and the poor. They should be used in combination to make more sense. For example, combining with Maslow's hierarchy of needs and the reality of social development and changes.

Table 5.11 Overview of the World Economic Outlook Projections①

(Percentage change, unless noted otherwise)	Year over Year								
				Difference from April 2020			Q4 over Q4 2/		
			Projections		WEO Projection 1/		Projection		
	2018	2019	2020	2021	2020	2021	2019	2020	2021
World Output	3.6	2.9	−4.9	5.4	−1.9	−0.4	2.8	−3.5	4.6
Advanced Economies	2.2	1.7	−8.0	4.8	−1.9	0.3	1.5	−7.2	5.1
United States	2.9	2.3	−8.0	4.5	−2.1	−0.2	2.3	−8.2	5.4
Euro Are	1.9	1.3	−10.2	6	−2.7	1.3	1	−8.6	5.8
Germany	1.5	0.6	−7.8	5.4	−0.8	0.2	0.4	−6.7	5.5
France	1.8	1.5	−12.5	7.3	−5.3	2.8	0.9	−8.9	4.2
Italy	0.8	0.3	−12.8	6.3	−3.7	1.5	0.1	−10.9	5.5
Spain	2.4	2	−12.8	6.3	−4.8	2	1.8	−11.4	6.3
Japan	0.3	0.7	−5.8	2.4	−0.6	−0.6	−0.7	−1.8	0
United Kingdom	1.3	1.4	−10.2	6.3	−3.7	2.3	1.1	−9.0	6.9
Canada	2	1.7	−8.4	4.9	−2.2	0.7	1.5	−7.5	4.6
Other Advanced Economies 3/	2.7	1.7	−4.8	4.2	−0.2	−0.3	1.9	−5.1	5.5
Emerging Market and Developing Economies	4.5	3.7	−3.0	5.9	−2.0	−0.7	3.9	−0.5	4.2

① Note: Real effective exchange rates are assumed to remain constant at the levels prevailing during April 21—May 19, 2020. Economies are listed on the basis of economic size. The aggregated quarterly data are seasonally adjusted. WEO = World Economic Outlook.

1/Difference based on rounded figures for the current and April 2020 WEO forecasts. Countries whose forecasts have been updated relative to April 2020. WEO forecasts account for 90 percent of world GDP measured at purchasing-power-parity weights.

2/For World Output, the quarterly estimates and projections account for approximately 90 percent of annual world output at purchasing-power-parity weights. For emerging market and developing economies, the quarterly estimates and projections account for approximately 80 percent of annual emerging market and developing economies' output at purchasing-powerparity weights.

3/Excludes the Group of Seven (Canada, France, Germany, Italy, Japan, United Kingdom, United States) and euro area countries.

4/For India, data and forecasts are presented on a fiscal year basis and GDP from 2011 onward is based on GDP at market prices with fiscal year 2011/12 as a base year.

5/Indonesia, Malaysia, Philippines, Thailand, Vietnam.

6/Simple average of growth rates for export and import volumes (goods and services).

7/Simple average of prices of UK Brent, Dubai Fateh, and West Texas Intermediate crude oil. The average price of oil in US dollars a barrel was \$61.39 in 2019; the assumed price, based on futures markets (as of May 19, 2020), is \$36.18 in 2020 and \$37.54 in 2021.

8/The inflation rate for the euro area is 0.2% in 2020 and 0.9% in 2021, for Japan is −0.1% in 2020 and 0.3% in 2021, and for the United States is 0.5% in 2020 and 1.5% in 2021.

9/Excludes Venezuela.

Continued

(Percentage change, unless noted otherwise)	Year over Year								
	Difference from April 2020						Q4 over Q4 2/		
			Projections		WEO Projection 1/		Projection		
Emerging and Developing Asia	6.3	5.5	−0.8	7.4	−1.8	−1.1	5	2.4	3.9
China	6.7	6.1	1	8.2	−0.2	−1.0	6	4.4	4.3
India 4/	6.1	4.2	−4.5	6	−6.4	−1.4	3.1	0.2	1.2
ASEAN-5.5/	5.3	4.9	−2.0	6.2	−1.4	−1.6	4.6	−1.4	6.1
Emerging and Developing Europe Russia	3.2	2.1	−5.8	4.3	−0.6	0.1	3.4	−7.0	6.6
Russia	2.5	1.3	−6.6	4.1	−1.1	0.6	2.2	−7.5	5.6
Latin America and the Caribbean	1.1	0.1	−9.4	3.7	−4.2	0.3	−0.2	−9.0	4.1
Brazil	1.3	1.1	−9.1	3.6	3.8	0.7	1.6	−9.3	4.5
Mexico	2.2	−0.3	−10.5	3.3	−3.9	0.3	−0.8	−10.1	4.8
Middle East and Central Asia	1.8	1	−4.7	3.3	−1.9	−0.7	…	…	…
Saudi Arabia	2.4	0.3	−6.8	3.1	−4.5	0.2	−0.3	−4.4	4.1
Sub-Saharan Africa	3.2	3.1	−3.2	3.4	−1.6	−0.7	…	…	…
Nigeria	1.9	2.2	−5.4	2.6	−2.0	0.2	…	…	…
Sourth Africa	0.8	0.2	−8.0	3.5	−2.2	−0.5	−0.6	−2.1	−2.8
Memorandum									
Low-Income Developing Countries	5.1	5.2	−1.0	5.2	−1.4	−0.4	…	…	…
World Growth Based on Market Exchange Rates	3.1	2.4	−6.1	5.3	−1.9	−0.1	2.3	−4.9	4.8
World Trade Volume (goods and services)6/	3.8	0.9	−11.9	8	−0.9	−0.4	…	…	…
Advanced Economies	3.4	1.5	−13.4	7.2	−1.3	−0.2	…	…	…
Emerging Market and Developing Economies	4.5	0.1	−9.4	9.4	−0.5	−0.7	…	…	…
Commodity Prices (U.S. dollars)Oil 7/	29.4	−10.2	−41.1	3.8	0.9	−2.5	−6.1	−42.6	12.2
Nonfuel(average based on World commodity import weights)	1.3	0.8	0.2	0.8	1.3	1.4	4.9	−0.8	1.3
Consumer Prices									
Advanced Economies 8/	2	1.4	0.3	1.1	−0.2	−0.4	1.4	−0.1	1.5
Emerging Market and Developing Economies 9/	4.8	5.1	4.4	4.5	−0.2	0	5	3.1	4

Continued

(Percentage change, unless noted otherwise)	Year over Year								
	Difference from April 2020						Q4 over Q4 2/		
			Projections		WEO Projection 1/		Projection		
London Interbank Offered Rate(percent)									
On U.S. Dollar Deposits(six month)	2.5	2.3	0.9	0.6	0.2	0	…	…	…
On Euro Deposits (three month)	−0.3	−0.4	−0.4	−0.4	0	0	…	…	…
On Japanese Yen Deposits(six month)	0	0	0	−0.1	0.1	0	…	…	…

Source: World Economic Outlook, June 2020.

Table 5.12 General Government Fiscal Balance and Gross Debt, 2018—2021: Overall Balance and Gross Debt①

(Percent of GDP) International Monetary Fund, June 2020

	Overall Fiscal Balance						Gross Debt					
			Current Projections		Difference from Projections				Current Projections		Difference from Projections	
	2018	2019	2020	2021	2020	2021	2018	2019	2020	2021	2020	2021
World	−3.1	−3.9	13.9	−8.2	−4	−2	81.2	82.8	101.5	103.2	5.1	6.6
Croup of Twenty(G20)	−3.7	−4.5	−15.4	−9.1	−4.6	−2.2	88.6	90.4	111.2	113.3	5.7	7.5
Advanced Economies	−2.7	−3.3	−16.6	−8.3	−6	−2.8	104	105.2	131.2	132.3	8.8	10.4
Advanced G20	−3.3	−4	−18	−9.1	−6.5	−3	111.6	113.2	141.4	142.9	9.6	11.5

① Note: All country averages are weighted by nominal GDP converted to US dollars (adjusted by purchasing power parity only for world output) at average market exchange rates in the years indicated and based on data availability. Projections are based on IMF staff assessments of current policies. In many countries, 2020 data are still preliminary. For country-specific details, see "Data and Conventions" and Table s A, B, C, and D in the April 2020 Fiscal Monitor Methodological and Statistical Appendix. MENAP = Middle East, North Africa, and Pakistan; WEO = World Economic Outlook.

1 For cross-country comparability, expenditure and fiscal balances of the United States are adjusted to exclude the imputed interest on unfunded pension liabilities and the imputed compensation of employees, which are counted as expenditures under the 2008 System of National Accounts (2008 SNA) adopted by the United States but not in countries that have not yet adopted the 2008 SNA. Data for the United States in this table may thus differ from data published by the US Bureau of Economic Analysis.

2 Including financial sector support.

3 For cross-economy comparability, gross debt levels reported by national statistical agencies for countries that have adopted the 2008 System of National Accounts (Australia, Canada, Hong Kong SAR, United States) are adjusted to exclude unfunded pension liabilities of government employees' defined-benefit pension plans.

4 Gross debt refers to the non-financial public sector, excluding Eletrobras and Petrobras, and includes sovereign debt held by the central bank.

Continued

	Overall Fiscal Balance						Gross Debt					
			Current Projections		Difference from Projections				Current Projections		Difference from Projections	
	2018	2019	2020	2021	2020	2021	2018	2019	2020	2021	2020	2021
United States[1,3]	−5.8	−6.3	−23.8	−12.4	−8.4	−3.7	106.9	108.7	141.4	146.1	10.4	14.2
Euro Area	−0.5	−0.6	−11.7	−5.3	−4.2	−1.7	85.8	84.1	105.1	103	7.7	7.4
Germany	1.9	1.5	10.7	−3.1	−5.2	−1.9	61.9	59.8	77.2	75	8.6	9.3
France	−2.3	−3	−13.6	−7.1	−4.5	−0.8	98.1	98.1	125.7	123.8	10.2	7.4
Italy	−2.2	−1.6	−12.7	−7	−4.4	−3.5	134.8	134.8	166.1	161.9	10.6	11.4
Spain[2]	−2.5	−2.8	−13.9	−8.3	−4.4	−1.6	97.6	95.5	123.8	124.1	10.4	9.5
Japan	−2.5	−3.3	−14.7	−6.1	−7.6	−4.1	236.6	238	268	265.4	16	17.8
United Kingdom	−2.2	−2.1	−12.7	−6.7	−4.4	−1.3	85.7	85.4	101.6	100.5	5.9	4.7
Canada[3]	−0.4	−0.3	−12.6	−5.8	−0.8	−1.9	89.7	88.6	109.3	108.8	−0.3	0.3
Australia	−1.2	−3.9	−8.6	−8.4	1.1	−1	41.5	45	56.8	64.3	−2.5	0.3
Kkrea	2.6	0.4	−3.6	−2.4	−1.7	−0.8	40	41.9	49.5	53.4	3.2	4.3
Emerging Market Economies	−3.8	−4.9	−10.6	−8.5	−1.5	−1	48.9	52.4	63.1	66.7	1.1	2.1
Excluding MENAP Oil Producers	−4	−5	−10.6	−8.5	−1.6	−1.1	50.4	53.9	64.4	68.1	0.9	2
Emerging G20	−4.3	−5.4	−11.3	−9.1	−1.6	−1	49.4	53	64.1	68.3	0.8	1.8
Asia	−4.5	−6	−11.4	−9.8	−1.5	−1.3	49.3	53.5	64.9	70.3	0.8	2.3
China	−4.7	−6.3	−12.1	−10.7	−0.9	−1.1	47	52	64.1	70.7	−0.8	0.6
India	−6.3	−7.9	−12.1	−9.4	−4.6	−2.1	69.6	72.2	84	85.7	9.6	11.9
Indonesia	−1.8	−2.2	−6.3	−5	−1.3	−1	30.1	30.5	37.7	40.3	0.8	2.8
Eurpoe	0.4	−0.6	−6.9	−4.8	−0.7	−0.6	29.3	29	36.4	37.1	0	0.8
Russia	2.9	1.9	−5.5	−3.9	−0.6	−0.9	13.5	13.9	18.5	18.8	0.6	1.7
Turkey	−3.7	−5.3	−8.4	−7.5	−0.9	−0.8	30.4	33	40.4	42.2	1.1	1.5
Latin America	−5.2	−4	−10.3	−4.8	−3.6	−0.9	66.6	70.6	81.5	79.7	3.6	3.6
Brazil[4]	[4] −7.2	−6	−16	−5.9	−6.6	0.2	87.1	89.5	102.3	100.6	4.1	2.4
Mexico	−2.2	−2.3	−6	−4	−1.8	−1.8	53.6	53.7	65.9	66.3	4.6	7.3
MENAP	−2.9	−3.9	−9.8	−7.8	0	−0.1	40.1	44.7	55.2	56.4	4	3.6
Saudi Arabia	−5.9	−4.5	−11.4	−5.6	1.2	3.4	19	22.8	35.2	36.8	1.1	−1.9
South Africa	−4.1	−6.3	−14.8	−11	−1.5	1.6	56.7	62.2	79.9	84.6	2.5	−1
Low-Income Developing Countries	−3.8	−4.1	−6.1	−5.1	−0.4	−0.2	42.9	43.1	48.2	49	0.8	1.3
Nigeria	−4.3	−5	−7.3	−5.7	−0.9	0.2	27.7	29.1	36.5	36.8	1.2	−0.1
Oil Producers	−0.6	−1	−8.4	−5.5	−0.8	−1	42.7	45.1	56.1	56.6	1.5	2.2

Continued

	Overall Fiscal Balance						Gross Debt					
			Current Projections		Difference from Projections				Current Projections		Difference from Projections	
	2018	2019	2020	2021	2020	2021	2018	2019	2020	2021	2020	2021
Memorandum												
World Output(percent)	3.6	2.9	−4.9	−5.4	−1.9	−0.3						

Source：IMF staff estimates and projections.

The Chapter's Referential Questions　本章参考题

(1) How is the economic growth of the world's major economies in recent years?
世界主要经济体近几年经济增长状况如何?

(2) How is the World Bank's standard for national income divided?
世界银行关于国家收入的标准是怎么划分的?

(3) According to Rostow's theory of stages of economic development，what stage is China's economy currently in?
按照罗斯托经济发展阶段理论,中国经济目前处于哪一阶段?

(4) Since urbanization is an inevitable trend，how can Chinese companies entering the international market grasp this trend?
既然城市化是必然趋势,中国企业进军国际市场应如何把握这一趋势?

Further Reading
拓展阅读

Chapter 6

The Political Environment of International Marketing
国际市场营销的政治环境

Learning Objectives
本章学习目标

(1) Type of government.
政府的类型。
(2) The political risk and how to avoid it.
政治风险及如何规避。
(3) Risks related to government economic policies.
与政府经济政策有关的风险。
(4) The impact of terrorism on international political stability.
恐怖活动对国际政治稳定性的影响。

Key Words
关键词

Political Stability; Political Risks; Nationalism; Confiscation; Expropriation; Nationalization; Domestication; Violence; Civil unrest

6.1 Uncertainty ahead, Trade Tensions Threaten Political Stability
未来不确定性、贸易紧张威胁政治稳定

Case Studies 6.1

Businesses have arguably never faced such a breadth of challenges as they do today. From emerging economies to mature ones, business and trade are increasingly susceptible to uncertainty, with political risks posing a threat to their business interests.

Businesses operating in both developed and emerging markets face a complex and often volatile political risk landscape in 2020. Issues related to global trade will continue, resulting in persistent political and economic uncertainty for businesses.

Rising geopolitical tensions, commodity-price volatility, political violence, and separatist movements are exacerbating political risks globally for foreign investors.

As the geopolitical landscape becomes increasingly uncertain, multinational organisations and financial institutions have elevated their awareness of the challenges inherent challenges in operating in areas of concern. Seemingly tranquil countries and regions can erupt quickly, and the nature of events is increasingly unpredictable. The risk of business interests being concentrated in just one, or a few, regions is an issue among companies that operate in emerging risk areas.

Rising geopolitical and geo-economic tensions represent the "most urgent global risks at present", according to the World Economic Forum's Global Risks Report 2019. Marsh's Political Risk Map 2019, based on data from Fitch Solutions, highlights changes from 2018 and looks ahead to ongoing risks, including continuing US-China tensions, trade wars, Brexit and changes within the Eurozone, the future of Iran's and North Korea's nuclear programs, and tensions between Russia and the West.

The transition to a more multi-polar world order protectionism is likely to continue. While the US, China, Russia, and to a lesser extent, the EU and Japan, will remain the most powerful players, emerging powers such as India, Iran, Saudi Arabia, Turkey and Brazil will be increasingly important players.

The US and China are intensifying geopolitical rivaly in the Indo-Pacific region, with both stepping up military activities in the South China Sea, an unintended military clash is possible. Meanwhile, Russia's relations with the West will remain tense in 2019 as a result of the Kremlin's alleged interference in US and EU domestic politics, the Skripal poisoning incident in the UK, laboratory hacking in Switzerland and conflicts in Syria and Ukraine. All of these could lead to more US and/or EU sanctions on Russia. Former president of US——Donald Trump's withdrawal from the 1987 US-Soviet Intermediate Range Nuclear Forces Treaty also raises the possibility of a new missile build-up in Europe.

As Fitch Solutions note, 2019 will be a busy year for auctions in emerging markets and some developed countries, which is likely to add to the buoyant mood globally.

Isolationist and protectionist sentiments and practices have been raized in some countries, halting, at least momentarily, the process of globalization. Actions in one economy create reactions in others. Against this backdrop, it could be proved more difficult for nations to make collective progress on global challenges.

Global trade is increasingly afflicted by uncertainty, with perhaps the biggest current cause being the ongoing trade dispute between the US and China. An export-heavy economy such as Germany is inevitably influenced. This uncertainty is compounded by Brexit, the exact nature and effects of which are still unclear. At the same time, there is a "fear factor" rippling through the global economy, and in some cases, there has been a retrenchment of liberal values and a political shift to the right.

Economic uncertainty can play a social and cultural role, and can easily change its forms and spread across continents. For example, disruptions to supply chains and/or economic slowdown in individual economy may well be recongized far beyond their own borders. More than ever, political risks in one part of the world or sector are likely to spill over into other regions or sectors, often causing unexpected harm.

What is most noticeable today is how many of the macro threats are in so-called developed economies as opposed to emerging markets. Vigilance and broad, systemic risk analysis will be vital to minimizing these risks.

The transition toward a multipolar world order in 2019—with multiple challenges to multilateralism and free trade is expected. Although the US and China have reached a "phase one" trade deal, it is unlikely to permanently resolve their trade dispute. The two countries are likely to remain strategically at odds over issues such as protection of intellectual property and state support for certain industries. Indeed, the World Economic Forum's Global Risks Report 2020 states: "Economic confrontations between major powers is the most concerning risk for 2020."

Sino-American rivalry is expected to deepen in 2020, particularly as the US presidential election approaches in November. The tech industry is expected to emerge as a particular battleground for the two countries, as both look to reduce technological dependence on the other. Businesses will be caught up in this rivalry, as the two countries politicize trade and investment relationships. Chinese telecoms firm Huawei embodies these challenges—the US has increased pressure on allies to not use the company's technology—a situation that is unlikely to change in 2020. Economies globally will increasingly have to choose between US and Chinese technology partners.

Geopolitics will dominate the risk environment in the Middle East. Iran and the US appear to be seeking a de-escalation following a significant flare-up in early 2020, which saw the targeted killing of an Iranian general by the US followed by ballistic missile launches against US facilities in Iraq. However, the US-Iran relationship is unlikely to improve and will generate instability in the region. Iran's accidental shooting down of a passenger plane during the recent incidents with the US is likely to strain relations with the international community, while European governments have formally triggered a dispute mechanism in the 2015 nuclear deal, increasing pressure on its sustainability. Iran may use its asymmetric capabilities to retaliate against the US, using its proxies to carry out targeted attacks or bombings, including cyber-attacks, across the region. Iran may also seek to put pressure on the US' regional allies, asserting itself in the Strait of Hormuz, where any significant disruption could impact oil supplies and thus the global economy. Iraq is likely to be the immediate focal point for US-Iranian confrontations, elevating political risk in the country. For example, one result of the January clash between the US and Iran in 2020 has been increased calls within Iraq for US troops to leave the country, a move that could contribute to resurging terrorism risks in Iraq.

Elsewhere, tensions between Russia and the West are expected to continue in 2020. Russia's increased role in the Middle East will continue to grow, for example, its support for the Syrian government. As the US presidential election plays out, much attention will be placed on any Russian attempts to interfere as it did in the 2016 election, straining relations further. In Europe, although the UK left the EU on January 31,2020, its future relationship with the EU—from economic to political and security—will take years to address.

The 2020 election is also looming. The US electorate is highly polarized, with former President Trump's impeachment exacerbating divisions, despite his acquittal on February 5 of 2020. The election may also see deep fake media adding to the risks.

6.2 Government Types 政府类型

6.2.1 Division Basis 划分依据

From the government type definitions provided by the Economist Intelligence Unit (EIU), based on country scores from its annual Democracy Index. The four types of regimes are defined as:

① Full democracies: Countries in which basic political freedom and civil liberty are respected by the government, people and the culture. Elections are free and fair. The government is generally well functioning and mostly free from bias and corruption due to systems of checks and balances.

② Flawed democracies: Countries in which elections are free and fair and basic civil liberty are respected. There may be significant weaknesses in other areas of democracy, such as problems in governance, minimal political participation or infringement on media freedom.

③ Hybrid regimes: States that hold elections that are not necessarily free and fair. There may be widespread corruption and weak rule of law, with problems regarding government functioning, political culture and political participation. The media and

the judiciary are likely to be under government influence.

④ Authoritarian regimes: Countries in which political pluralism is absent or severely limited, many of which can be characterised as dictatorships. Corruption, infringement of civil liberty, repression and censorship are common. The media and the judiciary are not independent of the ruling regime.

6.2.2 Government Performance 政府表现

Authoritarian regimes were the only type of government to register a fall in civil unrest. The largest number of incidences occurred in flawed democracies and hybrid regimes over the period 2011 to 2018. They also had the highest rates of violence, with riots making up 37 percent of all incidents of unrest in hybrid regime countries.

Civil unrest also increased the most in flawed democracies, followed by hybrid regimes. Figure 6.1 gives the trends in total civil unrest by regime type. Events include riots, general strikes, and non-violent anti-government demonstrations. The rate of civil unrest events per country increased tenfold in flawed democracies.

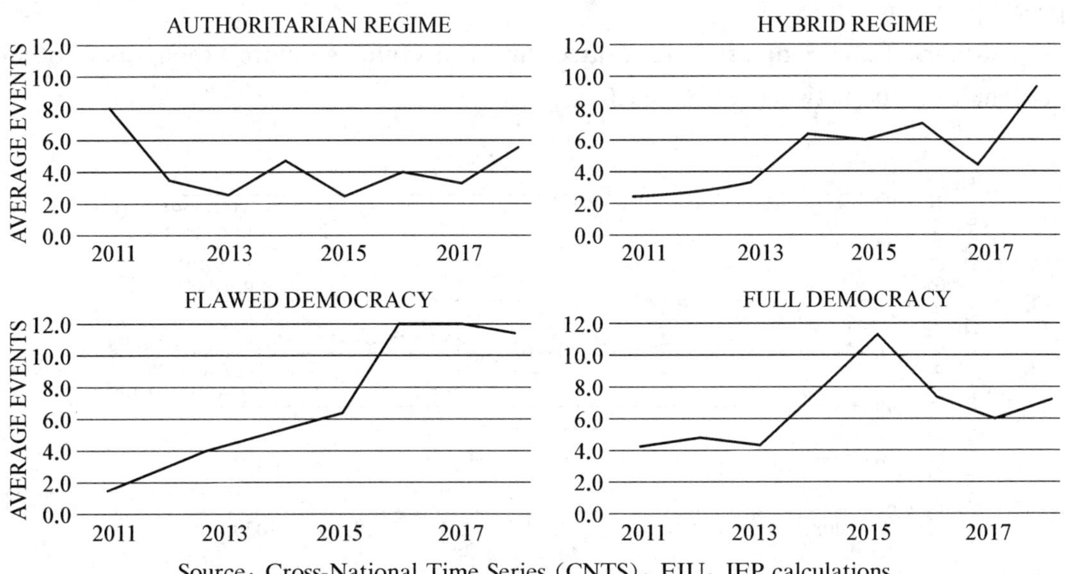

Source: Cross-National Time Series (CNTS), EIU, IEP calculations.

Figure 6.1 Civil Unrest by Government Type, 2011 to 2018

The rate of civil unrest in authoritarian regimes declined 30 percent from 2011 to 2018, with the sharpest fall occurring during the 2012 Arab Winter. However, the trend rose substantially for the other three government types. The largest increase occurred in flawed democracies, where the rate of demonstrations increased tenfold. Levels nearly quadrupled in hybrid regime countries and nearly doubled in full democracies.

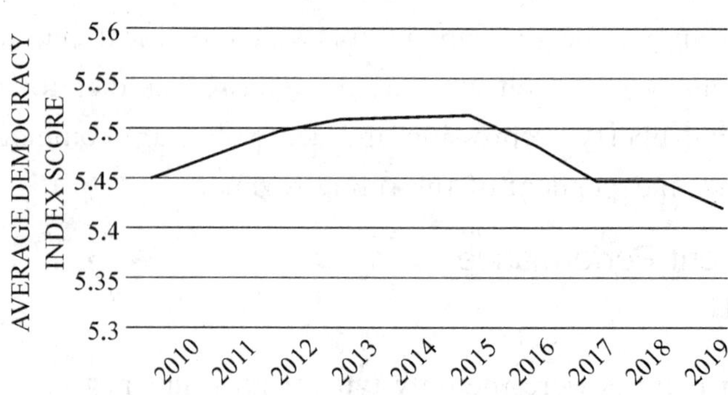

Source: EIU democracy index.

Figure 6.2 EIU Democracy Index Average Score, 2010—2019

Coinciding with the increase in protests around the world, the strength of democratic institutions continued to fall, as shown in Figure 6.2. The average country score on the democracy index is now at its lowest point in 14 years. From 2011 to 2019, the number of riots, general strikes and anti-government demonstrations around the world increased by 244 percent. As civil unrest has been increasing, democracy has been decreasing while.

Authoritarian regimes deteriorated in peacefulness more than any other government type between 2008—2020.

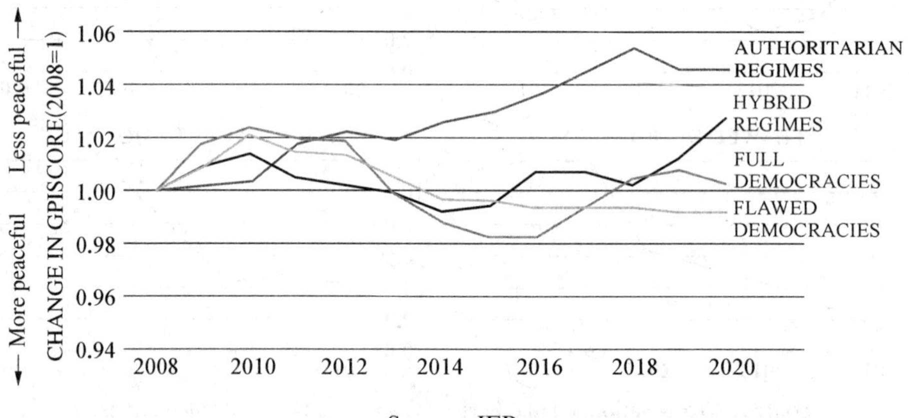

Source: IEP.

Figure 6.3 GPI Overall Trend by Government Type, 2008—2020

The 25 least peaceful countries deteriorated in peacefulness by an average of 12.9 percent, while the most peaceful improved by 2.1 percent.

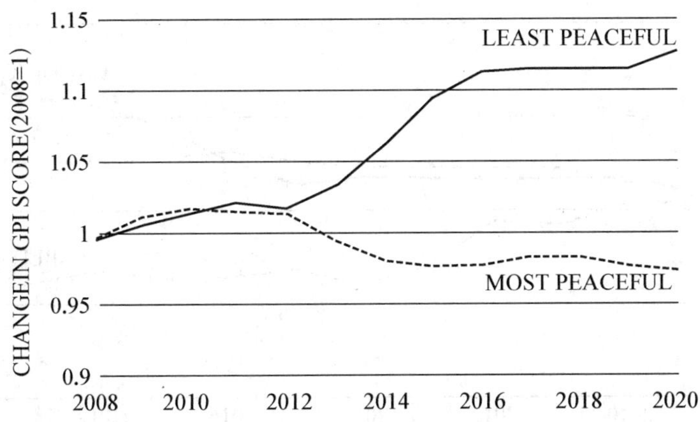

Figure 6.4 Trend in Peace 2008—2020, Most and Least Peaceful Countries

6.3 Evaluating on Political Risks 关于政治风险的评估

A company has several resources at its disposal to evaluate country risk: The Department of state, the Department of Commerce other governmental and non-governmental agencies provide data on country political risk that is current and continually updated to reflect new developments in each country around the world. Some examples of useful publications providing periodic information on country risk are:

① Business periodicals such as *The Economist* and *The Wall Street Journal*, particularly the European and Asian editions;

② Commercial sources, such as Country Report, the Economist Intelligence Unit, the World Business Intelligence. For example, they provide information on political developments, currency, and the regulatory insurance data and trade information, as well as a country risk rating on a scale from 1 to 10, and risk perception and collection experience for the previous 4 months.

6.3.1 Political Risk Signals 政治风险的信号

A number of country risk elements should be monitored on a regular basis to keep track of developments that might ultimately affect the international company. We focus on the GPI, which reflects, to some extent, some of the current signals on political peace.

Militarisation was the only domain to record an improvement since 2008.

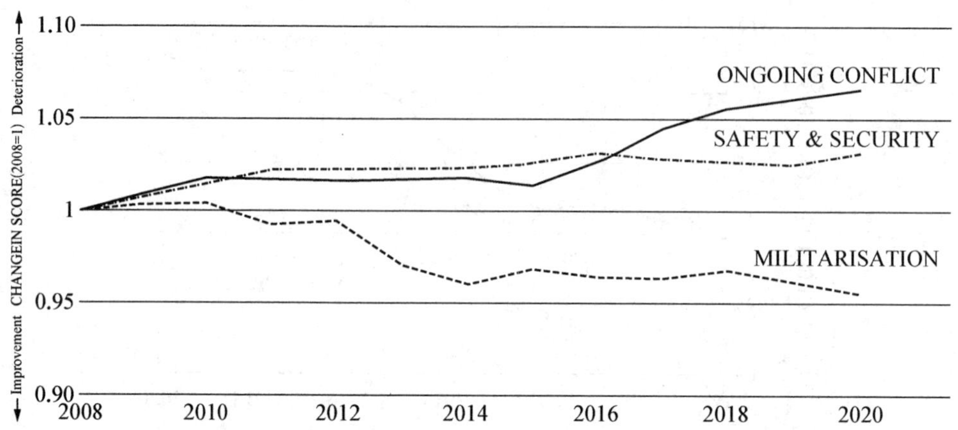

Figure 6.5 Indexed Trend in Peacefulness by Domain, 2008 to 2020 (2008=1)

The terrorism impact indicator had the largest overall change from 2008 to 2020.

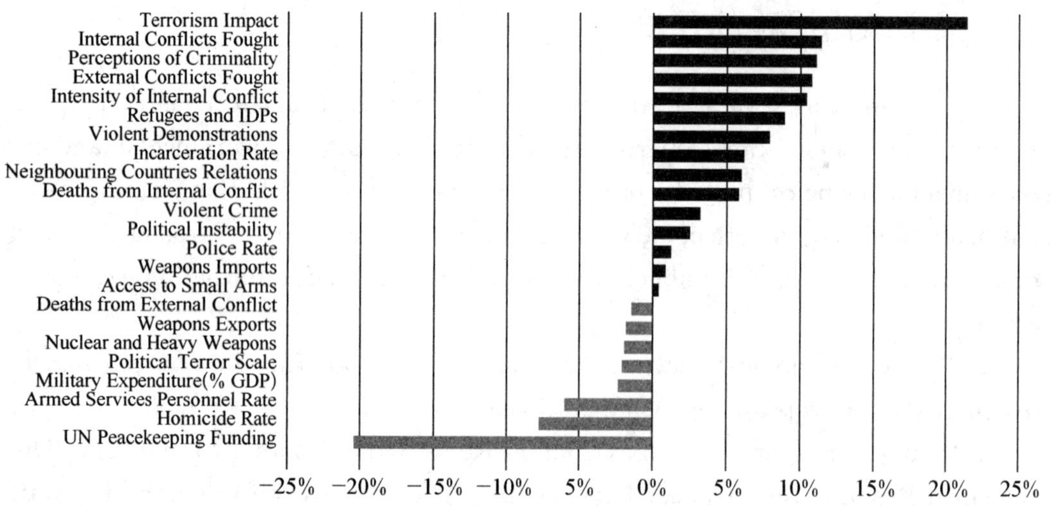

Figure 6.6 Percentage change by Indicator, 2008—2020

The Safety and Security domain deteriorated 3.3 percent between 2008 and 2020. Of the 11 domain indicators, nine deteriorated, with the largest number of countries deteriorating on the terrorism impact indicator. The homicide rate indicator had the largest improvement, with 123 countries recording an improvement. The refugees and IDPs indicator had the most significant change, with the total number of refugees and internally displaced people increasing from just under 25 millions in 2008, to over 65 millions in 2019.

Table 6.1 Safety and Security Domain-Top Five

Rank	Country	2020 Score	Score change	Rank change
1	Iceland	1.164	0.033	—
2	Singapore	1.224	−0.009	—
3	Japan	1.256	−0.021b	↑1
4	Norway	1.256	0.018	—
5	Switzerland	1.277	0.00c	↓1

Safety and Security Domain-Bottom Five

Rank	Country	2020 Score	Score change	Rank change
163	Afghanistan	4.275	0.072	—
162	Iraq	4.15	0.103	↓2
161	South Sudan	4.074	−0.01	↑1
160	Venezuela	4.034	0.364	↑5
159	Congo, DRC	3.982	0.001	—

While battle deaths have fallen since 2014, the total number of conflicts has increased.

Source: UCDP, EIU, IEP calculations.

Figure 6.7 Trends in Key Ongoing Conflict Indicators

Table 6.2 Ongoing Conflict Domain-Top Five

Rank	Country	2020 Score	Score change	Rank change
=1	Botswana	1	0	—
=1	Mauritius	1	0	—
=1	Singapore	1	−0.001	↑4
=1	Uruguay	1	0	—
5	Bulgaria	1.001	−0.001	↑1

Ongoing Conflict Domain-Bottom Five

Rank	Country	2020 Score	Score change	Rank change
163	Syria	3.828	0	—
162	Afghanistan	3.641	0	—
161	Yemen	3.621	0.118	—
160	Congo，DRC	3.379	0.03	↓1
159	Pakistan	3.35	−0.069	↑1

Both the armed forces rate and average military expenditure have fallen since 2008.

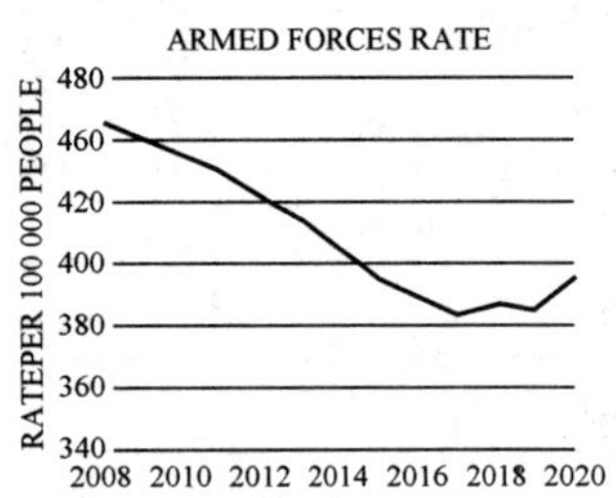

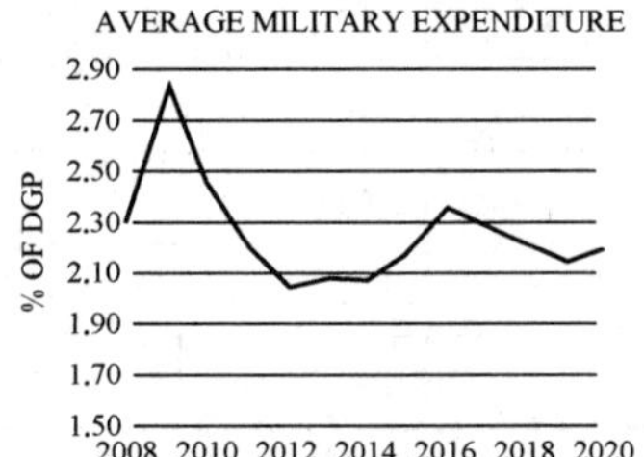

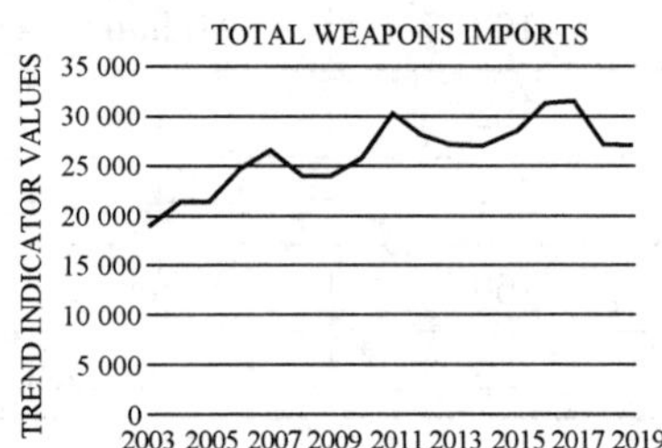

Source：IISS，SIPRI，IEP calculations.

Figure 6.8 Trends in key Militarisation Indicators

Table 6.3 Militarisation Domain-Top Five

Rank	Country	2020 Score	Score change	Rank change
1	Iceland	1.029	−0.003	—
2	Hungary	1.151	0	—
3	New Zealand	1.17	−0.016	↑1
4	Slovenia	1.17	−0.009	—
5	Moldova	1.236	−0.005	—

Militarisation Domain-Bottom Five

Rank	Country	2020 Score	Score change	Rank change
163	Israel	3.914	0.034	—
162	Russia	3.241	−0.011	—
161	North Korea	3.224	0.167	↓1
160	United States	3.06	−0.013	↑1
159	France	2.767	0.001	—

6.3.2 Economic Performance 经济运行

A poor economic performance and disruption are likely to lead to greater level of unrest in the country. Or of particular concern are high rate of inflation and unemployment, both of which could lead to political instability.

General business performance is also important. Commercial payment terms and collection experience indicate the availability of hard currency reserves and access to hard currency. Default on loans is likely to be a threat to companies contemplating entrance into the market. Finally, an increase in regulatory restrictions on investment, capital, or trade flows should be closely monitored.

6.4 Nationalism 关于民族主义

The expression of fierce nationalist sentiment, or nationalism, in a country where the company is operating could constitute a cause for concern to the international company. The expression of nationalist feelings, such as pride in a country's history and accomplishments, are common in most counties.

Nationalist sentiment may indicate an attempt at separation from or isolation of a particular segment of society, which could lead to political instability in the country; this is the case of the Tamil separatist movement in Sri Lanka, which led to economic chaos in the country. Particularly problematic for international business are expressions of anti-foreigner sentiment and anti-foreign business bias. In 1980s, the "buy American" slogans in the US echoing especially in the automobile and textile industries brought great concern to European and Asian business and private investors. Of special concern to international marketing managers is consumer ethnocentrism, the belief that buying foreign goods will drive local companies out of business and is, consequently, morally wrong. Countries where such beliefs predominate are more likely to erect barriers to international trade.

Thailand experienced a military coup in September 2006, resulting in new rules in foreign investment that frightened foreign investors. The military-appointed cabinet initiated more stringent laws of foreign ownership, requiring investors to sell holdings that exceed 50 percent ownership in companies based in Thailand and to give up voting rights in excess of 50 percent. U.S. firms are protected from this rule by a treaty with Thailand that dates back to the Vietnam War, but European and Japanese companies were seriously affected. The Foreign Business Act bans foreigners from taking majority shares in Thai businesses ranging from the media, rice farming, production of Buddha images, legal services, and construction.

6.5 Political Risks and Risk Management 政治风险及其管控

Nationalism and claims to national sovereignty can lead to protectionist measures on the part of the host country government, whereas political instability can lead to failure of the economy. All can harm the operations of the company in the respective country, from injuring its sales and overall prospects in the market to completely losing company assets.

"Risks Related to Government Economic Policy", "Risks Related to labor and Action Groups" and "Risks Related to Terrorism" are examples of risks a company can experience in international market.

6.5.1 Risks Related to Government Trade Policies 与政府对外贸易政策有关的风险

The host country government can erect trade barriers, imposing tariffs and non-tariff barriers on international business, such as exchange-rate controls, voluntary export restraints and other types of quotas, and export/import license requirements. The company could also find itself becoming victim to a trade war, in which the host country and home country reciprocally restrict the flow of goods. Or the company's home country government can impose embargoes and sanctions on the host country, which could force the company to exit the market.

6.5.2 Risks Related to Government Economic Policy 与政府经济政策有关的风险

Local government can use taxes as a means to control foreign investment. During downturns in the local economy, governments find that taxing foreign companies provides a source of huge revenue. Under more extreme conditions, especially if accompanied by a radical change in the political leadership, changes can lead to the (mainly involuntary) transfer of the firm's assets to local (national) ownership. Companies face the following types of risks:

(1) Confiscation 没收财产

Confiscation refers to the seizing of company assets and investors' assets without any compensation. In the 1940s and 1950s, most private companies operating in Central and Eastern Europe had their assets confiscated. More recently, all U.S. firms operating in Iran were confiscated when Shah Reza Pahlavi was dethroned. As a result of the confiscation of U.S. multinationals' assets in Iran after the Islamic Revolution United States imposed an embargo on trade with Iran.

(2) Expropriation 强力征用

Expropriation involves some reimbursement for company assets, usually not at market value. When Fidel Castro ascended to power in Cuba, the assets of U.S. multinationals and U.S. citizens were seized. The Castro government offered payment that was deemed inappropriate, and as a result, the United States imposed an embargo on trade with Cuba that is currently still in effect.

(3) Nationalization 收归国有

Nationalization involves a takeover by the local government with the aim of creating a government run industry. International law recongizes the ligitimacy of nationalization as long as it does the best interest of the public and it offers fair compensation to the international company and its investors. In 1997, the Korean government decided to nationalize the automobile Kia Motors by converting the state-run Korea Development Bank's debt into an equity stake in the company. In the aftermath of the Asian crisis, governments began nationalizing ailing banks across the region: In Indonesia, the government controls nearly all the country's biggest banks and has taken over around 75 percent of all bank assets; whereas in Japan, as a result of nationalization, the government, instead of markets, now plays a larger role in determining the flow of capital.

As mentioned earlier, Thailand now requires European and Japanese foreign investors to sell holdings such that they would ultimately own less than 50 percent of the company: The Foreign Business Act bans foreigners from owning majority shares in Thai businesses. In other examples, Venezuela's former president Hugo Chavez nationalized companies in the telecommunications and electricity industries and attempted to gain more control over natural gas projects. His goal was to change Venezuela into a socialist state with strong state oversight.

(4) Domestication 本土化

Domestication occurs when the local government requires a gradual transfer of ownership and management to locals. This transfer is usually completed over time, through consecutive government decrees aimed at reducing the presence of multinationals in non-essential local sectors (such as the consumer goods sector).

Companies can protect themselves against political instability by understanding the structure of the governments, the political parties, and the ideologies of the ruling party, as well as the competing ideologies of the opposition. As a first step, companies must make every attempt to be exemplary corporate citizens in every country where they operate. A solid reputation for product quality and community involvement can create a general environment that is favorable toward a company's local operations.

A company also can minimize its risk by partnering with local companies, creating local expertise in product manufacturing and management, and using local suppliers. McDonald's, for example, frequently stresses the use of local ingredients in all its products. Similarly, companies that produce products deemed essential to local development, such as industrial products, high-technology products, or pharmaceutical products, are less vulnerable to changes in government policies than companies that manufacture goods considered non-essential, such as consumer goods.

Companies can obtain insurance coverage against nationalization from private insurance sources. For example, companies such as Global Risk Advisors insure against confiscation, expropriation, and nationalization, in addition to providing insurance against war risk, localized or sub-national conflicts kidnapping, ransom, extortion, property terrorism and currency inconvertibility.

6.5.3 Risks Related to Labor and Action Groups 与劳工组织与行动团体相关的风险

In many countries, labor unions have a lot of power and can readily influence national policies. For example, layoffs in foreign companies can bring negative feelings that are likely to affect these companies in the long term. Boycotts initiated by action groups can also negatively affect the companies. Esso (Exxon) was the victim of a "Boycott Esso" campaign aimed at the United State's environmental policies. These actions are not usually sanctioned by national governments, but they are, nevertheless, legal.

Companies have some control over the actions of labor and action groups. Although they cannot control market demand and derived demand for labor, companies can provide severance packages that are fair, as well as invest in the services of job placement businesses in an effort to seek placement for the employees who have been terminated. To avoid negative public sentiment, companies must be politically neutral and keep a distance from local politics. Being too close to a regine can lead to negatire attitude about a company and its produnts. It is important for a firm to be perceived as a good citizen of the country where it operates because a company that has created opportunities for locals and that continues to see their interests.

6.5.4 Risks Related to Terrorism 恐怖主义导致的风险

International terrorist attacks against multinational interests gained worldwide attention with the September 11, 2001, attack on the World Trade Center in New York City. In the years preceding this attack, terrorist attacks steadily increased in frequency. Organizations or businesses with a U.S. connection alone were hit 206 times

in 2000, up from 169 in 1999; internationally, private-sector facilities were attacked 384 times, up from 276 in 1999, whereas only 17 government facilities and 13 military facilities were similarly hit around the globe. Terrorism was most lethal in Asia in the year 2000, with 281 of the 405 international victims perishing then. Africa had the second highest in total, with 73 in dead. In 2003, the number of people killed by terrorism was 625 (with 725 killed the preceding year); and 208 terror incidents took place, with 3,646 people injured.

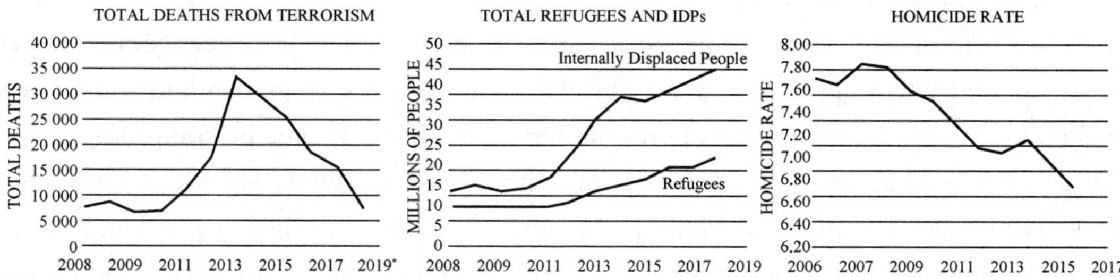

Source: GTD, UNHCR, IDMC, UNDP, IEP calculations.

Figure 6.9　Deaths from Terrorism are now at Their Lowest Level in a Decade

Companies have some control, however, in reducing their likelihood of becoming victims of terrorism by training employees in terrorism avoidance, such as briefing personnel on what to expect when entering high-risk areas and offering training for eluding roadblocks and avoiding hazardous encounters. Companies can also purchase insurance against terrorist acts from private insurance companies. For example, Cigna International's International Specialty Products & Services offers insurance products that cover kidnapping, detention (kidnapping without asking for ransom), hijacking, evacuation, business interruption and extra expenses, product recall expenses, and expenses arising from child abduction (such as hiring private investigators or posting rewards for information).

(1) Risks Related to Violence 暴力导致的风险

Military Expenditure accounts for the highest percentage of the economic impact of violence.The economic impact of terrorism decreased by 48 percent over the year of 2019. It causes a large loss of GDP(Table,见章末拓展阅读资源).

In Syria, Afghanistan and South Sudan, the economic cost of violence was equivalent to more than 50 percent of GDP. Looking at the top ten countries that have caused economic losses due to violence, Even in Sudan, the proportion is more than 20%.The global economic impact of violence improved for the second year in a row, decreasing by 0.2 percent or ＄29 billion from 2018 to 2019. The de-escalation of conflicts, particularly in the MENA region, contributed to the 1.8 percent decline in the global economic impact of violence from 2017(Figure,见章末拓展阅读资源).

Government spending on the military and internal security comprises almost three quarters of the global economic impact of violence. If these expenditures are used to revitalize the economy and people's livelihood, it will inevitably bring more positive contributions to world political stability and economic development.

Five of the nine GPI regions suffered an increase in their economic impact of violence from 2018. The most influential is the Asia-Pacific region, which caused economic losses of US $3,399.0 billion. At the same time, the problems in North America are also very serious.

Forced displacement accounts for nearly two thirds of the global economic impact of armed conflict. At present, various armed conflicts in Afghanistan and some parts of the Middle East have brought many disasters to civilians. Homicide comprises almost half of the global economic impact of interpersonal violence and Self-inflicted Violence. In recent years, especially in the United States, the shooting of blacks once caused turmoil in the United States. At the regional level, military expenditure accounts for between eight and 57 percent of the economic impact of violence. The de-escalation of conflicts, particularly in the MENA region, contributed to the 1.8 percent decline in the global economic impact of violence from 2017.

(2) Risks Related to Military 军事威胁导致的风险

On average, authoritarian regimes spend 3.7 percent of GDP on military expenditure. This is 2.3 percentage points more than the average military expenditure of full democracies, which spend 1.4 percent of GDP on average. As a percentage of GDP, full democracies on average spend 2.3 percentage points less than authoritarian regimes on their military. The military expenditure of China is higher than all the other countries in Asia-Pacific combined(Table,见章末拓展阅读资源).

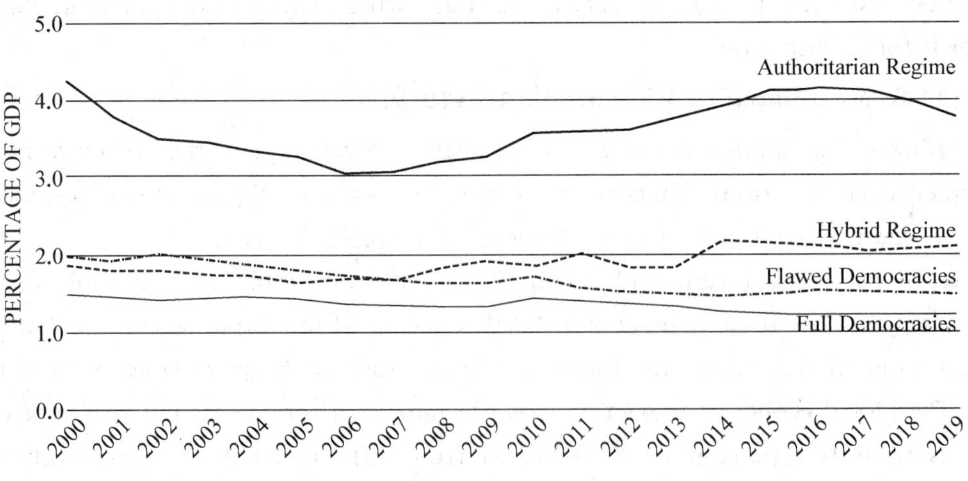

Figure 6.10 Average Military Expenditure by Government Type, 2000—2019

(3) Risks Related to Protest Movements and Civil Unrest
骚乱和抗议导致的风险

Protest movements and civil unrest had been on the rise for the previous decade, as shown in Figure 6.18. Incidents of civil unrest doubled over the last decade. In the eight years leading up to 2018, the available comparable global data shows a 102 percent increase in the number of riots, general strikes and anti-government demonstrations.

The number of both protests and riots roughly doubled, while the number of general strikes quadrupled, from 33 events in 2011 to 135 in 2018.

Every region of the world has experienced hundreds of civil unrest events over the last ten years, as shown in Figure 6.19. Europe had the highest incidence of unrest over the period, with over 1,600 anti-government demonstrations, general strikes and riots. The two regions with the largest increases in civil unrest were sub-Saharan Africa and Europe, although the vast majority of incidences in Europe were non-violent.

Global growth was driven by rises in seven of nine regions. Only MENA had fewer protests, riots and strikes in 2018, when compared to 2011, while levels in North America were stable. Sub-Saharan Africa had the greatest increase, followed by Europe, South Asia, South America, Central America and the Caribbean, Asia-Pacific and Russia and Eurasia. The MENA region had the most significant decline in violent demonstrations, with total unrest falling by 60 percent and the number of riots falling by 50 percent from 2011 to 2018. North America had fewer riots over the period, recording a decline of 27 percent. Incidents of civil unrest doubled over the last decade. The number and intensity of internal conflicts increased, but total conflict deaths fell.

The OECD indices of regulatory heterogeneity captures the regulatory heterogeneity in services. The indices are built from assessing—for each country pair and each measure—whether or not the countries have the same regulation. The regulatory heterogeneity indices take values between zero and one, where zero represents the same regulatory requirement and one indicates regulatory heterogeneity. To give an example, Australia and Austria do not have the requirement that the majority of board of directors must be nationals or residents, while Iceland and Norway do. The heterogeneity index will score the country pairs Australia/Austria and Iceland/Norway zero on this measure because they have the same answer, while Austria and Norway, Australia and Norway, Austria and Iceland, and Australia and Iceland will be scored one because they have different answers.

Table 6.10 illustrates the average regulatory heterogeneity across all services sectors in the database. The average regulatory heterogeneity is the lowest between OECD countries, while the regulatory requirements of China and Russia are relatively different compared with other economies.

Table 6.4 Regulatory heterogeneity is lowest among OECD countries[①]

	OECD	Brazil	China	Colombia	Costa Rica	India	Indonesia	Malaysia	Russian Federation	South Africa
OECD	0.24	0.33	0.41	0.30	0.29	0.40	0.41	0.30	0.37	0.29
Brazil	0.33		0.41	0.31	0.27	0.31	0.35	0.34	0.40	0.34
China	0.41	0.41		0.41	0.44	0.39	0.38	0.45	0.40	0.32
Colombia	0.30	0.31	0.41		0.23	0.36	0.39	0.30	0.36	0.30
Costa Rica	0.29	0.27	0.44	0.23		0.38	0.37	0.29	0.42	0.32
India	0.40	0.31	0.39	0.36	0.38		0.33	0.35	0.41	0.42
Indonesia	0.41	0.35	0.38	0.39	0.37	0.33		0.34	0.45	0.38
Malaysia	0.30	0.34	0.45	0.30	0.29	0.35	0.34		0.42	0.32
Russian Federation	0.37	0.40	0.40	0.36	0.42	0.41	0.45	0.42		0.36
South Africa	0.29	0.34	0.32	0.30	0.32	0.42	0.38	0.32	0.36	

Source: OECD regulatory heterogeneity index 2018.

Nordås and Kox (2009) estimate that if all economies harmonized or recognized each other's regulation to the extent that the heterogeneity index took its lowest bilateral value for all country pairs, total services trade through commercial presence in another country could increase by between 13 and 30 percent depending on the economy. More recently, Nordås (2016) shows that on average, a reduction in the regulatory heterogeneity by 0.05 points is associated with 2.5 percent higher services exports. Furthermore, improved regulatory coherence has a larger trade impact when the level of trade restrictiveness is low. For economies with an average score of the regulatory heterogeneity index (i.e. a heterogeneity index at 0.26), the trade costs amount to an ad valorem equivalent trade cost of between 20 percent and 75 percent at low levels of the STRI.

Conclusion 结语

The international political situation is changing rapidly. In particular, countries with backward economies and complex ethnic conflicts are more likely to attract the attention of international hostile forces. Therefore, to ensure the high-quality

① Note: The regulatory heterogeneity indices take values between zero and one. If two countries have the same answer on all the measures, their bilateral heterogeneity index is zero, and if they have a different answer to all measures, they have a heterogeneity index of one. The regulatory heterogeneity indices are aggregated by a simple average of the indices for different sectors. The indices for OECD countries are aggregated by taking the simple average of the indices for all OECD countries.

economic and social development of a country, a stable political environment is a prerequisite.

A stable, healthy, and prosperous international environment still faces many challenges, especially the threat of Western hegemonism(霸权主义). Therefore, the international political environment requires the cooperation of many parties to maintain and create.

Companies are not powerless in the face of the complex international political environment. One is to improve relations with local governments, and the other is to reduce political fragility.

The Chapter's Referential Questions 本章参考题

(1) According to EIU, what are the four types of government?
根据 EIU 的划分标准,四种政府类型分别是哪些?

(2) What are the basis for identifying the signals of political risk, how to judge?
识别政治风险的信号有哪些依据,如何判断?

(3) What are the manifestations of risks related to economic activities and how to prevent them?
与经济活动有关的风险表现在哪些方面,如何防范?

(4) How should multinational companies prevent and defuse political risks so as to improve their ability to adapt to the international market?
跨国公司应该如何防范和化解政治风险从而提高国际市场适应能力?

Further Reading 拓展阅读

Chapter 7

The Legal Environment of International Marketing 国际市场营销的法律环境

Learning Objectives 本章学习目标

(1) Three types of laws.
三种法律类型。

(2) How the international law, home-country law, and host-country law affect international marketing.
国际法律、母国法律及东道国法律如何影响国际市场营销。

(3) Main legal system.
主要的法律体系。

(4) Implementation and impact of antitrust law.
反垄断法的实施和影响。

Key Words 关键词

International Laws; Host-Country Laws; Home-Country Laws; Common Law; Code Law; Islamic Law; Mediation; Arbitration; Lawsuit; Jurisdiction; Intellectual Property Rights; Antitrust Laws; Article 301

7.1 Three Types of Law 三种法律类型

Case Studies 7.1

7.1.1 International Laws 国际法

It is refered to a body of rules and regulations that countries agree to abide by

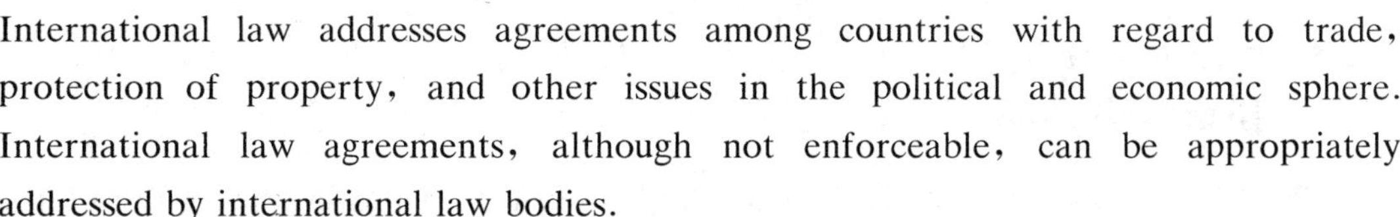

International law addresses agreements among countries with regard to trade, protection of property, and other issues in the political and economic sphere. International law agreements, although not enforceable, can be appropriately addressed by international law bodies.

7.1.2 Host-Country Laws
东道国的法律

These are the laws of the different countries where the company operates. The legal system in the host country could differ substantially from that of the company's home country.

7.1.3 Home-Country Laws
母国法律

The laws of the company's home country. Home-country laws follow the company all over the world. U.S. companies must abide by all three types of law. For example, they must abide by international trade laws and agreements, such as WTO trade regulations; they must abide by host-country laws governing every aspect of the company's operations; and they must abide by home-country laws, such as antitrust regulations and corrupt practice regulations.

7.2 Legal Systems
法律体系

Three legal systems are predominant: Common Law, Code law, and Islamic law.

7.2.1 Common Law
普通法

Common law is based on prior court rulings (legal precedent). It has its roots in English Common Law, on which U.S. law is based. This system of law is shared by many of the countries formerly colonized by the Great Britain.

7.2.2 Code Law or Civil Law
法典法或者公民法

It refers to comprehensive written laws that specify what constitutes legal and non-legal behaviors. Code law has its roots in Roman law. This system of law is shared by most of the places in the world, including most of Europe, Latin America, mainland China, Taiwan China, Japan, and South Korea.

7.2.3 Islamic Law 伊斯兰法

The Islamic law (sha'ria) is a system of law based on the interpretation of the Koran, Islam's holy book, and on interpretations of the practices and sayings of the prophet Muhammad. Islamic law establishes rules for business practices that can affect firms' operations. For example, it requires the sexes to be separated; in practice, this means that women cannot interact in any environment with men with whom they are not related. It bans the consumption of products such as pork and alcohol, it does not allow banks to offer or charge interest, and it requires Muslims to pray five times a day and to fast in the month of Ramadan.

All these factors have an impact on firms' local operations wherever Islamic law constitutes the basis of the legal system—in North Africa and the Middle East and in Pakistan and Malaysia, among others. For example, business activities must be arranged during daily prayer time. During Ramadan, business performance is generally low; in fact, many international businesses rely on the foreign, non-Muslim, workforce to carry out their firms' operations this month.

7.3 Jurisdiction 司法管辖权

Since legal systems differ around the world and international law home-country laws, and host-country laws which govern all aspects of doing business internationally, it is important to establish jurisdiction in international legal disputes. No automatic supranational jurisdiction is assigned to an international court, unless the dispute takes place between companies and/or countries in the European Union; in this case, jurisdiction lies with the European Court of Justice. Legal disputes that arise between governments are usually handled by the International Court of Justice in the Hague, under the United Nations system.

International commercial law is usually handled in the home or host country, or even in a third country, depending on where there is the place for the jurisdiction for the matter under litigation. Because jurisdiction is often difficult to determine, it is advisable that each contract specifies the venue for handling the dispute and the procedure avenue that is agreeable to all the parties involved. The contract should also specify whether the dispute settlement process will involve procedures other than litigation, which is often too costly and leads to negative perceptions in the international business community of the companies involved. Such procedures may be as follows:

① Mediation(调解).

It is a non-binding procedure that involves an independent third party. The disadvantage of mediation is that any decision of the mediator is non-binding. The perspective of a neutral third party, however, could provide better insights into how the issue is perceived by the larger business community; moreover, not accepting the terms of mediation could signal to firms outside the conflict that the firm seen as being at fault might not be a reliable future partner.

② Arbitration(仲裁).

It is a procedure that involves an independent third party; the outcome of arbitration is a binding decision. Agreeing to arbitration does not necessarily mean that the companies found to be at fault will adhere to the decisions; if they do not, however, their reputation in the international business community is likely to suffer. Arbitration is often preferred to litigation. It is a much faster procedure that is likely to cost the company much less than a lawsuit.

7.4 Intellectual Property Rights Protection 知识产权保护

Violation of intellectual property rights is the most significant threat to the competitiveness of companies involved in international business. Intellectual property is the result of ideas and creativity transformed into products, services, and experiences that are protected for a specified period of time from unauthorized commercialization. Companies from developed countries manufacturing brand name products are the primary victims of intellectual property rights infringement and are leading the fight against violations. Losses attributed to the violation of intellectual property rights are estimated to be \$60 billion a year, and its primary victims are the most innovative, fastest—growing industries such as software (with estimated annual losses at \$11.4 billion), pharmaceuticals (with estimated losses at \$ billion), and entertainment (with estimated annual losses at \$8 to \$10 billion and expected to rise due to Internet piracy).

7.4.1 Intellectual Property Protection Takes on Different Forms 知识产权保护的不同形式

Protection of the rights of the inventor or of the firm employing the inventor to use and sell the invention for a specified period of time—this type of intellectual property is known as a patent. In many countries around the world, multinationals are racing to local patent offices to apply for patents to protect and enforce their technology. In Korea, for example, local memory chip and electronics firms are embroiled in patent disputes, fending off lawsuits initiated by multinational firms such as IBM and NEC, and the stakes are high: losers will not only suffer financial setbacks in the form of paying royalties, but will also suffer the stigma of being labeled copycats. This situation will ultimately be rectified by the WTO, which will institute uniformed patent rules that all members are expected to follow.

Protecting the rights of an original work of art(literature, music, film, design, and other works) by allowing the owner the right to reproduce, sell, perform, or film the work-this is known as copyright. National and international associations are actively fighting copyright infringement. In the United States, such an organization is the International Intellectual Property Alliance, or IIPA. The IIPA was formed in conjunction with the Association of American Publishers. The Business Software Alliance, the Interactive Digital Software association the motion Picture Association of America, the national music publishers association, and the Recording Industry Association of America. In recent years, the IIPA filed petitions with the office of the U.S. Trade Representative to investigate copyright infringement in the CD and CD-ROM markets in Brazil, Costa Rica, Guatemala, Russia, and Uruguay.

Protection of a brand name, mark, symbol, motto, or slogan that identifies a particular manufacturer's brand and distinguishes it from the competitors' brands in the same product category—this is known as trademark. Trademark infringement occurs at many levels, from directly copying the product, as in the case of counterfeit Rolex watches and Gucci and Fendi purse selling for $30 in the streets of New York City, Hong Kong China, and Paris and in many bazaars in developing countries. Brand name counterfeiting involves using the brand name, but not necessarily the product design, as in the case of Oleg Cassini and Christian Dior plain Egyptian cotton t-shirts selling in the streets of Cairo.

Protection of unre gistered proprietary technology, formulas, and special blends that are not registered, and thus not protected by law-these are shared with licensees, franchisers, or other Partners and are known as trade secrets.

7.4.2 Factors Influencing Intellectual Property Rights Violations 知识产权侵犯的影响因素

The degree of intellectual property rights violation is influenced by a number of market factors, such as:

① Lack of appropriate legislation, e. g. for software;

② Lax enforcement, especially for local firms;

③ Unavailability of the authentic products, or when available, their high price provides justification for both the violators and the respective government to allow the practice.

Such violations are also influenced by cultural factors, such as:

① Values that perceive imitation as a high form of flattery;

② A culture characterized by interpersonal distrust and feelings of not getting a

fair deal;

③ A culture characterized by an emphasis on acquisition of material wealth at the expense of caring for others; in such a culture, the focus of acquisition is status brands consumed and or displayed publicly, rather than privately;

④ Beliefs that technology is in the common domain and that use of others' intellectual property is appropriate.

7.5 Home-Country Legislation Affecting Multinational Firms Operating Overseas 母国法律对跨国企业在海外市场运作的影响

7.5.1 Antitrust Laws 反垄断法

Antitrust laws of home and host countries are designed to prevent domestic anti-competitive activities, such as the creation of monopolies and cartels. The United States was among the first to impose its antitrust laws on firms in the United States and on its firms operating abroad. Increasingly, governments of other countries are enacting and enforcing antitrust legislation that affects multinationals worldwide. In fast antitrust enforcement in the United States often appears to be more lenient than in other developed countries, for example, the European commission vetoed mergers between competitors after the United States gave these mergers a green light, as in the case of General Electric failed takeover attempt of Honeywell and the MCI Worldcom and Sprint proposed merger.

The United States allows certain types of collusion in the case of small and medium sized firms that might not have the resources to embark on a successful export program. The U.S. Congress passed the Export Trading Company Act in the 1980s to encourage firms to join forces in exporting by exempting them from antitrust laws.

In 2016, the European Commission prosecuted a cartel case against major European truck producers that had colluded on pricing and the timing to introduce new emissions technologies—and had agreed to pass on the cost of such systems to buyers of trucks.59 Intermediate input suppliers may also collude to raise prices for parts needed by lead firms. Automotive parts makers in Europe were first investigated in 2010—2012, and eventually more than a dozen specific cartels for a range of car parts were identified by the authorities. The European Union alone imposed more than 2 billion in fines in 15 separate rulings pertaining to various car parts producers (Figure 7.1).

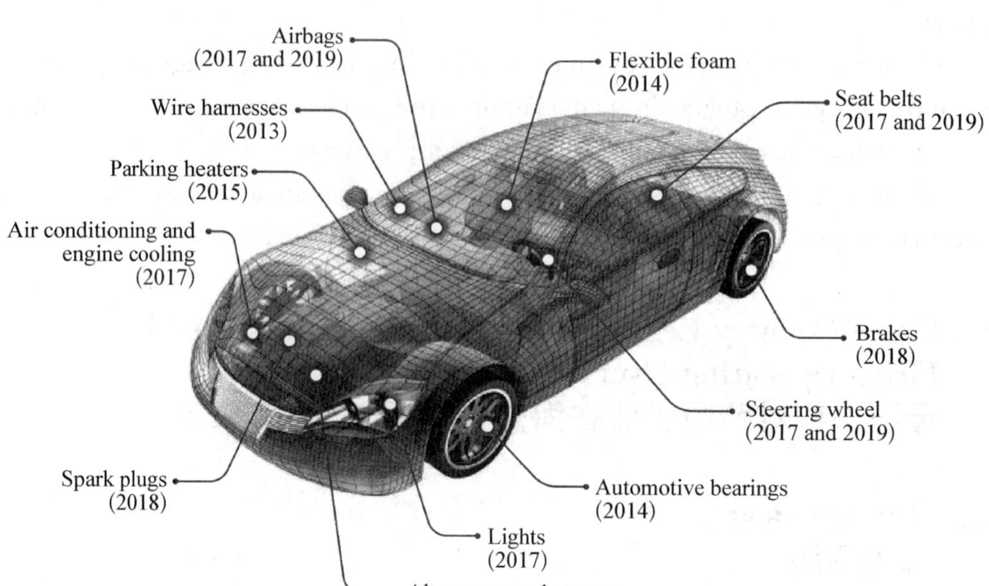

Source: European Commission 2019.

Figure 7.1 The European Commission Has Imposed Large Fines on Car Parts Cartels Since 2013

7.5.2 Corruption Laws 反行贿法

Corruption laws of home and host countries are designed to prevent multinational corporations from using unethical means to obtain competitive advantage in a particular market. The World Bank surveyed 3, 600 companies in 69 countries and found 40 percent paid bribes, and in the former Soviet Union, it increased to 60 percent. Similarly, the European Bank for Reconstruction and Development (EBRD), which encourages investments in the former Eastern Bloc, has called Eastern Europe's bribe-seeking a deterrent to 46 foreign investment.

The U.S. Foreign Corrupt Practices Act (FCPA) makes it illegal for companies and their representatives to bribe government officials and other politicians or candidates to political office. The Act also prohibits payment to third parties when the company has good reason to assume that part of that payment is being used for bribery purposes. U.S. multinational companies take such laws very seriously, and some even address their commitment to reject bribery and other corruption in their mission statement(Caterpillar does so, for example)—even though forbidding these practices places U.S. firms at a disadvantaged position. In a number of high-profile cases, investigators found that illegal payments were made by firms operating in Canada, Colombia Cook Islands, the Dominican Republic, Egypt, Germany, Iraq, Israel,

Jamaica, Mexico, Niger, Nigeria, and Trinidad and Tobago; these payments ranged from \$22, 000 to \$9.9 million and represented percentages of up to 20 percent of the business obtained. Seventeen companies have been charged under the FCPA, with fines ranging from \$10.000 to \$21.8 million.

The United States is not alone in the fight against bribery. The Organization for Economic Co-operation and Development (OECD), which consists of 30 primarily developed member countries adopted a Convention on Combating Bribery of Foreign Public Officials in International Business Transaction. Other signatories include non-member countries Argentina, Brazil, Bulgaria, and Chile. The purpose of the convention is to fight corruption in international business and to help improving the competitive field for companies.

7.6 The Framework of the U.S. Export Control Legal System 美国出口管制法律体系的框架

美国出口管制的法律体系主要包括《出口管理法》(EAA)、《武器出口管制法》(AECA)和《国际突发事件经济权利法》(IEEPA)三部法律,根据以上法律制定的《出口管理条例》(EAR)、《伊朗交易与制裁条例》(ITRS)和《武器出口管制法》(ITAR)三部管制法则,以及明确实施细则的《商业管制清单》(CCL)、《商业国家列表》(CCC)和《美国防务目录》(USML)等指引。

对于如何判定产品是否受美国出口管理条例(EAR)约束,BIS要求企业向被加入实体名单企业销售或转移受到EAR约束的物品前,需事先获得许可。

According to Section 3 of Part 734 of the EAR, projects subject to the EAR specifically include the following five categories:

① All products located in the United States (including the United States Foreign Trade Zone and transit within the United States);

② All products located outside the United States but originating in the United States;

③ "Foreign countries" that are not produced in the United States but contain "American ingredients" (including finished products, software, and technology) and reach a certain percentage (according to the nature and category of the product, there are three minimum standard lines of 0%, 10%, and 25%). Product, please refer to the following for the minimum standard line division;

④ Specific products produced using American technology or software;

⑤ Produced by a factory outside the United States, but the main components of the factory or factory are derived from American technology or software.

7.7 Article 301 of U.S. Trade Law 美国贸易法 301 条款

"301 条款"是美国《1974 年贸易法》第 301 条的俗称，一般而言，"301 条款"是美国贸易法中有关对外国立法或行政上违反协定、损害美国利益的行为采取单边行动的立法授权条款。根据这项条款，美国可以对它认为是"不公平"的其他国家的贸易做法进行调查，并可与有关国家政府协商，最后由总统决定采取提高关税、限制进口、停止有关协定等报复措施。

"Article 301" is the common name of Article 301 of the US *Trade Act of 1974*. Generally speaking, "Article 301" refers to the unilateral action taken in the US trade law against foreign legislative or administrative violations of agreements and harm to the interests of the United States. According to this Article, the United States can investigate the trade practices of other countries that it considers "unfair", and can negotiate with the governments of relevant countries. Finally, the President decides to take retaliatory measures such as raising tariffs, restricting imports, and suspending relevant agreements.

According to the Trade Facilitation and Trade Enforcement Act of 2015 signed by former US President Barack Obama, Section 301 was revised and the investigation of Section 301 was initiated again. At the end of 2016, the United States launched a related investigation on whether the retaliatory measures against EU beef were implemented. After Trump took office, in order to reduce the trade deficit of the United States and the trade protection practices implemented by the trade counterparts, the application of this clause has become more frequent, and even the scope of application of Clause 301 has been expanded and the scope of application has been specified. In addition, in accordance with the relevant provisions of the 2015 Trade Convenience and Trade Promotion Law, the scope of application of the revised Section 301 covers new areas that have not been covered by the WTO system but have recently been included in free trade agreements. These unilateral decisions and measures against foreign trade activities have been controversial so far, and they have posed a serious threat to the WTO system that emphasizes the settlement of multilateral trade disputes. In this situation, China, which continues to have a trade surplus with the United States, is particularly affected. In 2017, the United States again initiated the application of Section 301 against China. In March 2018, the United States released the so-called Section 301 investigation results on China's technology transfer and intellectual property protection. As a result, Sino-US trade frictions have escalated again and continue to escalate.

Conclusion 结语

International political relations affect the international legal environment. To engage in production and business activities in the host country, multinational companies must abide by the laws of the host country, especially in Islamic countries, and must not offend the laws and taboos of the host country. In recent years, due to trade frictions between the United States and China, many Chinese companies have been interfered and investigated by the U.S. government, which has brought great difficulties to the survival of Chinese companies in the United States. Therefore, in addition to implementing their own strategies, multinational companies must pay attention and adjust their activities overseas in time.

The Chapter's Referential Questions 本章参考题

(1) What is the legal environment of the international market? What legal aspects does it consist of?
什么是国际市场法律环境？它由哪些方面的法律构成？

(2) How does the host country's laws affect the company's international marketing?
东道国法律对企业国际营销产生何种影响？

(3) Please think about the legal issues that may be touched in the Sino-US trade friction.
请思考中美贸易摩擦中的可能触及的法律问题。

(4) How do you comment on the Canadian government's arrest of Chinese citizen Wanzhou Meng?
如何评价加拿大政府逮捕中国公民孟晚舟这件事情？

Further Reading 拓展阅读

Chapter 8

The Science and Technology Environment of International Marketing
国际市场营销的科技环境

Learning Objectives
本章学习目标

(1) Innovation and globalization.
创新与全球化。
(2) The influence of the internet on economic development.
互联网对经济发展的影响。
(3) Related industry and technology development trends.
相关产业和科技发展趋势。

Key Words
关键词

Innovation; R & D; EDI; GVCs; Digital; Internet; Emerging Science and Technology

8.1 The Overall Trend of Global Technological Development 全球科技发展总体态势

Case Studies 8.1

全球的科技环境变化非常迅速,新产品的开发日新月异。科技革命,尤其是互联网技术的应用已经彻底改变了跨国公司所处的环境和所实施的国际市场营销的面貌。

Worldpay recently released the "2019 US Consumer Behavior Report". The report found that nearly two-thirds (66%) of American consumers believe that smartphones will replace plastic credit and debit cards as the main payment method within the next five years.

New technologies on balance promote trade and GVCs. The emergence of new products, new technologies of production such as automation and 3D printing, and new technologies of distribution, such as digital platforms are creating both opportunities and risks. But the evidence so far suggests that on balance these technologies are enhancing trade and GVCs.

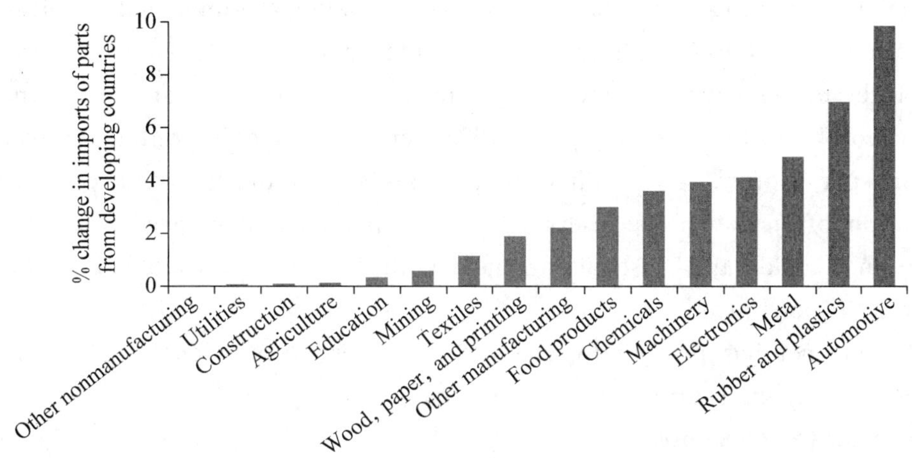

Source: Artuc, Bastos, and Rijkers 2018.

Figure 8.1 Automation in Industrial Countries has Boosted Imports from Developing Countries①

Innovation is leading to the emergence of new traded goods and services, which contributes to faster trade growth. In 2017, 65 percent of trade was in categories that did not exist in 1992.

Surprisingly, new production technologies are also likely to boost trade. Automation does encourage countries to use less labor-intensive methods and reduces the demand for the labor-intensive products of developing countries. However, the evidence on reshoring is limited, and the evidence on automation and 3D printing suggests that these technologies have contributed to higher productivity and a larger scale of production. As such, they have increased the demand for imports of inputs from developing countries.

Similarly, digital platform firms are reducing the cost of trade and making it easier for small firms to break out of their local markets and sell both goods and services globally. But there are signs that the rising market power of platform firms is affecting the distribution of the gains from trade.

Ad valorem equivalent trade cost reductions 2018—2040—different trends (averages across economies).

---

① Note: The figure depicts the automation-induced increase in industrial countries' imports of materials from developing countries by broad sector over 1995—2015. The change in imports of parts is measured in log points; a 0.10 increase in log points is roughly equivalent to a 10 percent increase in imports.

8.2 The Impact of the Internet on the Global Economy 互联网对全球经济产生的影响

The Internet allows for instant access to new international markets and creates potential for exchange that have never been previously imagined. Multinational corporations, as well as small and medium enterprises, benefit from the long reach of the Internet. The average amount of time each person spends on the Internet is 10 hours a month, visiting an average of 49 different sites, going online an average of 19 times per month. The United States and the Netherlands have the highest penetration of active home users up to 39 percent, compared with the total population. Canada and Australia are next with 34 percent, followed by the Great Britain at 30 percent.

The internet has profoundly changed the lives of individuals, but it has also changed the way international business is conducted.

Consider these examples:

① There are more than 4 million Web sites, with 235,000 new ones being added each month;

② There are 200 million email boxes in the United States;

③ People send more than 7 trillion E-mails each year in the United States;

④ The average e-mail user receives 31 E-mails per day;

⑤ The Business-to-business e-commerce in the United States totals \$1.3 trillion per year;

⑥ Business will place orders totaling \$3 trillion per year worldwide via the Internet;

⑦ Twenty-five percent of all business-to-business purchases are placed through some type of Internet connection;

⑧ Internet retail sales account for almost 2.5 percent of all retail sales.

Many American companies have been successful in selling to international clients through the Internet. Nevertheless, there are some pitfalls. For example, the company may need to make use of freight forwarders, who handle transportation insurance, and export documentation but also substantially increase the cost to the buyer. Companies must also determine the appropriate payment mechanisms. Countries differ not only with regard to the currency they use for transactions, but also in their methods of payments. For example, Europeans tend to use the Eurocard, which is a debit one and, for payments. Also, worldwide, there is a high rate of credit card theft, which increases the risks that sellers might face in the international market. Using the Internet to send Mother's Day flowers from the United States to one's mother-in-law in

Holland will become possible. Nevertheless, the online transactions never before thought possible are commonplace due to the advances in the past two decades.

Technology is permeating all services sectors and gradually transforming them. This is the result of the synergy between the telecom industry and its provision of high-speed connectivity such as 5G, the IT sector and its development of innovative industry-specific software, and robotics, thanks to a thriving R & D sector.

For example, the construction industry is increasingly using advanced technology in its operations, such as drones for the aerial surveillance of building projects, replacing land surveillance, and construction through automated modular 3D printing, to cut costs and compensate for skilled labor shortage. In addition, with prefabricated construction taking place indoors in factories and just assembly work onsite, the definition of construction as a service is becoming blurred. Currently, over 90 percent of construction and related engineering services are traded worldwide through a commercial presence abroad; however, it is already possible for construction to be traded across borders meanwhile.

However, innovation and creativity thrive in several developing economies, where the applications for patents, industrial designs and trademarks record outstanding growth (WTO, 2018). Digital communications, IT and electrical machinery were the main areas of technology for patent applications in China in 2017, while Singapore focused on IT, semiconductors, pharmaceuticals and biotechnologies. The Republic of Korea ranked third globally for applications for industrial designs, mainly in ICT and audio-visuals in the same year. Innovation has translated into a significant rise of developing Asia's IP-related services exports (17 percent on average per year since 2005).

In the Middle East, Israel is an international hub for research and innovation ranging from IT to medical technologies and pharmaceuticals. In 2017, Israel ranked first in the world for R&D expenditure (4.5 percent of GDP), and fourth for exports of R & D services, behind the European Union, the United States, and China.

Case Studies 8.2

8.3 Emerging Science and Technology Trends[①] 新兴科技趋势

The S & T Strategic Trends report in 2016 synthesizes 32 S & T forecasts that have

① Source: Office of the Deputy Assistant Secretary of American Army (Research & Technology); This report was prepared for the Deputy Assistant Secretary of the Army (Research & Technology) by FutureScout, LLC, a strategy and analytics firm specializing in helping organizations understand emerging trends and how to prepare strategically to thrive in the face of an uncertain future.

been published over the past five years by government agencies in the U.S. and abroad, industry leaders, international institutions, and think tanks. The objective was to identify trends that are most likely to generate revolutionary or disruptive change of interest to American Army over the next 30 years. 24 emerging science and technology trends were identified in the report. The first 15 areas are explained and forecasted from the three major aspects of Enabling S & T, Signal, and Impact. The 21～24 areas are only for reference because the current supporting data is not obvious. Learning and understanding the frontiers of science and technology is of great value for Chinese companies to participate in future competition and cooperation in the high-tech field. This part takes up a lot of space. Please scan the QR code next to it to continue learning.

Case Studies 8.3

Conclusion 结语

With the improvement of the technological level of developing countries led by China, the advantages of the more developed Western countries such as the United States will not be able to occupy a monopoly position for a long time. Therefore, competition in the field of science and technology is inevitable. Which country and enterprise will occupy the commanding heights of science and technology in the future will inevitably enhance its competitive advantage. As the Chinese market begins the process of innovation in China, the future service unicorn and super unicorns companies will surely lead the world. Chinese multinational companies should improve their competitiveness in the global market through active innovation.

The Chapter's Referential Questions 本章参考题

(1) Pharmaceutical companies have always maintained a high return on investment. List the listed companies with international pharmaceutical technology strength you are familiar with.
医药公司一直保持较高的投资回报率,列举你所熟知的国际医药类科技实力较强的上市公司。

(2) As far as you know, many Chinese multinational companies are currently being suppressed by the United States. What are the main technical issues involved?
据你所知,目前很多中国跨国公司遭到美国政府的打压,主要涉及哪些技术问题?

(3) Referring to the 24 emerging technology Sectors given in the textbooks, in which

fields do you think Chinese companies can gain competitive advantages at international level?
参考教材上给定的 24 个新兴科技领域，你认为中国企业在哪些领域能够获得国际竞争优势？

Further Reading 拓展阅读

Chapter 9

The Natural Environment of International Marketing 国际市场营销的自然环境

Learning Objectives 本章学习目标

(1) Regional conflicts caused by shortage of natural resources.
自然资源短缺引发的地区冲突现象。

(2) The impact of natural resource constraints on economic development.
自然资源约束对经济发展的影响。

(3) The various factors of the natural environment impose restrictions on multinational companies.
自然环境的各因素给跨国公司带来的限制。

Key Words 关键词

Water safet; Resource; Ecological Risks; Environmental; Hydrology; Natural Resources; Climate; Food security

本章将介绍对国际市场营销产生影响的自然环境。因为,一个国家的地理位置决定跨国公司进入这个国家的最佳路径,地理因素会决定其在整个国际市场的位置,气候和自然资源情况会直接影响如何安排生产。

Case Studies 9.1

The natural environment of international marketing poses challenges to businesses: geology and the shortage of natural resources, coupled with a high population growth, can negatively affect market potential. Similarly, topography can affect access, and hydrology and climate can affect economic development. Phenomena such as a shortage of natural resources, the energy crisis, and the environmental quality crisis affect the business environment.

Population displacement from natural disasters was greater than displacement from armed conflict. The number of natural disasters has quadrupled in the last four decades.

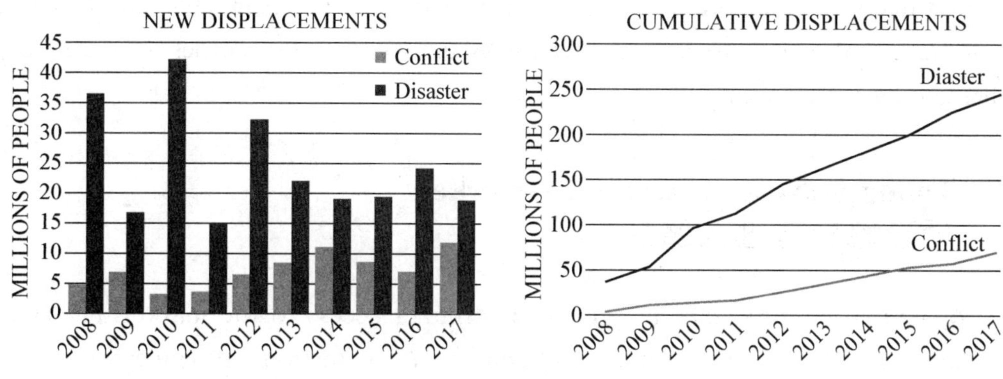

Source: IDMC.

Figure 9.1 Population Displacement from Conflict and Natural Disasters, 2008—2017

The natural environment of international marketing addresses the relationship between natural resources worldwide and marketing. A country's geographic location determines how its key markets can be optimally accessed. Its climate determines its production and even its productivity capability. Geography facilitates or impedes relationships with other international markets.

National boundaries determine access to the local market and the movement of goods, access to natural resources, and overall, the potential for economic development.

9.1 Geology and Natural Resources 地理环境和自然资源

A country's access to natural resources determines whether or not it can become a viable trade partner in the international market. Its geology determines the natural resources available in the country and its potential for prosperity. For example, oil in North Africa and the Middle East has brought prosperity to countries where the climate is a challenge and whose terrain contains a large desert expanse. Countries in Sub-Saharan Africa that have survived at subsistence level for centuries have found new prosperity from mining gold and diamonds. Botswana and the Central African Republic have attracted markets that are actively courted by multinationals.

A shortage of raw materials is slowly reverberating in most world markets, including the markets of industrialized countries. Prices of oil are steadily increasing, whereas access to oil sources is becoming more and more limited due to geologic and political factors. This shortage is translating to higher prices charged to consumers, which, in the long term, will lead to changes in consumption patterns. In the case of oil, it may mean that Northern Europeans will no longer count on their Southern European and North African vacations, which will, in turn, hurt tourism in Southern Europe and North Africa. Consumers in the United States may have to trade in their gas-guzzling monster trucks and sports utility vehicles for fuel-efficient smaller and hybrid vehicles.

9.2 Topography and Access to Markets 地形地貌与进入路径

Topography is important because it determines access to the market and affects distribution decisions. For example, Holland has a flat terrain, allowing for efficient transportation. Holland has also altered its topography to increase access by creating an effective network of man-made canals that cross the country in every direction allowing for easier access to markets.

On the other hand, a mountainous terrain limits market access. The Andes, for example, allow minimal access to local consumers, which can only be accomplished at great company expense. These restrictions are especially difficult to surmount in low-income countries; high-and middle-income countries have devised sophisticated access to the more remote areas, such as the canyons in Utah, the peaks of the Alps, or across the Brahmaputra mountains.

Tibet was initially reached only by air or by road from the rest of China. There is now a railway that facilitates access. Nevertheless, the Brahmaputra mountain chain presents a challenge to the movement of goods and access to the market.

9.3 Hydrology and Economic Development 水文条件与经济发展

Hydrology determines access to local markets as well. Ocean access allows for the affordable shipping of goods to the local target market, Rivers and lakes offer access as well as potential for the development of agriculture and manufacturing. Hydroelectric power is essential for local development. In general, economic development is related to hydrology.

Water-related risks are highest in the Middle East and North Africa, where almost a third of catchments were rated to be extremely high risk.

Water risks, food insecurity and sea level rising are threating catastrophic levels of impact across 44, 30 and 19 countries, for each of the risks respectively.

Table 9.1 Catastrophic Ecological Risks

INDICATOR	CRITERIA FOR CONSIDERING CATASTROPHIC	COUNTRIES
Water stress	Score of 3 on scale of 1 to 5. This is a measure of the severity of the unmet demand for water	In 2016: 44 of 164 (27%)
Food insecurity	≥25% pop food deficient	In 2017: 30 of 137 (21%)
Population at risk due to rising sea level	>10% of pop at risk of rising sea level	Projected for 2100: 19 of 91 (20%)

Source: IEP.

9.4 Climate 气候

Climate is also an essential determinant of economic development. Arid lands, such as the desert lands of the Sahara and the southwestern United States, are inhabitable only at a very high cost. In other areas, excessive rain and hurricane activity often lead to flooding and the destruction of the local infrastructure. On the other hand, a mild climate year round brings tourists to the Amalfi Coast of Italy, the islands of Hawaii, the beaches of the Caribbean, the shores of Tunisia, and the Sinai.

From 1901 to 2015, the global temperature increased by 1.21 degrees Celsius. The increase during the 15-year period from 2000 to 2015 accounted for 38 percent of the total rise.

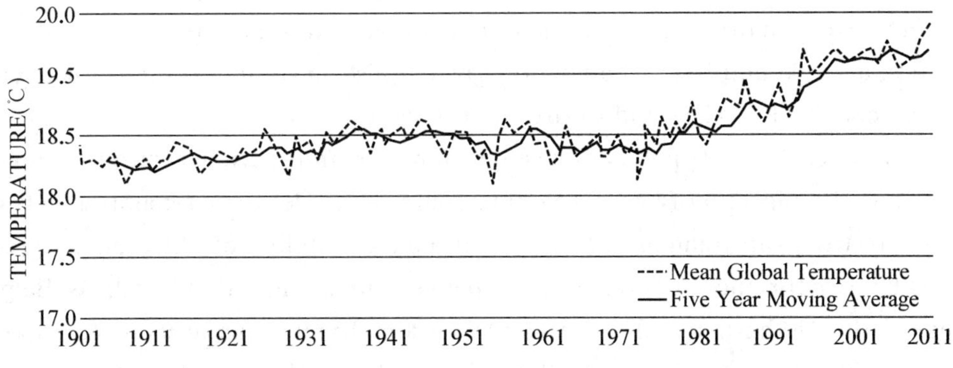

Figure 9.2 Mean Global Temperature, 1901—2015

Climate change is narming the atmosphere and oceans, reducing snow and ice and raising sea levels. The effects of these trends pose a major challenge to peace in the coming decades, as the increasing scarcity of resource will have an import on livelihood.

The impacts of different climate change hazards on food security and water scarcity have already emerged in many regions and countries. The World Economic Forum believes that by 2050, climate change induced environmental risks will have a greater negative impact than any other economic, geopolitical, societal, or technological changes. Countries those fail to adapt will be facing the biggest risks.

The severity and impacts of environmental risks vary across geographic regions. Some regions face multiple ecological threats. However, other areas might face a single climate related hazard.

9.5 Population and Human Capital 人口与人力资源

Case Studies 9.2

As mentioned earlier, one relevant aspect of the natural environment is the scarcity of natural resources, especially raw materials, in light of today's high population growth. High population growth in spite of limited natural resources has led to famine and precipitated conflict in Ethiopia, Somalia, Rwanda, and Burundi in sub Saharan Africa. In these markets, the overall infrastructure is inadequate and cannot meet the basic needs of the population. The concentration of population in large cities of millions of inhabitants, such as Mexico City and Cairo, has taxed the infrastructure and impeded the optimal functioning of business. Most importantly, today, the world's population exceeds 7 billion and is growing rapidly, particularly in developing countries.

Population growth determines the types of markets that multinational companies, as well as small and medium enterprises, can target. In the high-income countries, marketers have a more mature market to contend with-markets with a substantial population aged 65 and older. Population growth also has implications with regard to access to goods and services and to the environment.

The implications of population migration for international business are also considerable. Immigration from developing countries to developed countries has often resulted in strong anti-immigrant sentiment and instability of different degrees in counties known for their tolerance and openness to immigration, such as Belgium, Denmark, the Netherlands, France, and Sweden. Immigrants account for about 12 percent of Sweden's population of 9 million and, of those, 450,000 are Muslim. Immigrants in Sweden, as in much of Western Europe, often live in run-down immigrant neighborhoods, are less likely to learn Swedish, and are more likely to go to all-immigrant schools and remain unemployed and poor. Countries that have, historically, encouraged immigration are now struggling to absorb their large immigrant populations. Most Western European countries have now enacted laws restricting immigration.

The new immigrants are not fully aware of their rights or of their obligations to their adoptive country, as such, they end up in an ambiguous situation. The issues that Sweden is grappling with are not unusual. The European mass media regularly address issues related to anti-immigrant sentiment that can, potentially, lead to destabilization. France's 2006 student riots ultimately resulted in anti-immigrant rhetoric from government officials. The mayor of Berlin, on the occasion of the 2006 World Cup, increased security to a high alert and advised all foreign visitors to stay away from neighborhoods in eastern Berlin, to avoid attacks by radical nationalists.

One aspect of migration that has important economic consequences for the country affected is "brain drain", the migration of trained professionals. Historically, this migration has been mostly from developing to developed countries, this migration has created shortages of qualified medical personnel in many countries in Eastern Europe, for example. More recently, open borders in the European Union have created a brain drain phenomenon for countries with high taxation and unemployment. For example, the brain drain from Germany, a country with a rapidly shrinking population, has become an issue of concern to business executives and government leaders. More professionals are leaving today than in the past years. A popular show on German television is Goodbye Deutschland. The show portrays emigrants to South Africa and Spain. About 150,000 emigrate yearly, and only about 50,000 return. The emigrants who leave are doctors, lawyers, and scientists. France has many emigrants leaving for Britain. Adding to the burden of brain drain is the fact that Germany and France are less attractive to people seeking for jobs in medicine, academic research, and engineering. The reasons emigrants give for leaving are high taxes, chronic unemployment, a rigid labor market, a stifling bureaucracy, and the hierarchical structure of some professional environments such as academia and medicine. As a new employee, you have little time to pursue research and are under the thumb of your director.

9.6 Environmental Quality 环境质量

Concerns about the effects of the overall population growth and industry on the natural environment have led to the active regulation of business, especially in industrialized countries. For example, the European Union actively promotes normones in beef and antibiotics in livestock. It continues to raise taxes on gasoline to reduce consumption and encourage the use of public transportation. It charges localities huge sums for refuse and actively encourages recycling at both individual and community level.

Worldwide, there is a concerted effort to reduce air and water pollution, to control the amount and disposal of nuclear waste, to reduce deforestation and land erosion, and to limit fishing and hunting activity to preserve a viable natural habitat. The effort to preserve environmental quality limits infrastructure development in protected areas and charges businesses to take responsibility of consumption by encouraging bottle reuse and recycling, by limiting packaging to its more basic forms, and by producing products that can be consumed with minimal harm to the environment.

Vehicular emissions are rising in almost every European country and across the globe. Greenhouse gases are increasing even in countries where industry pollution is decreasing, because of increased car and truck use, according to the European Environment Agency. And this is happening in spite of the invention of environmentally friendly automobiles: hybrid cars and ethanol buses do not compensate for the effect of the large number of vehicles on the road.

Increasingly, environmental pollution is also attributed to developing countries. For example, in many developing countries, cheap diesel generators from China are a preferred mode for providing electricity. They power home appliances, irrigation systems, allowing many in rural villages to grow crops and to connect to the world through television. Demand for energy is increasing in these rural areas, and smoke spewing diesel generators are bumming all day long, creating pollution in areas that used to have none. In remote and roadless areas in India, Bangladesh, Nepal, as many as half of the households have television sets and pay 40 cents every few days to the owner of the generator supplying the electricity for their bamboo hut. Diesel is cheap, owing to lavish government subsidies, making it difficult to introduce alternative renewable energy technologies. Efforts on the part of local government and international development organizations such as the United Nations Development program to introduce expensive renewable energy have been successful for urban areas; however, the investment is not warranted in remote villages. China is offering a successful alternative: cheap roof-top water heaters that channel water through thin pipes crisscrossing a shiny surface. More than 5, 000 small Chinese companies sell these water heaters to more than 30 million households. Today, China accounts for 60 percent of the market for solar water heaters. One such water heater costs $330, and it pays for itself in 2 years.

9.6.1 Climate Change 环境变化

By 2050, the average global surface temperature is estimated to rise by 2.5 to

5.4 degrees Fahrenheit.① Sea levels could rise up to five feet by the end of the century,② leading to increased flooding. Many coastal areas will become inundated with water, transforming coastlines around the world and adversely affecting millions of people living in coastal cities. Temperature change will also affect global weather patterns, leading to more frequent and severe weather events in many parts of the world. Desertification will accelerate, leading to a decline in agricultural output. Agriculture in equatorial regions will be particularly affected, potentially causing food shortages across North Africa and the Middle East. Oceans, which absorb a large amount of atmospheric carbon dioxide, will experience increased acidification of up to 70% by 2050.③ Acidification will cause potentially devastating ripple effects throughout the oceanic ecosystem, causing a decline in global amount of fish and other aquatic food stocks and increasing food stress in many regions of the world. At the same time, melting of polar ice will open vast new regions to exploration for energy and minerals. The Arctic is already becoming a focus of strategic maneuvering for the U.S., Russia, and Europe, and expanded access to polar resources could trigger interstate conflicts.④

Most experts agree that we are unlikely to entirely avoid the negative effects of climate change, even if aggre ssire action was taken today to reduce greenhouse gas emissions. Therefore, science and technology will likely play an important role in climate change adaptation. For example, analytics could be used to predict flooding hazards based on near-term meteorological data and long-term climate modeling. This would enable proactive responses by government planners and emergency services that mitigate threats to residents, buildings, and infrastructure. Agricultural technologies such as vertical farming could enable cities to meet food demand locally through farming methods that are more resilient to drought and other climate influences. And while a certain amount of warming is already locked into the global climate, clean energy technologies could mitigate the severity of future warming by reducing

① IPCC, 2014: Summary for policymakers. In: Climate Change 2014: Impacts, Adaptation, and Vulnerability. Part A: Global and Sectoral Aspects. Contribution of Working Group II to the Fifth Assessment Report of the Intergovernmental Panel on Climate Change [Field, C.B., V.R. Barros, D.J. Dokken, K.J. Mach, M.D. Mastrandrea, T.E. Bilir, M. Chatterjee, K.L. Ebi, Y.O. Estrada, R.C. Genova, B. Girma, E.S. Kissel, A.N. Levy, S. MacCracken, P.R. Mastrandrea, and L.L.White (eds.)]. Cambridge University Press, Cambridge, United Kingdom and New York, NY, USA, pp. 1-32. Available from http://www.ipcc.ch/pdf/assessment-report/ar5/wg2/ar5_wgII_spm_en.pdf.

② Jevrejeva, S., Moore, J. C., & Grinsted, A. (2012). Sea level projections to AD2500 with a new generation of climate change scenarios. Global and Planetary Change, 80, 14-20.

③ Orr, J. C., Fabry, V. J., Aumont, O., Bopp, L., Doney, S. C., Feely, R. A., ... & Key, R. M. (2005). Anthropogenic ocean acidification over the 21st century and its impact on calcifying organisms. Nature, 437(7059), 681-686.

④ UK Ministry of Defense (2015). Future Operating Environment 2035. Available from https://www.gov.uk/government/publications/future-operating-environment-2035.

greenhouse gas emissions from burning fossil fuels.

9.6.2 Resource Constraints 资源约束

Over the next 25 years, The world of food, water, energy and material resources demand will likely continue to rise dramatically. Global fresh water demand is projected to grow by 55% by 2045,① and unless specific measures are taken to mitigate water shortages, around 3.9 billion people—over 40% of the world's population—could experience water stress. Food supplies will come under pressure from population growth and declines in agricultural output due to climate change and mismanagement of arable land (some estimates indicate that up to 25% of farmland is already degraded due to overuse of chemical fertilizers and poor crop management practices).② While China and other industrialized nations are beginning to their transition to renewable energy sources, global energy demand is expected to double by 2045, with supply continuing to undershoot demand.③ Global reserves of materials such as copper and lithium, which are essential to the digital economy, are falling as demand increases. In 2030 it is predicted that 83 billion tons of minerals, metals and biomass will be extracted from the earth: 55 percent more than in 2010.④ Countries that control large resource reserves are likely to gain immense control over the global economy. For example, China currently supplies 97% of global demand for rare earth metals. The Chinese government has already tightened rare earth exports, driving up prices for electronic components and boosting its own domestic electronics industry.

Resource constraints will be a powerful driver of global research and technology development. Water harvesting and recycling technologies, such as efficient desalination and water vapor farming, will reduce water stress. Agricultural output will benefit from new advances in transgenic crops, micro-irrigation, and autonomous systems. New manufacturing methods such as 3D and 4D printing will reduce waste and make use of recycled materials. Further afield, it is possible that by 2045, advances in space technologies could open the door to asteroid mining and a potentially enormous new source of raw materials. We have already seen early signs of an emerging off-planet mining industry: in 2015, the Washington-based space mining company

① OECD (2012). Environmental Outlook to 2050. Available from http://www.oecd.org/env/indicators-modelling-outlooks/oecdenvironmentaloutlookto2050theconsequencesofinaction.htm.

② Godfray, H. C. J. (2014). The challenge of feeding 9～10 billion people equitably and sustainably. The Journal of Agricultural Science, 152(S1), 2-8.

③ International Energy Agency (2016). World Energy Outlook. Available from http://www.worldenergyoutlook.org/.

④ KPMG International, De Boer, Y., & van Bergen, B. (2012). Expect the unexpected: Building business value in a changing world. KPMG International.

Planetary Resources launched the first in a series of probes from the International Space Station that are designed to scout asteroids in near-Earth space and the asteroid belt for water and precious metals.①

9.7 Food Security Issues 粮食安全问题

Trends in food security started to deteriorate in 2017 after decades of improvement. Globally, 873 million people experienced hunger and food insecurity in 2017. This number increases to two billion people when moderate levels of food insecurity are factored in.

Food security requires availability, access and utilisation of sufficient food to meet dietary needs for a productive and healthy life. Food security is affected by numerous factors, such as climate change, depletion of water tables, economic development, technology, social and political stability and the overall resilience of a society in the face of shocks. Many countries might not be able to ensure food security due to inappropriate agricultural technologies or practice, lack of natural resources or productive land, or emergency situations like natural disasters.

Conclusion 结语

With the rapid development of the global economy and society, the contradiction between economic development and self-construction of resource constraints has become increasingly prominent. Due to lack of resources, conflicts have erupted in Africa and the Middle East. With the global warming, bio-diversity is being challenged, food crises and floods continue to threaten various regions and the process of globalization. Under the constraints of carbon neutrality and carbon peak targets, China's market environment will also undergo tremendous changes, which will pose challenges to multinational companies. Therefore, in addition to improving adaptability through technological innovation and industrial upgrading, international companies should also actively pay attention to changes in the global ecological environment and natural environment to make optimal decisions.

---

① http://www.space.com/30213-asteroid-mining-planetary-resources-2025.html

The Chapter's Referential Questions　本章参考题

(1) As far as you know, which regions in the world may cause the entry risks to bring to multinational companies due to the deterioration of the natural environment?
据你所知,目前全球哪些地区可能由于自然环境恶化会导致跨国公司进入产生一定的风险?

(2) In light of international news trends, what are the inducing factors for regional tensions in recent years?
结合国际新闻动态,近年来地区紧张局势的诱导因素有哪些?

(3) How does the natural environment of a country affect the international marketing of a company?
一个国家的自然环境如何影响企业的国际市场营销?

Further Reading 拓展阅读

Part 3

International Market Analysis

国际市场分析

There are two chapters in this part. Firstly, Understand the basic situation of the international market, starting from the regional market, and then in-depth study from the four dimensions of the international goods and services market, intercontinental market, the industrial market, and the national market. Secondly, Learn the knowledge of international market research and forecasting. This part of the study will lay a good foundation for the fourth part of the international market strategy study.

本部分有两章学习内容。首先了解国际市场基本情况，从区域市场入手，然后从商品与服务市场、洲际市场、产业市场、国家市场四个维度深入学习。然后学习国际市场调研和预测知识。通过这一部分的学习，为第四部分国际市场战略部分的学习打下良好的基础。

Chapter 10
International Market
国际市场

Learning Objectives
本章学习目标

(1) The connotation of the international market.
国际市场的内涵。
(2) International regional market and intercontinental market.
国际区域市场与洲际市场。
(3) International commodity market and international service market.
国际商品市场和国际服务市场。
(4) Major economies of the world.
世界主要经济体。

Key Words
关键词

International Market; Global Market; Regional Market; NAFTA; EU; ASEAN; RCEP; MERCOSUR; AEC; Service Trade Market; Emerging Market; BRI

Case Studies 10.1

10.1 Overview of International Markets 国际市场概述

10.1.1 Definition of the International Market 国际市场的含义

The international market is the product of the expansion of the commodity exchange in the space, indicating that the commodity exchange relationship breaks through the boundaries of a country. At the same time, the international market is

multi-dimensional concept from the civilization, culture in time and space intertwined.

10.1.2 Types of International Markets 国际市场的类型

(1) Classified by Historical Evolution 按历史演进分类

According to the evolution of historical logic and the size of the space involved in international market exchange relations, international market can be divided into three different levels: foreign markets, international regional markets and world markets. Among them, the foreign market refers to the market that the scope of commodity exchange breaks through the boundaries of countries, and the commodity exchange relationship with a certain foreign country constitutes a market. Generally, foreign markets refer to country markets, such as the U.S. market, Japanese market, etc.; international regional markets refer to the further expansion of commodity exchange relations and a unified market composed of several countries or regions, such as the European Union, North American Free Trade Area, etc.; the world market refers to a global unified market, which is a unity formed by the exchange of commodities, exchanges of labor services and resource allocation among all countries or regions in the world on the basis of international division of labor. According to the regional division, it can be divided into the European market, the North American market, the Asian market, the African market, the Latin American market and the Oceania market.

(2) Classified by Country Type 按国家类型分类

According to different types of countries, it can be divided into developed capitalist countries, developing countries, socialist countries, and so on.

(3) Classified by Economic Group 按经济集团分类

According to the division of economic groups, it can be divided into European Union market, Central American market, Southeast Asian Union market, the West African Economic Community market and the Arab Common Market, etc.

(4) Classified by Product Structure 按商品结构分类

According to the composition of commodities, it can be divided into an industrial finished product market, a semi-finished product market and a primary product market. The manufactured goods market can be divided into the mechanical product market, the electronic product market, and the textile market.

(5) Classified by Transaction Partner 按交易对象分类

According to the transaction object, it can be divided into commodity market, labor market, technology market, capital market, etc.

(6) Classified by Degree of Monopoly 按垄断程度分类

According to the degree of monopoly, it can be divided into monopoly market, semi-monopoly market and non-monopoly market.

10.1.3 The Characteristics of the International Market 国际市场的特点

① The size of the international market has expanded rapidly.

② The international market is more complex.

③ International market monopoly continues to increase.

④ The rise of trade protectionism.

⑤ International market develped increasingly to the legalization, treatyization, standardization.

10.1.4 The Significance of International Market Analysis 国际市场分析的意义

① Help to grasp the more diverse needs of foreign consumers.

② Grasp the changing trade patterns, changes in the characteristics of the international market.

③ Help enterprises to develop market strategies and tactics correctly, make full use of resources in the international market to be successful.

10.2 International Regional Market 国际区域市场

区域是一个相对的概念,本节讲的国际区域市场和后面讲到的洲际市场、国家市场实际上都是区域的概念,只是从不同视角展开的。本节的国际区域市场主要从市场类型划分标准的经济集团来介绍,后面的国际洲际市场主要是按照自然地理位置以洲为单位。

The regional market is actually a concept of a modern marketing segment market, or a segmented customer group theory.The regional market is a geographical concept which are relative and versatile.

The development characteristics of the regionalization of the international market can be summarized in four aspects: ① Increasing international regional markets. ② International regional markets have a certain degree of cross.③ The international regional market is expanding.④ The international regional market develop to the direction of high development.

Since economic globalization has become an irreversible trend, regional economic integration is the inevitable choice to achieve global economic integration. Regional economic integration is also called "regional economic grouping". Two or more countries in the same region gradually transfer part or all of their economic sovereignty, adopt a common economic policy, and form an exclusive economic group. Its organizational forms are ranked from low to high degree of integration, including preferential trade arrangements, free trade areas, customs unions, common markets, economic unions, and complete economic integration. The regional economic group with the highest degree of integration is the European Union.

In the process of global economic integration, more and more regions are actively forming regional economic organizations based on the advantages of their natural geographical proximity to enhance their regional influence in the global market. Many regional economic organizations have gradually emerged, such as NAFTA, EU, ASEAN, AEC, MERCOSUR, RCEP, etc.

10.2.1 NAFTA 北美自由贸易协定

The North American Free Trade Agreement (NAFTA) is an agreement on comprehensive trade between the three countries signed by the United States, Canada, and Mexico on August 12, 1992. The North American Free Trade Agreement is not an agreement that overrides the national government and national laws, which is different from the EU. The North American Free Trade Agreement came into effect on January 1, 1994. At the same time, the NAFTA Area was officially established. The NAFTA Area has a population of more than 400 million, a gross national product of more than 20 trillion US dollars, and an annual trade volume of more than 4 trillion US dollars. It is one of the largest regional economic integration organization in the world.

NAFTA is the first regional market composed of developing and developed countries. Because the three-country market in the North American Free Trade Zone is mainly dominated by the United States, the characteristics of the regional market mainly reflect the characteristics of the American market, which mainly has the following characteristics:

① The market capacity is large.

② Diversification of demand.

③ The market is open.

④ The market is fiercely competitive.

⑤ Excellent infrastructure conditions.

⑥ Rich in natural resources.

⑦ Social and cultural diversity.

10.2.2 EU 欧洲联盟

The full name of the EU is the European Union. In 2013, it reached to 28 member states. With a land area of 4 million square kilometers, the population exceeded 513 million in 2019, accounting for about 9% of the world's total population. The total global GDP in 2018 was US$ 85.8 trillion. The EU accounted for 21.8% of the global GDP, second only to the United States, which accounted for 23. 8% of the global GDP.

The current membership of the European Union is also unstable. The United Kingdom has announced its withdrawal from the European Union in 2019. In January 2020, the European Union formally approved Brexit.

The EU market has the following characteristics:

① Large market size.

② High degree of market integration.

③ More market demand levels.

④ High market consumption.

⑤ More market restrictions and high requirements.

⑥ Advanced market infrastructure.

10.2.3 ASEAN 东南亚国家联盟

The full name of ASEAN is the Association of Southeast Asian Nations. It was announced on August 8, 1967 in Bangkok, Thailand. Initially there were only five countries. Since then, some countries have been recruited. By the end of April 1999, Cambodia officially joined the alliance and ASEAN formed 10 countries then. The composition of ASEAN. With 4.5 million square kilometers, the population of more than 600 million in 2019, accounting for 10% of the world's total population, it is the most promising market for economic development.

The ASEAN market has the following characteristics:

① The market capacity is large.

② Market control is loose.

③ There is a large gap in the level of economic development, and there are many levels of demand for commodities.

④ The market system has a clear gap.

10.2.4 RCEP 区域全面经济伙伴关系

The Regional Com-prehensive Economic Partnership (RCEP), initiated by the ten

ASEAN countries, invites China, Japan, South Korea, Australia, and New Zealand to participate ("10 + 5") to reduce tariffs and non-tariff barriers to establish a free trade agreement for a unified market in 15 countries. If RCEP is negotiated, it will cover about 3.5 billion people, and the total GDP will reach 23 trillion US dollars, accounting for 1/3 of the global total, and its covered area will become the world's largest free trade zone. On November 4, 2019, India announced that it would not join the ASEAN RCEP agreement. Held on November 15, 2020, the ten ASEAN countries and 5 countries including China, Japan, South Korea, Australia and New Zealand formally signed the Regional Comprehensive Economic Partnership Agreement (RCEP), marking the official conclusion of the world's largest free trade agreement.

10.2.5 AEC 非洲经济共同体

The African Economic Community (AEC) is an international organization established by the member states of the African Union to promote the economic development and integration of most African countries. The African Economic Community was established on June 3, 1991. The organization's regular goals include the establishment of a series of free trade zones and customs unions, the same single market, central bank, and currency union, which led to the establishment of this economic and currency union.

There are currently many regional groups in Africa. They are called Regional Economic Communities (RECs). Many African countries have joined more than one regional economic community. These regional economic communities are mainly composed of trade groups, and they also include cooperation in the political and military fields.

10.2.6 MERCOSUR 南方共同市场

The Southern Common Market (MERCOSUR) is the largest economic integration organization in South America and the first common market in the world composed entirely of developing countries. On March 26, 1991, the presidents of Argentina, Brazil, Uruguay and Paraguay signed the Asuncion Treaty in Asuncion, the capital of Paraguay (the treaty entered into force on November 29 of the same year), announcing the establishment of the Mercosur. Since then, the Mercosur has successively accepted Chile (October 1996), Bolivia (1997), Peru (2003), Ecuador (December 2004) and Colombia (December 2004) as its associate countries. The purpose of the organization is to promote the scientific and technological progress of member countries through effective use of resources, protect the environment, coordinate macroeconomic policies, strengthen economic complementarity, and ultimately achieve economic and political integration.

10.3 International Goods and Services Trade Market 国际商品与服务贸易市场

10.3.1 Globalization of Services 服务全球化

Services are becoming a key driver of global trade. Services have already transformed national economies at a massive scale. Not only are services indispensable to running our increasingly complex and sophisticated industrial economies—from logistics, to finance, to informatics—but the services sector is the fastest growing economic segment in its own right—from business services, to healthcare, to entertainment. Services generate more than two-thirds of economic output, attract over two-thirds of foreign direct investment, and provide almost two-thirds of jobs in developing countries and four-fifths in developed ones.

Services now seem to be transforming international trade in similar ways. Although they still account for only one fifth of cross-border trade, they are the fastest growing sector (WTO, 2017). While the value of goods exports has increased at a modest 1 percent annually since 2011, the value of commercial services exports has expanded at three times that rate, 3 percent (Figure 10.1). The services share of world trade has grown from just 9 percent in 1970 to over 20 percent today.

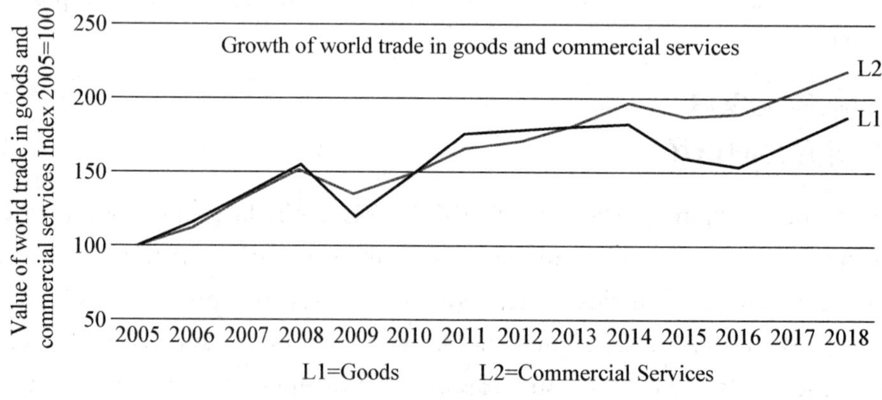

Source: WTO-UNCTAD-ITC estimates.

Figure 10.1 Trade in Goods Has Grown More Slowly than Trade in Commercial Services[1]

---

① Note: World trade is calculated as the average of world exports and world imports.

There is a common perception that globalization is slowing down. But if the growing wave of services trade is factored in—and not just the modest increases in merchandise trade—then globalization may be poised to speed up again.

We can find from the figure(见章末拓展阅读资源) that Number of services RTAs notified to the WTO, by year of entry into force (left) and proportion of RTAs notified to the WTO that cover trade in services, by year of entry into force (right).

In addition, across the world, the share of services employment in total employment is on the rise. Structural change due to innovation, changing demographics, rising incomes, and other factors, continues to pull workers into the services sector, as Figure(见章末拓展阅读资源) illustrates. This implies, for instance, that in high-income economies, services trade has the potential to benefit a larger share of workers than trade in goods and an increasing share of workers in low-and middle-income economies.

10.3.2 Proportion of Service Industry in the Global Regional Market 全球区域市场服务业占比

Trade in services is more resilient than trade in goods to foreign income shocks. For instance, according to Ariu (2016), trade in services was far less affected by the global financial crisis in 2008—2009 than merchandise trade. His explanation is that services represent essential inputs for the production process, that their flow must be continuous, and that they cannot be stored, nor can they easily be modified in reaction to fluctuations in output. Therefore, even during the crisis, firms continued importing services that provided fundamental production inputs(Figure,见章末拓展阅读资源).

Emerging economies, are becoming more services-based—in some cases, at an even faster pace than advanced ones. Despite emerging as the "world's factory" in recent decades, China's economy is shifting dramatically into services. Services now account for over 52 percent of GDP—a higher share than manufacturing—up from 41 percent in 2005. In India, services now make up almost 50 percent of GDP, up from just 30 percent in 1970. In Brazil, the share of services in GDP is even higher, at 63 percent (World Bank, 2019). Between 1980 and 2015, the average share of services in GDP across all developing countries grew from 42 to 55 percent (UNCTAD, 2017) (Figure,见章末拓展阅读资源).

10.3.3 The Performance of Service Trade in Different Economies 服务贸易在不同经济体的表现

From the perspective of the three industries of transportation, communications, and finance and insurance, the three industries in developed economies are relatively even, while the growth in service trade brought about by the reduction of service trade barriers in developing countries is the most.

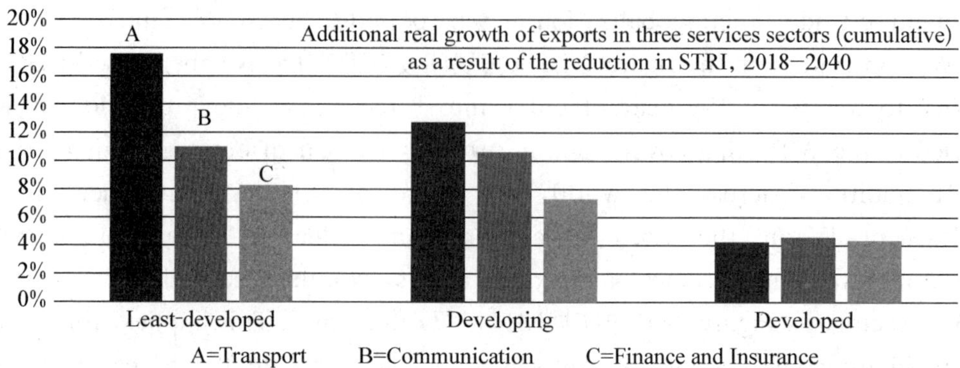

Source: Simulations with WTO Global Trade Model.

Figure 10.2 Projected Services Trade Growth Associated with Reductions in Services Trade Barriers is Highest in Least-developed Countries①

Judging from the actual performance in recent years, more and more developing countries have joined various service trade agreements, which is very important for developing countries to improve the level of service trade.

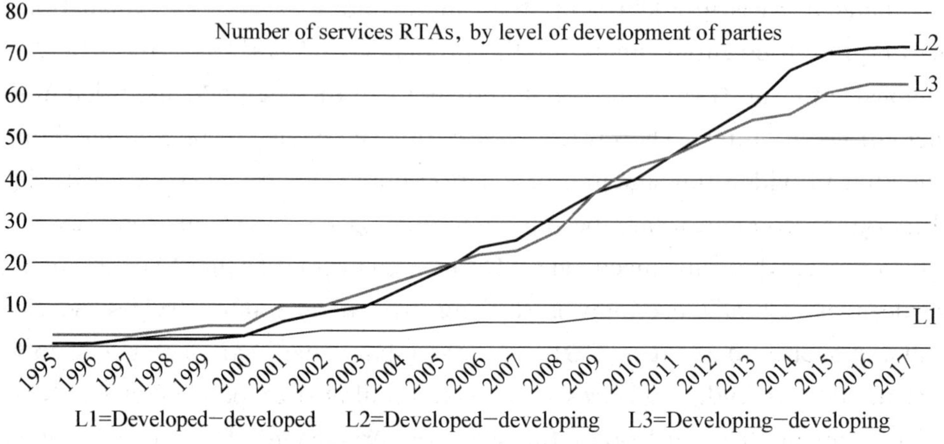

Source: WTO Secretariat, December 2018.

Figure 10.3 Developing Countries are Increasingly Parties to Services RTAs

This is the result of substantial investment flows in services, with branches and subsidiaries estblishe by the five major developing economics not only in other developing regions but also in developed economies. For example, US services

① Notes: The figure displays the cumulative additional growth in real exports from 2018 until 2040 under the scenario of a reduction in the STRI towards the median of the lowest quartile of STRI scores across economies. Regional averages are calculated based on trade weighted averages.

imports through foreign-controlled affiliates of the five economies are rising. Between 2014 and 2016, distribution services, financial services and transport services imports through China's affiliates established in the United States doubled, although on a small scale, while IT services imports through affiliates of Indian companies grew by 12 percent on average annually. In the same period, the Republic of Korea held a 13 percent share in total US imports of distribution services through a commercial presence (US Bureau of Economic Analysis, 2018, WTO calculations).

Apart from the five leading developing economy traders, the other 125 developing economies export services differently (Figure,见章末拓展阅读资源). These other developing economies, some 125 in number, spread across all regions, have relatively fewer financial resources to set up affiliates abroad. According to estimates, in 2017 less than one-third of their services exports took place through a commercial presence. This share is 23 percentage points lower than in the five leading developing economies. For these 125 developing economies, cross-border trade is the predominant mode to export services such as in professional and other business services.

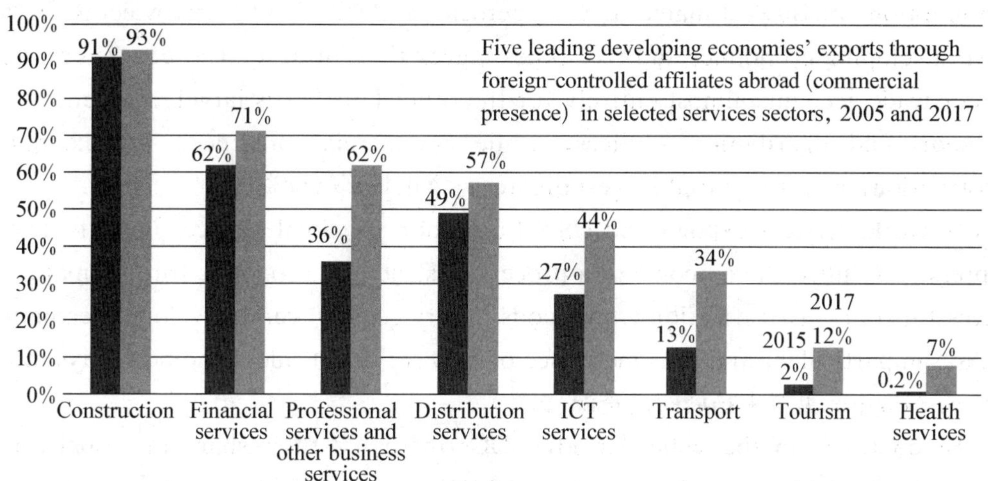

Figure 10.4 For the Top Five Developing Economies, Commercial Presence is the Dominant Mode for Exporting Services

Turning to LDCs, since 2005, their services exports have been rising by almost 11 percent on average per year, albeit from a very low base, with growth led by tourism. Boosted by intensified intra-regional arrivals in recent years, tourism represents an important source of revenue for LDCs and is the only services sector in which the group's participation in global exports exceeds 1 percent (at 1.3 percent).

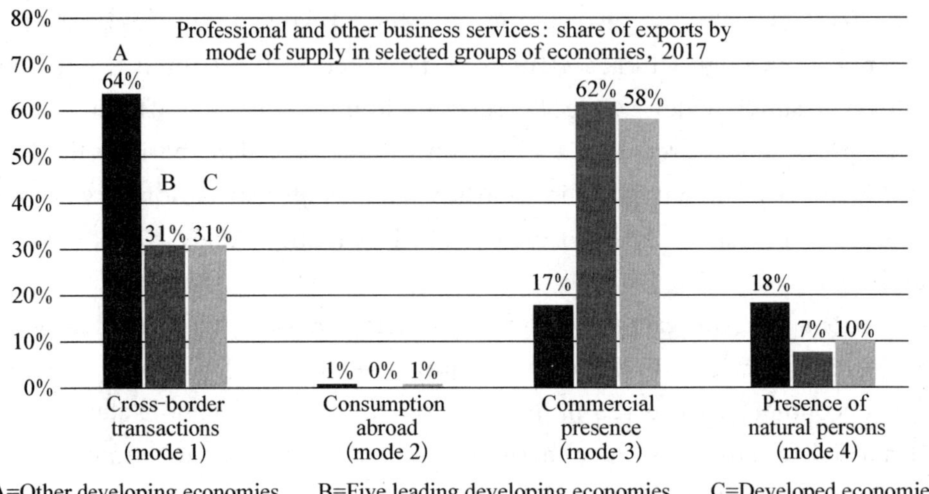

Figure 10.5 The Other 125 Developing Economies Export Services Differently

However, LDCs' services exports are unbalanced. With tourism as the largest sector (34.4 percent of services exports), the share of LDCs' services exports through consumption abroad, estimated at 43.1 percent in 2017, is at least twice as big as in most developing economies and five times bigger than in developed economies. Cross-border trade accounts almost entirely for the other half but is largely concentrated on transport and distribution services, while commercial presence, for example in construction, is in the initial stages(Figure,见章末拓展阅读资源).

In world services exports and US $ 4.5 trillion in global services imports. Such an impressive result is the outcome of a process of structural economic transformation and successful trade diversification from goods to services in several developing economies, in Asia in particular, and the emergence of new services traders and new ways to trade services(Figure,见章末拓展阅读资源).

By contrast, in the same period, LDCs increased their share in global services exports by 0.1 percentage point. In 2017, LDCs accounted for only 0.3 percent of world services exports, or US $ 38.3 billion, and in imports, their participation was at less than 1 percent, with services imports totalling US $ 124.1 billion. Commercial services production in LDCs is, on average, 40 percent of GDP, well below middle income economies (over 50) and high income economies (generally above 70%).①

We can find share of developing countries (left panels) and least-developed countries (right panels) in total trade (upper panels) and services trade (lower

① Notes: The figure displays the average yearly real trade growth of services from 2018 until 2040 under the different scenarios in the different regions. Region averages are calculated based on trade-weighted averages.

panels), 2018—2040. The share of developing and least-developed countries in services trade rises in scenarios with trade cost reduction(Figure,见章末拓展阅读资源).

10.3.4 Service Trade Cost Difference 服务贸易成本差异

However, the cost of internal trade in the service industry is still different. There are many low-cost service industries, such as maritime transport. From an industry perspective, the cost of many fields is still rather high, such as real estate(Figure,见章末拓展阅读资源).

10.3.5 Service Industry Value Added Performance in Various Fields 服务业增加值在各行业表现

Providing a decomposition of manufacturing exports by value-added and origin (Figure, 见章末拓展阅读资源). illustrates the importance of services for manufacturing. In developed economies, because of a higher degree of servicification, services value-added accounted in 2015 for 33 percent of manufacturing exports compared to 29 percent in developing countries. The decomposition for the three manufacturing hubs—Asia, Europe and North America—in 2015 shows that Europe had the highest services content (34 percent), followed by North America (31 percent) and Asia (29 percent). While the aggregate services value in manufacturing exports remained stable for developed countries between 2005 and 2015, it increased in Asia, particularly due to the strong increase of the domestic services content in China's manufacturing exports. More heterogeneity is observed at the level of individual economies.

The decomposition at the sector level shows that services exports rely to a large extent on services inputs from within the same sector as compared to inputs from other services sectors. The share of intra-sectoral value-added in exports is highest for the following sectors: real estate (78 percent); public, health, education and social (71 percent); finance and insurance (71 percent); other business services (71 percent). In contrast, intersectoral services value-added is important for the exports of sectors such as construction (32 percent), information and communication services (30 percent), and accommodation and food (28 percent)(Figure,见章末拓展阅读资源).

Despite speculation about automation and reshoring, there is no sign indicating a shortening of GVCs. Figure 10.6 shows that overall share of foreign services value-added in world gross exports shows no significant decline and is slightly increasing.

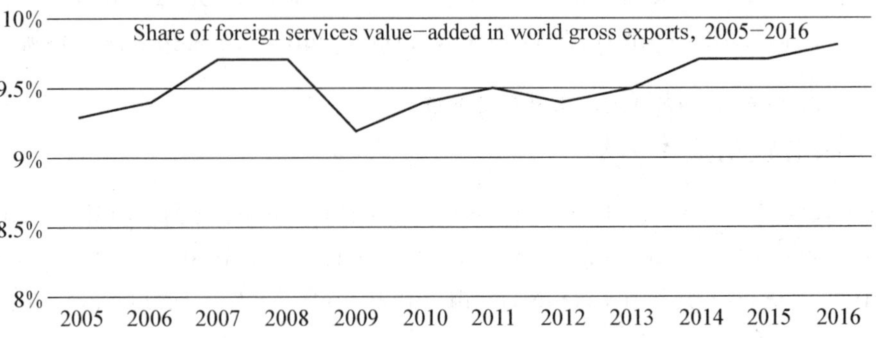

Source: Trade in Value-Added (TiVA) database.

Figure 10.6 The Share of Foreign Services Value-added in World Gross Exports is Stable and is even Slightly Increasing

10.3.6 The Rapid Growth of Cross-border Service Trade 跨境服务贸易迅速增长

If one takes all the 43 economies of Figure (见章末拓展阅读资源) in 2014, the simple average import share in services is only 9.8 percent compared to 48.4 percent in goods. In other words, services are only about one-fifth as traded across borders as goods. These calculations suggest that increased cross-border tradability can unlock potentially large welfare gains for many economies.

The results of the calculations are shown in Figure (见章末拓展阅读资源). During the period 2000—2014, cross-border trade in services led to an average increase in GDP per capita of 6.3 percent for the economies in the sample. In the last decade, the GDP per capita of many economies rose as a result of more cross-border trade in services(Figure,见章末拓展阅读资源).

Descriptive statistics highlight that services trade supports a large number of jobs in some developing countries; for instance, the ICT sector in India employs 3.5 million workers. Figure (见章末拓展阅读资源) shows the number of jobs supported by services exports relative to the total number of jobs and the number of jobs in the services sector. In several economies, including Chile, Costa Rica, India, South Africa and Turkey, exports account for more than 10 percent of employment in services. Obviously, these numbers do not indicate whether services exports increase the number of jobs or just absorb resources from other sectors, but they illustrate the importance of services trade for domestic employment(Figure,见章末拓展阅读资源).

10.3.7 Performance of Various Sub-Fields of International Service Trade 国际服务贸易各细分行业表现

This section introduces the development of various industries in the field of service trade in recent years, and will not repeat the introduction in the section on the international industry market later, and jointly observe the current development trend of new international industries.

(1) International Tourism Market 国际旅游市场

As the number of international tourist arrivals worldwide rose to some 1,330 million in 2017, up from 809 million in 2005 (UNWTO, 2018), world trade in tourism reached US $ 1,029 billion, almost doubling its 2005 value. International tourism is the most inclusive service sector with participation in trade by economies at all levels of development. In developing economies, the tourism and travel-related industry records the highest contribution in exports by micro, small and medium-sized enterprises (MSMEs) and by women (WTO estimates based on World Bank Enterprise Surveys). The new trend towards sustainable and green tourism will offer further export opportunities to areas not yet touched by tourism development(Figure,见章末拓展阅读资源).

Foreign travelers' expenditure during stays abroad enters the tourism value chain directly via the hospitality sector, transport, retail, entertainment and cultural activities, etc. Tourism indirectly contributes to the development of other sectors such as conference and event management or communications. It also drives the construction of infrastructure and accommodation.

(2) International Construction Trade Market 国际建筑贸易市场

In 2017, trade in construction reached US $ 445 billion, with an average annual growth of 7 percent since 2005, and a share in global services trade of 3.4 percent. The last decade has seen the emergence of China as a global construction exporter, involved in large infrastructural building projects (Figure,见章末拓展阅读资源). China, whose exports reached US $ 188 billion and accounted for over one-third of global construction exports (37.3 percent) in 2017, up from 8.4 percent in 2005, ranked the second largest exporter in the world right after the European Union.

Chinese firms are actively engaged in the construction of bridges, harbours, roads and railways, in Africa and other developing regions. China's construction exports are expected to rise further with the "Belt and Road Initiative", an initiative launched in 2013 by the Chinese government, aiming at infrastructure development and investment in many economies.

(3) Global Information Technology Market 国际信息技术市场

IT firms in India and other economies are increasingly expanding their core services including product development. This segment, which include new technologies such as the Internet of Things, cloud analytics and artificial intelligence, is expected to boost not only the IT industry and global trade in computer services, but also trade in intellectual property (IP)-related services in the next few years(Figure,见章末拓展阅读资源).

(4) International Intellectual Property Market 国际知识产权市场

IP-related services cover, for example, fees for the reproduction and distribution of copyrights on computer software, audio-visuals, books, broadcasting and recording of live performances. Fostered also by mobile technology and digital means, trade in IP-related services is growing rapidly. In the last five years, the boom of on-demand music and video streaming, such as through online platforms, has turned audio-visuals into the most dynamic segment of the United States' IP-related services exports (Figure,见章末拓展阅读资源).

IP-related services cover also fees relating to the international use of patents, outputs from R & D, industrial processes and designs, as well as franchises and trademarks. In general, cross-border trade in IP-related services, estimated overall at US $ 396 billion, is dominated by flows between developed countries (92 percent of exports and 75 percent of imports).

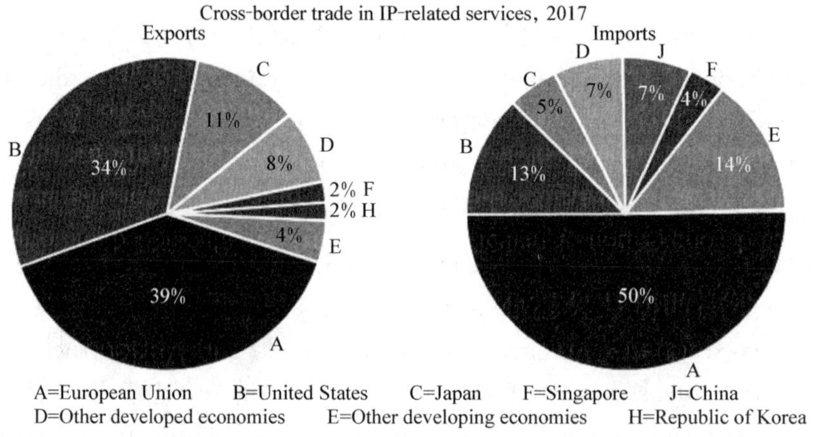

Figure 10.7 Trade in IP-related Services is Dominated by Developed Economies

(5) International Education Market 国际教育市场

Thanks to more than 5 million international students worldwide in 2017, trade in educational services recorded dynamic growth (7 percent on average annually since 2005), and a value of US $ 111 billion, or 0.9 percent of world trade in services. developed English-speaking economies, such as the United States, the United Kingdom, and Australia are the main destinations for foreign students but developing economies are no longer only sending their students to other economies. China, Malaysia and India, among others, are emerging as exporters of educational services, attracting students mainly from other developing regions (UNESCO, 2019).

Educational services are predominantly traded through overseas consumption. However, online distance education is growing thanks to the thousands of educational platforms flourishing on the web, addressing a variety of educational needs from primary school students to graduates. Several leading universities offer online courses in subjects from sciences to the humanities, with online tutors available to assist students. Online distance learning represents a cheaper and more flexible alternative for students worldwide who, due to financial constraints or for other reasons, are unable to travel abroad to pursue higher education. New technologies are increasingly making it possible to integrate virtual reality into education and training, thereby making e-learning an ever more thorough experience for online students.

(6) International Medical Service Market 国际医疗服务市场

Cases Studies 10.2

Trade in medical services, ranging complex surgery to rejuvenation treatments, was estimated at US $ 54 billion in 2017, with a share in world trade in services of only 0.4 percent but recording an annual average growth of 11 percent since 2005. Globally, over 72 percent of health services were traded primarily by developed economies through affiliated hospitals and medical centres in other countries, and 22 percent exported to foreign patients during their stay abroad.

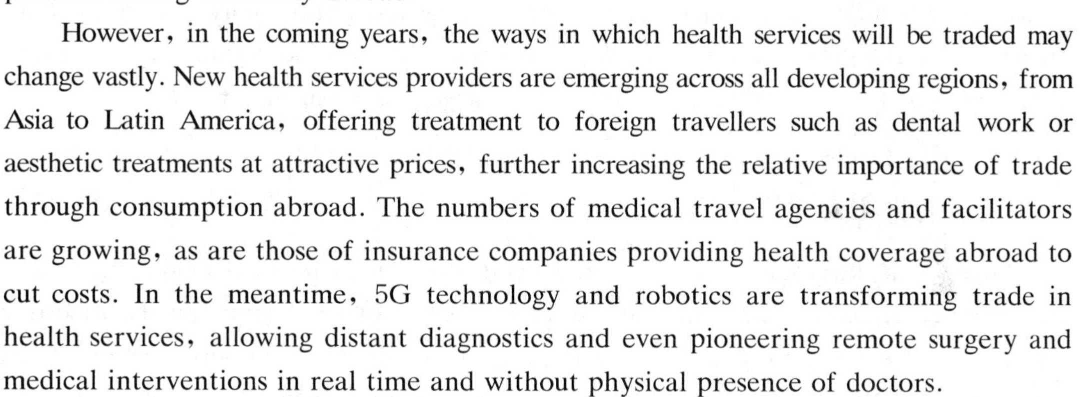

However, in the coming years, the ways in which health services will be traded may change vastly. New health services providers are emerging across all developing regions, from Asia to Latin America, offering treatment to foreign travellers such as dental work or aesthetic treatments at attractive prices, further increasing the relative importance of trade through consumption abroad. The numbers of medical travel agencies and facilitators are growing, as are those of insurance companies providing health coverage abroad to cut costs. In the meantime, 5G technology and robotics are transforming trade in health services, allowing distant diagnostics and even pioneering remote surgery and medical interventions in real time and without physical presence of doctors.

As healthcare demand outpaces healthcare supply in developed countries, supply of these services is likely also to come from developing countries where there is a large working-age population. Mobility of people and the increasing remote delivery of health services through digital technologies are likely to satisfy this demand.

(7) International Environmental Services Trade Market 国际环境服务贸易市场

According to preliminary estimates, some US $ 20 billion of environmental services, including waste disposal, recycling, sanitation and cleaning of pollution were traded in 2017. Environmental services account for just 0.2 percent of services trade; however, growing environmental concerns and ensuing regulatory initiatives, such as those which aim to reduce pollution by plastics, are boosting demand for these services worldwide, and their trade is growing (4 percent on average annually since 2005).

10.4 Intercontinental Market 洲际市场

10.4.1 African Market 非洲市场

Growth in Sub-Saharan Africa is estimated at 2.5 percent for 2018, down from 2.6 percent in 2017. Although expected to rebound to 2.9 percent in 2019, growth remains insufficient to reduce poverty significantly. Although the poverty rate declined from 54 percent in 1990 to 41 percent in 2015, population growth at 2.6 percent per year has offset these gains, resulting in 130 million more poor people. Please refer to Table 10.1 (Africa Regional Snapshot) for relevant information on the African market as of 2019.

Volatility in the global environment—trade tensions, protectionism, and recovering but uncertain commodity prices—continues to have a negative impact on African economies. Holding back growth within the region are macroeconomic instability, including poorly managed debt, inflation, and deficits; political and regulatory uncertainty; and conflict and fragility. For example, fragility in a few countries is costing the region nearly a half a percentage point of growth per year, or 2.6 percentage points over five years.

10.4.2 East Asia and Pacific 东亚和太平洋

Growth in developing East Asia and Pacific remained resilient at 6.3 percent in 2018. Domestic demand has remained resilient in much of the region, partly offsetting the impact of slowing exports. Despite the recent slowdown, the region remains a key driver of the global economy, accounting for around one-third of global growth, mainly due to China. For East Asia and Pacific market related information, please refer to Table (East Asia and Pacific,见章末拓展阅读资源).

China's growth slowed moderately to 6.5 percent in 2018, after growing faster than anticipated in 2017. In Thailand and Vietnam, growth was robust at 4.1 percent and 7.1 percent respectively. Indonesia's growth picked up slightly at 5.2 percent, credited to improved prospects for investment and private consumption. Growth in the Philippines slowed to 6.2 percent, but the planned expansion of public investment is expected to boost it over the medium term. In Malaysia, growth eased at 4.7 percent, with the slowing of export growth and public investments.

In the region's smaller ecnomic exercise, growth prospects remained robust in 2018, averaging over 6.5 percent annually in Cambodia, Lao People's Democratic Republic, Mongolia, and Myanmar. In Timor-Leste, growth is expected to resume in

2019 following the resolution of a political impasse, while prospects in Papua New Guinea were affected by a large earthquake in 2018. Growth in the Pacific Island countries is expected to remain relatively stable, although highly vulnerable to shocks from natural disasters.

The region has made significant progress in eliminating extreme poverty. The percentage of people living on less than ＄1.90 a day is now estimated at less than 1.5 percent (3.8% percent excluding China). This number is expected to reach 1 percent by 2021 (2.7% percent excluding China). Nonetheless, an aging population, rapid urbanization, slowing growth in global trade, and rapidly advancing technologies present new challenges to sustainable progress in the region.

In 2019, the East Asian market has a population of about 1.5 billion, accounting for 10.5% of the world's total population. China, Japan, South Korea, North Korea and Mongolia are among the world's largest regional markets. The average GDP growth is higher than the average growth rate of world GDP. The region with the strongest economic growth in the world is a big market with great appeal to countries all over the world.

10.4.3 Europe and Central Asia 欧洲和中亚

Economic growth in Europe and Central Asia slowed to 3.1 percent in 2018. It is projected to decline further to 2.1 percent in 2019, amid a global downturn and uncertain prospects. For information about the Europe and Central Asia market, please refer to Table (Europe and Central Asia,见章末拓展阅读资源).

Growth in countries across the region varied, with Russia, the largest economy, contributing robustly to regional growth, alongside Albania, Hungary, Poland, and Serbia. Regional growth is expected to pick up modestly in 2020—2021, as anticipated gradual recovery in Turkey offsets moderating activity in Central Europe. The region's long-term challenges, remain formidable however.

The share of the working-age population in the region has fallen dramatically, largely due to declining fertility rates in the 1990s. Productivity slowed to 0.8 percent per year between 2013 and 2017. Investment growth has slowed sharply, from an average of above 15 percent in the five years prior to the global financial crisis to an average of just 1.6 percent in 2014—2018. Parts of the region—particularly Central Asia and the Western Balkans—are highly vulnerable to climate change impacts, including droughts, flooding, and other frequent natural disasters.

10.4.4 Latin America and the Caribbean 拉丁美洲和加勒比

Growth in Latin America and Caribbean was 1.6 percent in 2018 and is estimated to rise to 1.7 percent in 2019. Our aim is to expand upon the profound social transformation during the first decade of the 21st century, when the commodity boom and widespread growth cut the region's poverty rates in half. Between 2003 and 2016, the share of the population living in extreme poverty in the region fell from 24.5 percent to 9.9 percent. Since then, however, economic prospects have dimmed, and many people are at risk of slipping back into poverty. For information about the Latin America and the Caribbean market, please refer to Table (Latin America and the Caribbean,见章末拓展阅读资源).

Much of this poverty reduction was due to the favorable phase of the economic cycle rather than an improvement in the underlying, long-term economic structure of the region. It remains a challenge for countries to overcome these limitations to support stronger and inclusive growth.

10.4.5 Middle East and North Africa 中东和北非

Growth in the Middle East and North Africa is expected to be a modest 1.5 percent in 2019, down from 1.6 percent in 2018, largely due to weaker global growth and global financial market volatility. Real per capita growth across the region will be −0.1 percent, improving slightly on 2018's decline of −0.2 percent. For Middle East and North Africa market related information, please refer to Table 10.5 (Middle East and North Africa,见章末拓展阅读资源).

Conflict continues in the Republic of Yemen and Libya and, though diminished, in Syria as well. This has contributed to an increase in the region's extreme poverty rate, which nearly doubled from 2.7 percent in 2011 to 5 percent in 2015. Iraq's recovery and reconstruction efforts are moving forward, if slowly. The Arab Republic of Egypt, with strong reforms on the fiscal and energy fronts, will post a growth rate of 5.5 percent in 2019. Jordan and Lebanon, still bearing the cost of millions of refugees, are preparing to embark on significant economic reforms, while in Tunisia, upcoming parliamentary and presidential elections have slowed the reform agenda. Morocco remains stable, though with slow growth. Djibouti's 7 percent growth rate for 2019 is the region's fastest, though it has had little impact on the country's high level of poverty. Growth in the Gulf Cooperation Council (GCC) remains around 2 percent, with reforms in many countries, most notably Saudi Arabia.

We believe that the Middle East refers to the entire West Asia and North Africa region connecting Europe, Asia and Africa, including Iran, Iraq, Saudi Arabia, Kuwait, Bahrain, Qatar, UAE, Oman, Yemen, Jordan, Syria, Lebanon, Israel, and Palestine. Turkey, Egypt, Libya, Tunisia, Algeria, Morocco and Sudan, as well as Cyprus, because of its accession to the European Union, statistics do not include the country, a total of 21 countries. The ethnic composition of the Middle East is complex, with Arabs, Turks, Greeks and pure Persians. 80% of people believe in Islam, and the Middle East is rich in oil. The oil reserves account for 66% of the world total.

The Middle East market involves in 21 countries in the Middle East (except Cyprus) with a total land area of about 14 million square kilometers and a population of more than 500 million. The vast majority of countries in the Middle East are buried in oil. The per capita annual income ranges from 3～4 million U.S. dollars in the United Arab Emirates and Kuwait to Iran, Iraq, Yemen and other countries with annual per capita income ranging from 5 to 6 thousand US dollars. These Arab countries have light labor, daily use, electronics, and clothing. Relying on imports, the price requirements of the products are medium and low, and the grades are not very high. At the same time, these areas are almost completely characterized by pure consumption.

Characteristics of Middle East market:

① The market is highly dependent on imported products.

② The market has few restrictions on imports, low tariffs, and fierce market competition.

③ Market demand hierarchy diversity.

④ The market has strong demand for labor products.

⑤ Market products are greatly influenced by religious culture.

⑥ The market has a large demand for agricultural products and live sheep products.

The population of Africa has exceeded 1 billion, accounting for about 15% of the world's total population. It is expected to reach 2 billion in 2050. There are 54 countries in Africa with an area of about 30.2 million square kilometers. The area and population are second only to Asia, ranking second in the world. Africa's natural resources, proven mineral resources, large reserves, platinum, manganese, chromium, antimony and other mineral deposits account for more than 80% of the world's total reserves, phosphate, palladium, gold, diamonds, cobalt and vanadium, etc. More than half of the mineral deposits are abundant in oil and natural gas; Africa is the region with the lowest level of economic development in the world, and most countries are economically backward.

Characteristics of African market:

① Great market potential and abundant resources.

② Intense market competition.

③ Economic backwardness, low per capita income.

10.4.6 South Asia 南亚

South Asia remains the fastest-growing region in the world, projected to grow by 6.9% in 2019, 7.0% in 2020, and 7.1% in 2021, driven by tepid private consumption, recovering in exports, and investments due to policy reforms and infrastructure upgrades. The region has also experienced political stability, with democratic and peaceful transition of governments in most countries. Risks to the outlook mainly stem from domestic factors, including weak exports, slow progress on fiscal consolidation, high deficits, and disruptions due to natural disasters. For South Asia market related information, please refer to Table (South Asia,见章末拓展阅读资源).

Robust growth has translated into reduction poverty and impressive improvements in health and education. But as of 2015, the proportion of people living on less than \$ 1.90 a day was still an estimated 12.4%, or about 216 million people1—a third of the global poor—and multidimensional poverty is higher than the global average. Many countries in the region also suffer from extreme forms of social exclusion and significant infrastructure gaps. The region has also seen one of the largest refugee inflows in modern times, with more than 740, 000 Rohingya refugees fleeing to Bangladesh since August 2017, according to UN estimates.

10.5 International Industrial Market 国际产业市场

10.5.1 World Infrastructure Investment Market 世界基础设施投资市场

According to the World Bank's Private Participation in Infrastructure (PPI) Database, approximately 10,000 infrastructure projects were launched between 1990 and 2018, and only 2.2 percent of these projects have been carried out.

Figure (10.32,见章末拓展阅读资源) shows the amount of investment in infrastructure in each region. Latin America and the Caribbean received 34.3 percent of the total amount of investment in infrastructure, followed by East Asia and the Pacific (27.6 percent), South Asia (15.8 percent), Europe and Central Asia (13.4 percent), sub-Saharan Africa (6.5 percent) and the Middle East and North Africa (2.4 percent).

10.5.2 Mobile and Broadband User Market 移动和宽带用户市场

A reliable, comprehensive and affordable high-speed broadband network is central to competitiveness in the digital era. Developing countries have been fast catching up on broadband networks. Figure (10.33,见章末拓展阅读资源) shows the evolution of mobile and fixed broadband subscriptions by development level from 2005 to 2017. Active mobile subscriptions in developing countries increased exponentially from 43 million to nearly 3, 371 million between 2007 and 2018, and mobile subscription in LDCs also increased from nearly zero to 291 million during the same period. Similarly, from 2005 to 2018, fixed broadband subscriptions experienced an impressive growth in developing countries, from 71 million to 661 million.

In 2018, fourth-generation (4G) services became the leading mobile technology, with 3.4 billion subscribers. As growth continues, particularly across developing markets, 4G is expected to reach 60% of total mobile services in use by 2023. Meanwhile, great hopes are pinned on fifth-generation (5G) high-bandwidth mobile technology as a means of better quality connection of developing countries to the global economy that will allow them to enhance participation in e-commerce, trade in services and global value-chains. Following commercial launches in the United States and South Korea towards the end of 2018, 16 more economies will have launched 5G networks by the end of 2019. By 2025, 5G services are predicted to be available in 116 markets (GSMA, 2019). The wide penetration of mobile devices, coupled with the development of mobile broadband, could bring new development opportunities.

10.5.3 E-Waste Market 电子废物市场

The United Nations University conservatively estimated the value of recoverable materials of e-waste to be $55 billion in 2019, or more than the 2016 gross domestic product of most countries. Some countries such as Japan have e-waste management laws that make manufacturers and retailers responsible for taking back used home appliances, recycling them, and publishing the costs of recycling. E-waste flows should be viewed as sources of inputs for next-generation products.The global trade in plastic waste grew in lockstep with the expansion of GVCs through the 1990s and 2000s. In 1990, worldwide imports of plastic waste were worth less than $1 billion, and by 2010, they had peaked at around $10 billion. In the last decade, they have begun to level off and even decline. Meanwhile, plastic and microplastic waste have proven to be a major challenge for solid waste management and have become a global crisis for the environment, especially the oceans. In 2018 the Center for Biological Diversity estimated that swirling convergences of plastic make up about 40% of the world's ocean surfaces and that at current rates they could outweigh all the fish in the sea by 2050.

10.5.4 Solar Photovoltaic 太阳能光伏产业①

Figure 10.39 illustrates the supply chain of a PV company. Solar cell production is

① Note: Solar cell production is primarily concentrated in China and elsewhere in Asia and is dependent on the production of components from several countries. Europe and the United States lead upstream service provision, including shipping, distribution, installation, and recycling.

concentrated primarily in China and elsewhere in Asia and is dependent on the production of components from several countries. Europe and the United States lead upstream service provision, including shipping, distribution, installation, and recycling. Large parts of the supply chain have generally been located in countries or regions with strong demand, such as the European Union. Low labor costs, natural resources, and government policies have driven some production to China.

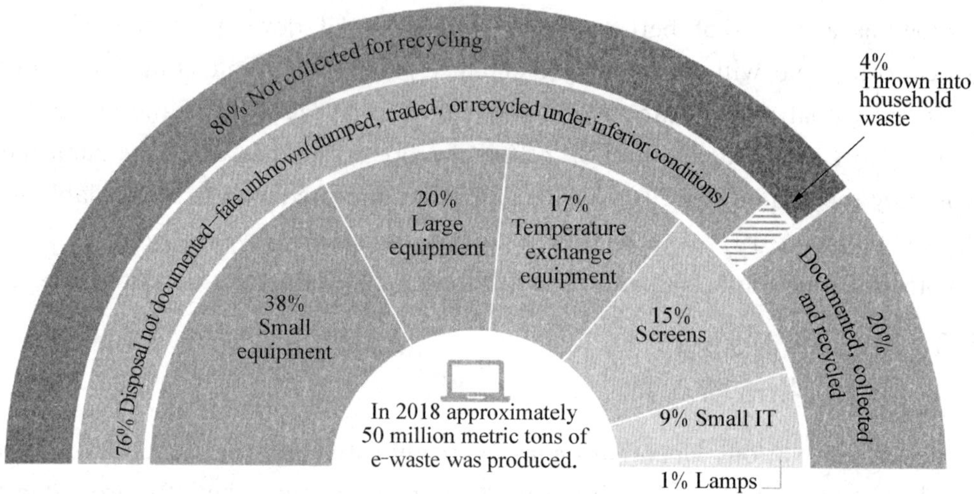

Source: World Development Report 2020.

Figure 10.8 The World Produced 50 Million Metric Tons of E-waste in 2018

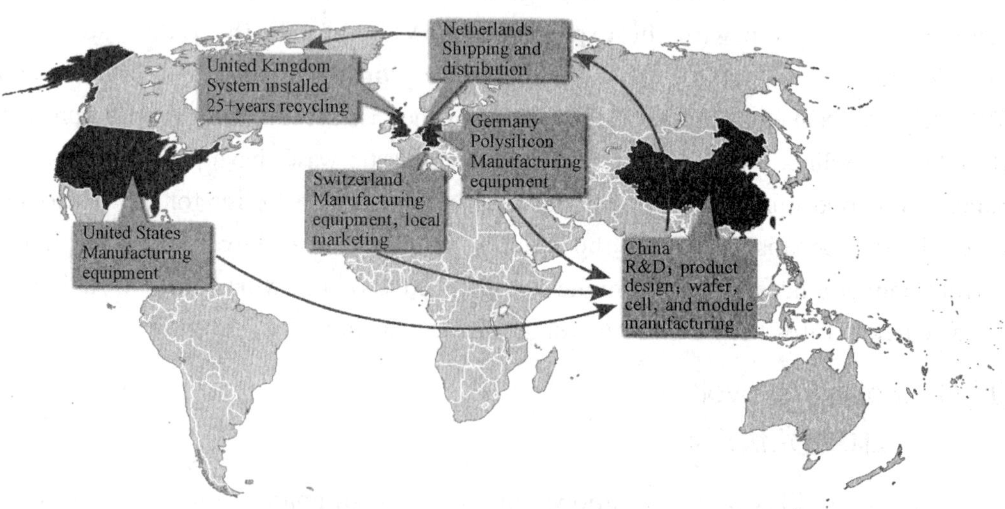

Source: European Commission 2016.

Figure 10.9 Supply Chain of a Solar Photovoltaic Company

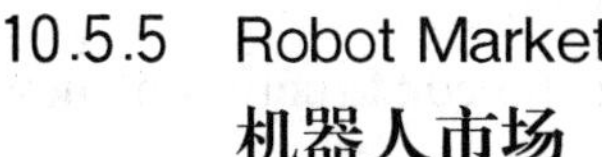

10.5.5 Robot Market 机器人市场

Robotization is on the rise, raising concerns about the future of GVCs. The spread of new production technologies, such as advanced robotics and 3D printing, has raised concerns about the future of trade and of GVCs. Robotics technology, having advanced greatly in the last two decades, is predicted to develop further in the coming years. The average price of an industrial robot has fallen by half in real terms and even more relative to labor costs. Global sales of industrial robots reached a record 387,000 units in 2017, up 31 percent from 2016. Figure 10.36 shows that robotization is higher in countries with higher income per capita, where wages are higher, and in sectors in which robotization is feasible.

Robots are used predominantly in high-wage countries in Asia, North America and Western Europe (panel a). In recent years, China, which has gone through the fatest growth in industrial robot demand and was projected to have the largest operational stock of robots by the end of 2018, but still relatively low robot density. Robotization is most pronounced in the automotive, rubber and plastics, metals, and electronics sectors, reflecting differences in the feasibility of automation (panel b). It is still limited in traditionally labor-intensive sectors such as textiles, suggesting that export-led industrialization in these sectors is still a viable development path. Robot adoption is projected to increase greatly over the coming decade, reflecting further reductions in quality-adjusted robot prices.

10.6 Selected Country Markets 主要经济体

10.6.1 Chinese Market 中国市场

After 70 years of development, China has become the only country in the world with all the industrial categories in the United Nations Industrial Classification. Of the more than 500 major industrial products in the world, China's output ranks first in the world for more than 220 industrial products.

China's industrial added value increased from 12 billion yuan in 1952 to more than 30 trillion yuan in 2018, an increase of about 971 times at constant prices, an average annual growth rate of 11%. According to World Bank data, in 2010, China's manufacturing value added surpassed the United States to become the largest manufacturing country. In 2018, the added value of China's manufacturing industry accounted for more than 28% of the world's share, becoming an important engine driving global industrial growth.

At present, China is developing in step with the world in the construction of new infrastructure such as 5G, industrial Internet, and artificial intelligence, and even has a partial lead; at the same time, new business models and new models continue to emerge, giving birth to world-class brands such as Huawei, Alibaba, and Tencent. Of companies have spawned new business formats such as e-commerce and sharing economy, and applications in areas such as autonomous driving, smart home appliances, VR/AR, distance education, and telemedicine are in the ascendant.

According to the *Global Business Environment Report 2020* released by the World Bank, the top ten economies in the global business environment in 2019 are New Zealand, Singapore, Hong Kong China, Denmark, South Korea, the United States, Georgia, the United Kingdom, Norway, and Sweden. Among the 190 economies, China ranked 31st, a significant jump from 2018 (ranked 46th) and 2017 (ranked 78th).

In recent years, China has also been committed to optimizing the business environment, and the continuous rise in China's business environment rankings released by the World Bank report is undoubtedly a recognition of China's continuous efforts to optimize the business environment. As China continues to open up and optimize its business environment, foreign companies will have more confidence and a greater sense of gain in investing in China in the future.

"The Belt and Road" (B & R) is the abbreviation of "Silk Road Economic Belt" and "21st Century Maritime Silk Road", respectively proposed by Chinese Chairman Xi Jinping in both September and October 2013. Although the scope of the BRI is still taking shape, it is structured around two main components, underpinned by significant infrastructure investments: the Silk Road Economic Belt (the "Belt") and the New Maritime Silk Road (the "Road"). The overland Belt will link China to Central and South Asia and onward to Europe, and the maritime Road will link China to Southeast Asia, the Gulf countries, East Africa and North Africa, and on to Europe.

Improved internationaly connected transport in frastruc ture can have a significant impact on international trade and GVC (Global Value Chain) integration. By one estimate for a sample of 126 countries, a one-day delay in shipping time reduces trade by at least 1 percent.The World Trade Organization (WTO) argnes that delays and border costs can be equivalent to a 134 percent ad valorem tariff on a product in high-income countries and a 219 percent tariff equivalent in developing countries.

An analysis of the impacts of transport projects linked to the Belt and Road Initiative reveals the relevance of international cooperation in infrastructure for GVCs. For economies along the Belt and the Road, as well as for non-Belt and Road countries, the effects of infrastructure investment on GDP are larger when the model accounts for cross-border input-output linkages. When a sector experiences a decrease in the price of its imported inputs as shipping times and trade costs fall, it passes on the associated reduction in production costs to downstream industries, propagating the benefits across the world. These input-output linkages lead to a potentially complex reallocation of comparative advantage, production, and trade, thereby increasing welfare.

Figure 10.38 shows the household services consumption composition for China in 2017, with the largest services consumption being housing, transport and communication.

Although the Chinese market has become the most attractive market in the world, the Chinese market has exposed a series of problems due to regional differences and rapid economic development. For example, many family residents have a relatively large burden on housing and children's education.

10.6.2 US Market 美国市场

The United States has an area of 93,761,14 square kilometers, accounting for 6.3% of the world's total, ranking fourth in the world. The national administrative division is divided into 50 states and a direct jurisdiction, including 48 states and the District of Columbia, and two overseas states. In 2020, the United States had a population of 331 million, accounting for 5% of the world's total. The gross domestic product was 21.4 trillion US dollars, accounting for 25% of the world. It is the most powerful country in the world.

The US market has the following characteristics:

① The market system is developed and the legal system is sound.

② Large market capacity and rapid change.

③ High quality requirements.

④ More market demand levels.

⑤ Unblocked market channels.

⑥ Seasonal sales in the market.

⑦ Commodity advertising has a big impact on the market.

From the perspective of age distribution and expenditure structure, the proportion of expenditures in the real estate, insurance, and telecommunications sectors of American consumers is relatively large, and the trend of younger ones is relatively obvious(Figure 10.39).

In the United States, five of the top ten fastest growing occupations are related to healthcare, and these occupations include home health aides, personal care aides, physicians' assistants and nursing practitioners (US Bureau of Labor Statistics, 2019), as highlighted. A similar trend is also observed in the European Union, where employment of health associate professionals is expected to increase by 10.38 percent between 2016 and 2030.

10.6.3 Japanese Market 日本市场

Japan has a land area of 377,800 square kilometers, a population of 124 million (2019), and a GDP of 5.21 trillion US dollars in 2019. It is the economic power after the United States and China,It is a country with strong economic strength and strong scientific and technological strength.

In 2019, Japan's GDP reached 5.08 trillion U.S. dollars. This is the first time that Japan's GDP has exceeded 5 trillion U.S. dollars after a lapse of six years. In fact, Japan has been hovering around 5 trillion U.S. dollars for the past 30 years.

Japan's GDP has two historical peaks: First, it reached 5.45 trillion U.S. dollars in 1995, while the United States accounted for 7.63 trillion in the same year. Japan accounted for 71.4% of the United States. China has not yet reached this level; the second is 6.2 trillion U.S. dollars in 2012. This is the highest value of Japan's dollar nominal GDP.

The Japanese market has the following characteristics:

① Market monopoly.

② Large market capacity and high quality requirements.

③ The market is export-oriented.

④ Market openness has improved.

⑤ Intense market competition.

⑥ Market circulation channels are long and complicated.

⑦ Increase in the proportion of manufactured goods from goods.

10.6.4 German market 德国市场

As of 2020, Germany's GDP has reached 3.806 trillion U.S. dollars and continues to remain the fourth place in the world, with a total of 83 million people. Among them, it ranks 17_{th} in the world's population. Germany has an area of 357,114 square kilometers. It is the most populous country in the European Union, with a population density of 226 people per square kilometer, making it one of the most densely populated countries in Europe. The main ethnic group is German, with a small number of Danes and Sorbians, who are commonly spoken in German.

Germany is a highly developed capitalist country, the largest economy in Europe, the top of the four major European economies, and one of the founding members of the European Union. It is also a member of NATO, the Schengen Convention, the Group of Seven, and an important member state of the Organization for Economic Cooperation and Development. Its social security system is sound, and its citizens have

an high standard of living. The high-end manufacturing industry represented by automobiles and precision machine tools is also an important symbol of Germany.

10.6.5 Russian Market 俄罗斯市场

On August 19, 1991, the Soviet Union declared its disintegration. Russia became a completely independent sovereign state, which was called the Russian Federation.

Russia is located across Europe and Asia. Its eastern part is in Europe and the north is in Asia. It covers an area of 17.08 million square kilometers, accounting for 11.4% of the world's land area. It is the country with the largest land area in the world. Russia is surrounded by the sea on three sides. About 40,000 kilometers, the land border is more than 10,000 kilometers long, and it is adjacent to 14 countries. There are thousands of kilometers along the border with China.

Russia has a population of 146 million (2019) and is sparsely populated. 74% of the population is in cities and 26% are in rural areas. The population distributed in some parts of Europe is more than the Asian part. There are more than 130 ethnic groups in Russia, and the level of economic development among different ethnic groups is very different.

The terrain of Russia is mainly plain, accounting for 70% of the country's land area. There are many inland rivers and lakes, 3 million large and small rivers, more than 2 million large and small lakes, and abundant fresh water resources. Russia is rich in resources, with many types of resources and large reserves. The proven reserves of oil are 6.5 billion tons, accounting for more than 12% of the world's proven reserves, ranking second in the world. The proven reserves of natural gas are 48 trillion cubic meters, accounting for 28% of the world. More than 1/3 of the world ranks first in the world, with a forest coverage rate of over 40% and a wood stock volume of 80.7 billion cubic meters. The coal reserves are 200 billion tons, ranking second in the world. Nuclear power accounts for 10% of the electricity supply. It has various metal deposits and abundant reserves. Many of its mineral resources are among the highest in the world.

The Russian market has the following characteristics:

① The market capacity is large.

② Market imports are biased towards light industry and agricultural products.

③ Consumers prefer products from Europe, America and Japan.

④ The market is fiercely competitive.

10.6.6 Other Countries 其他国家

(1) Emerging Economies 新兴经济体国家

Counties with emerging markets present great potential to international firms.

Their attractiveness lies primarily in their rate of economic growth up to 7 percent per year, in the past 20 years, compared with about 2 percent for Western Europe and North America. The following countries have been identified as emerging markets by The Economist in its regular reports on emerging markets:

In Asia: China, India, Indonesia, Malaysia, the Philippines, Singapore, South Korea, Thailand.

In Africa and the Middle East: Israel, South Africa.

In Europe: The Czech Republic, Poland, Russia, Turkey.

In Latin America: Argentina, Brazil, Chile, Mexico, Venezuela.

Other countries are likely prospects for the emerging market category on the basis of their economic policies and performance in the past 20 years. Among them are Slovenia, Slovakia, Croatia, Romania, Bulgaria, the Ukraine, Latvia, Estonia, Lithuania and Belarus in Central and Eastern Europe and Colombia, Paraguay Peru, and Uruguay in Latin America. These countries are rapidly privatizing their economics and adopting the economic reforms necessary to create a stable growing economy.

Counties with emerging markets that are expected to have a successful economic future share a number of traits:

—High political stability.

—A sound currency.

—A low level of inflation.

Privatization policies that reduce government deficit, create first time share owners who vote for pro-business conservative policies, and diminish the power of trade unions.

—Policies that facilitate repatriation of dividends and capital.

—Policies that are in line with international accounting standards.

Open disclosure of directors interests Policies that stress regular reporting of earnings and sales figures.

—A sound and comprehensive system of corporate law.

—A liquid and well-traded securities market reflecting fair prices.

—A high savings rate.

—Strong government support for internationalization.

A people characterized by integrity, a strong work ethic, and respect for the law of interest to multinationals are what the United States Department of Commerce refers to as big emerging markets (BEMs). These markets share all the traits of emerging markets and present the most potential because they are large, have large population, and consequently, set the pace for the economy in the region. Among these countries are China and India (both with populations exceeding 1 billion), South Korea, Argentina, Brazil, Mexico, South Africa, Poland, and Turkey.

The big emerging markets are developing rapidly and making rapid strides toward industrialization. However, breakneck growth can be problematic, as in the case of India.

(2) African Countries 非洲国家

A survey of GVC sectors across 14 countries in Sub-Saharan Africa found that just 43 percent of lead firms outsourced critical business and technical services, with the majority choosing to bring the required expertise in-house. 29 Results from the survey suggest that this choice is driven in part by lack of access to a sufficient breadth of quality suppliers (reflecting barriers to trade and investment in services, among other things). Weak legal and regulatory enforcement mechanisms also contribute significantly to the underdevelopment of local markets for services. Share of "other business services" in intermediate inputs is low in poor countries

Many African countries already faced food insecurity before the COVID-19 crisis. A score of 100 indicates the highest possible food availability, affordability and quality.

Table 10.1 Food Security Index—Top and Bottom Ranks, 2019

Top 15 Food Security Ranks			Bottom 15 Food Security Ranks		
RANK	COUNTRY	SCORE (OUT OF 100)	RANK	COUNTRY	SCORE (OUT OF 100)
1	Singapore	87.4	99	Sudan	45.7
2	Ireland	84.0	100	Angola	45.5
3	United States	83.7	101	Zambia	44.4
4	Switzerland	83.1	102	Togo	44.0
5	Finland	82.9	103	Haiti	43.3
6	Norway	82.9	104	Malawi	42.5
7	Sweden	82.7	105	Mozambique	41.4
8	Canada	82.4	106	Sierra Leone	39.0
9	Netherlands	82.0	107	Syria	38.4
10	Austria	81.7	108	Madagascar	37.9
11	Germany	81.5	109	Chad	36.9
12	Australia	81.4	110	Congo (Dem. Rep.)	35.7
13	Qatar	81.2	111	Yemen	35.6
14	Denmark	81.0	112	Burundi	34.3
15	Belgium	80.7	113	Venezuela	31.2

Source: The Economist Intelligence Unit and Corteva Agriscience.

Because bilateral trade protection among African countries affects backward and forward participation in agriculture and food GVCs, the immediate challenge for AfCFTA negotiations for GVC integration is to address the distortions created by traditional barriers to trade within Africa. Existing trade agreements in Africa are relatively shallow.

Conclusion 结语

The first three technological revolutions were the rise of the United Kingdom, the United States, and Germany. The fourth wave of technological revolutions has come. New industries and companies will emerge in the fields of artificial intelligence, biotechnology, and new energy. An attractive market, through reform and opening up, market-oriented operation, and insistence on innovation and development, has shown strong competitiveness. As China's economy catches up with the United States and China's per capita income level increases, Chinese companies are determined to enter the international market at the same time. We cannot abandon the large market of China's domestic internal circulation. Under the Belt and Road Initiative, a growing number of Chinese companies will penetrate into various nodes of the global value chain.

The Chapter's Referential Questions 本章参考题

(1) Discuss on the advantages and disadvantages of the establishment of RCEP to Chinese companies.
谈一下 RCEP 的建立对中国企业带来的机遇与挑战。

(2) In the global service trade market, which Chinese companies have firmly occupied the high end, and which areas are worthy of further exploration by Chinese companies?
在全球服务贸易市场,中国企业有哪些已经牢牢占据高端,还有哪些领域值得中国企业去深入挖掘?

(3) Investigate 15 years of China-US GDP data, and use the dot-and-line method to predict when China's economic aggregate will surpass the United States, and in which areas will Chinese companies inevitably rise?
调研近 15 年中美 GDP 数据,用描点连线法预测中国经济总量何时赶超美国,中国企业在哪些领域也将必然崛起?

Further Reading 拓展阅读

Chapter 11

International Market Research and Forecast
国际市场调研与预测

Learning Objectives
本章学习目标

(1) Methods of international marketing research.
国际市场营销调研的方法。
(2) Concept of international marketing research decision support system.
国际营销调研决策支持系统的概念。
(3) How to make sales forecasts.
如何进行销售预测。

Key Words
关键词

Research; Consumer Behavior; Qualitative Research; Quantitative Research; Primary Data; Secondary Data; Forecasts

Case Studies 11.1

International marketing managers operating in unfamiliar environments need to have a thorough understanding of their target market if their marketing efforts are to be successful. Numerous marketing plans fail due to an incomplete understanding of the market. Companies selling consumer products are especially prone to experiencing difficulties in foreign markets. Many such examples exist: European and U.S. multinationals have entered many low and medium-income markets with large and expensive bottles of cleaning products and tubes of toothpaste, only to find that consumers will not purchase them, in spite of the fact that they prefer Western brands. As soon as those products were packaged in cheap sachets. Consumers started purchasing large volumes. As we see in earlier edition of Chapters, sales of Coke packaged in 200 ml recyclable bottles took off instantly in India. Unlike in the U. S., where 24 packs of any drink fly off the shelves, internationally, products sell better when they come in smaller packages. In fact, smaller-sized products do better in general.

Companies must conduct research in local markets to understand consumers, their needs, and consumption patterns. This chapter defines marketing research and examines its broad scope across all components of the marketing mix (product, place, price and promotion). The Chapter addresses the international marketing research process and the complexities of the process in an international environment.

11.1 The Need for International Market Research 国际市场调研的必要性

《孙子兵法》曰,"知己知彼者,百战不殆",只有通过科学的市场调研才能做到熟悉海外目标市场。由于国际市场调研非常复杂,营销人员会遇到与本国国情大不相同的问题和困难。

Marketing managers need to constantly monitor the different forces affecting their international operations. Marketing information, which should constitute a basis for all executive action, must be taken into consideration to improve the chances of success in a complex global environment. Such information, although amply available in highly developed industrialized nations, still needs to be carefully evaluated and viewed in light of the purpose for which it was collected. In developing countries, relevant data may not be available at all, and if available, it is often questionable in terms of both quality and integrity. For example, production and sales data reported may be tainted by pressures of governments on factories to exceed unrealistic plans or production quotas.

International marketing research is especially complex. International managers are likely to encounter not only the obstacles they have learned to master when conducting research in their own countries, but also obstacles laden with the specifics of the international market where they are conducting the research, specifics that may differ substantially from those of their national market. Consider, for instance, a male marketing researcher working for a hair care firm interested in launching its lines in the beauty salons of the Middle East. In the United States, it is perfectly appropriate for this individual to assess interest in the company's product line by collecting data in beauty salons. In most countries in the Middle East, however, Woman's Beauty Parlors cater exclusively to women (Man's Barber Shops cater exclusively to men), and the presence of males in this environment would constitute a breach of Islamic law, which forbids males from seeing a woman's hair if they are not closely related.

Another aspect of the difficulty of engaging in research internationally is readily observable in Eastern Europe, where consumers remain suspicious of attempts by foreigners and locals to investigate local markets and related consumer behavior. Consumers are simple not accustomed to responding to opinion polls and regard such attempts as an intrusion or as suspect. And, since the transition to a market economy, prospective respondents are also likely to promptly demand payment for any time and effort demanded by the investigation.

These and many other environmental factors encountered in international market research complicate the task of marketing researchers, who should not only have an expertise in the most advanced techniques of scientific inquiry, but also have a profound understanding of the markets under investigation.

11.2 Defining the International Marketing Research 国际市场调研的定义

国际市场调研是指系统地设计、搜集、记录、分析、整合和报告与本企业国际化运营中的特定营销决策有关的数据和信息，从而把握目标市场变化规律，为企业的国际市场营销决策提供可靠的客观依据。

We define international marketing research as follows：

International marketing research is the systematic design, collection, recording, analysis, interpretation and reporting of information pertinent to a particular marketing decision facing a company operating internationally.

This definition of international marketing research contains a caveat also present in the general definition of marketing research: an acquired understanding of the market environment. In an international setting, the environment is particularly complex, and it displays obvious and important subtle differences in culture, religion, customs and business practices, and general market characteristics from the environment of the company's home country.

11.3 The Scope of International Marketing Research 国际市场调研的范围

国际市场调研同本土市场调研相比具有更大、更广范的领域，营销人员需要通过专业的方法获取额外的数据和信息，并进行分析和处理，提供给管理者制定国际营销战略。

International marketing research has a broader scope than domestic research: Managers need additional information to compensate for lack of familiarity with the foreign environment. Sections 11.3.3 to 11.3.6 describe some general research categories.

11.3.1 On Industry, Market Characteristics, and Market Trends 关于行业发展、市场属性和市场趋势的调研

Studies of industry, market characteristics, and market trends, often in the form of acquisition, diversification, and market-share analyses-are conducted regularly by marketing research suppliers and shared with subscribers. Export research is yet another type of research in this category; it is prompted by the shortening of the product life cycle and the intensity of international competition, as well as by the rapid technological change that increases the need to segment markets more frequently. The research techniques range from formal methods, such as focus groups and concept testing, to more informal approaches.

Figure 11.1 Maslow' Hierarchy of Needs

11.3.2 Buyer Behavior Research 关于购买行为

Examining brand preferences and brand attitudes falls into the category of buyer behavior research. To the uninformed, China is an emerging market that cannot afford many luxuries. However, buyer behavior research found that the Chinese luxury market is growing, and this market is demanding. Researchers at General Motors (GM) know that well. According to Maslow's Hierarchy of Needs, consumer needs are hierarchical. Before low-level needs are met, high-level needs cannot become dominant ones.

Case Studies 11.2

11.4 The International Marketing Research Process 国际市场调研的步骤和方法

在国际市场,营销人员会遭遇太多的问题,因此从事国际市场调研,必须学习并掌握一整套科学的步骤和方法,如根据特定的问题设定调研目标、制定调研计划、确定信息来源、如何搜集和处理信息等。

Researchers attempting to obtain accurate and reliable information regarding a problem experienced in the firm's international operations are likely to encounter a number of difficulties, such as translation and cross-cultural comparison complications, which do not, as a rule, affect firms engaging only in domestic research. These difficulties will be addressed for each step in the subsections titled "International Constraints".

11.4.1 Defining the Research Problem and Research Objectives 明确调研的问题和目的

The first step in the international marketing research process requires the international marketing managers and marketing researchers to define research questions and jointly agree on the research objectives. The complexity of the environment of international operations does not allow marketing researchers the opportunity to obtain a clear idea of the specifics that the research study should examine. Instead, they may need to engage in exploratory research into the problem to define the relevant dimensions of the problem investigated. Exploratory investigations may help to further define the problem, suggest hypotheses, or even actually identify additional problems that need to be investigated, Descriptive research, on the other hand, portrays a situation-for instance, how frequently shoppers in Cairo shop for food items; whether they prefer to shop for meat products in state stores, which are cheaper but offer inferior-quality products, or in private stores, which are more expensive but offer a higher quality and assortment of meat products, Finally, causal research examines cause-and-effect relationships, such as the extent to which Sony's offer of financial incentives to electronics sales staff in Ahmadabad, India, is likely to increase sales of the Sony brand.

11.4.2 Developing the Research Plan 制定调研计划

The research plan is a blueprint for the study, indicating all the decisions to be made with regard to information sources; research methods; data collection instruments; sampling procedures; data collection methods; data analysis; and based on these decisions, the projected costs of the research.

11.4.3 Deciding on Information Sources 确定信息来源

After the international manager and researcher define the problem and set the objectives, the researcher must determine the extent to which available information may shed further light on the problem at hand. The researcher starts by identifying useful information pertaining to the issue that has been collected either by the company itself (internal) or by some other firm or agency (external) secondary data. The secondary data may, if needed, help the researcher more clearly define the problem and set better objectives. It also helps the researcher pinpoint the type of information that needs to be gathered for the goals articulated.

(1) Secondary Data 二手数据

Researchers first must determine whether information is available, and if so, how much. Doing so may aid in gaining insights into the problem at hand. Secondary data are defined as data collected for a problem other than the problem at hand.

Secondary data are typically examined first, and they offer the advantage of low cost and ready availability in many of the more-developed countries. Secondary data can be categorized as internal, collected by the company to address a different problem, or collected by the company to address the same problem but in a different country, or external, collected by an entity not affiliated with the company.

(2) Secondary Data Sources 二手数据来源

Researchers must check established sources of information on countries, regions, markets, competitors, and consumers. As a first step, researchers can conduct online searches using search products such as Dialog, Lexis-Nexis, and others, as well as Google, Yahoo, and other similar search engines or portals. They provide sufficient country background information, information on the people, language, customs, lifestyles, government, economy, and other important facts useful for a summary country analysis (www. culturegrams.com).

As a second step, researchers can access various publications and both national and international marketing associations.

(3) International Constraints 国际市场调研的限制性因素

In many international markets, information sources may be limited and inaccurate. Although information accuracy is usually closely linked to the level of country development, the data collected may have shortcomings attribute to factors other than development, such as translation, correspondence, and so forth.

1) Dada Inavailability 信息不便性

In many markets, the detailed data readily available in developed countries may not exist in numerous regions in developing countries, where for example, population censuses are frequently collected based on estimates made by village elders. If, for instance, demographic information—reliable and readily available in developed countries—is deemed important to the project but it not available for the local market to be researched, the researcher may have to collect this type of data. Also, data on income and sales from tax returns can be inaccurate in countries where this information is not declared. Finally, state-run research organizations are often reluctant to disclose the details of the data collection method and process used; no information may be available on response rates, questionnaire development, and the nature of the sample.

2) Lack of Primary Data 缺少一手数据

Primary research is used internationally far less than it should be cost-benefit analyses suggest that spending on research in to remote markets of questionable value is unwise; consequently, the temptation is to use secondary date to serve all research functions.

In its April 2020 World Economic Outlook, the International Monetary Fund predicts that major industrialized economies will contract sharply in 2020 and then rebound in the second year. This seems to be a very optimistic situation. China and India are the only major economies that are not expected to contract. But at the March 2021 contract, after revising previous data, Indian officials also announced economic data for the full year of 2020: an actual decrease of 7% year-on-year.

Table 11.1 GDP Forecasts

	Annual Change in Real GDP (%)		
Region	2019	2020(f)	2021(f)
World	2.9	−3.0	5.8
Advanced Economies	1.7	−6.1	4.5
of which			
US	2.3	−5.9	4.7
Germany	0.6	−7.0	5.2
France	1.3	−7.2	4.5
Italy	0.3	−9.1	4.8
Spain	2.0	−8.0	4.3
UK	1.4	−6.5	4.0
Japan	0.7	−5.2	3.0
Emerging Markets and Developing	3.7	−1.0	6.6
of which			
China	6.1	1.2	9.2
Russia	1.3	−5.5	3.5
Brazil	1.1	−5.3	2.9
India	4.2	1.9	7.4
ASEAN-5	4.8	−0.6	7.8
Middle East and Central Asia	1.2	−2.8	4.0
Sub-Saharan Africa	3.1	−1.6	4.1

Source: IMF World Economic Outlook April 2020.

3) Lack of Marketing Infrastructure 缺少市场信息专业机构

The costs of collecting primary data in foreign markets are likely to be much higher, given the lack of a marketing infrastructure. Many markets do not have research firms or field-interviewing services; consequently, the sponsoring firm would have to invest in developing sampling frames and training interviewers.

4) Infrastructure Factors 基础设施落后

Research using the telephone as the contact method has changed greatly in the past decade alone. It used to be that, in many countries, the use of telephones limited the data collection to a handful of individuals who had access to a landline.

Using mail surveys is problematic in many international markets where mail is unreliable and slow.

In the lowest-income countries, another obstacle to the mail survey approach is the low literacy rate, which eliminates most potential respondents. Here, a telephone or personal interview is the preferred approach of data collection.

Finally, the sampling frames needed for data collection (mailing lists, telephone books, or other relevant databases) may not be available. In business-to-business research, sampling frames such as industry-association directories are often used.

5) Language Barriers 语言障碍

Instruments developed in one country require translation into the language of the country where they will be administered. Many concepts, however, are likely to lose some of then meaning when translated into another has language. Idioms are particularly problematic, and their literal translation has led to numerous marketing blunders.

In cross-cultural research, all steps should be performed by individuals fluent in both the original language of the questionnaire and the one of the country where it will be administered.

11.4.4 Determining Research Approaches 确定调研的路径和方法

When collecting primary data, researchers may use both qualitative and quantitative research approaches. Qualitative research method typically have some of the following characteristics:

① Fewer respondents belonging to a no random sample.

② Open-ended answer format.

③ Non-systematic observation.

④ Researcher involvement as participants.

(1) Qualitative Research 定性调研

Qualitative research is particularly useful as a first step in studying international marketing phenomena. When conducting exploratory research or as one of the methods to explore the problem at hand in a multiple method approach. Focus group research and observation fit in this category. In certain countries, such as France and Italy, there is a preference for qualitative data as a complement to quantitative data, whereas in others, such as Germany, the United States and Scandinavian countries, quantitative data are deemed as most valuable.

1) Focus Group Interviews 小组座谈法

Focus group interviews typically involve 6 to 12 participants recruited to meet some previously decided characteristics for instance, ethnic background, specific age group, social class, tribal allegiance, and use of certain products and a moderator who guides the discussion based on a certain discussion agenda. Often, representative from the sponsor observe the group's deliberations through a one-way mirror or on closed circuit television. A video camera or tape recorder may also be used to record the group's deliberations on a certain topic of interest to the sponsor. The participants are typically given a small financial reward for participating in the study or products such as free beer and food, product samples.

Depth interviews are one-on-one attempts to discover consumer motivations, feelings, and attitudes toward an issue of concern to the sponsor using a loose and unstructured question guide. They are typically used if the issue under study is a complex behavioral or decision-making consideration or an emotionally laden issue.

2) Observation 观察调研法

One type of observation research which is particularly useful in international research is naturalistic inquiry. Naturalistic inquiry requires the use of natural rather than contrived settings because behaviors take substantial meaning from their context. The researcher is the date collection instrument and part of the behavior-verbal and nonverbal. The analysis performed by the researcher is inductive, rather than deductive; that is, unlike in conversation research methods, the researcher does not rely on previous theory in the process of developing hypotheses, but, rather, theories are developed from date.

Table 11.2 Planning Primary Data Collection

Research Approaches	Contact Methods	Sampling Plan	Research Instruments
Observation	Mail	Sampling unit	Questionnaire
Survey	Telephone	Sample size	Mechanical instruments
Experiment	Personal online	Sampling procedure	

Other observation methods, such as the study of garbage (garbology); physiological measurement method, which measures a respondent's non-voluntary responses to stimuli; eye tracking, which is used in packaging research and advertising; and response latency, which measures the time interval between the question and the response to that question are used only to a limited extent in international research, usually in developed countries. They are costly because they require sending expensive experts to the research site abroad and obtaining data only on limited, usually no representative samples.

Table 11.3 Strength and Weaknesses of Contact Methods

	Mail	Telephone	Personal	Online
Flexibility	Poor	Good	Excellent	Good
Quantity of data that can be collected	Good	Fair	Excellent	Good
Control of interviewer efffects	Excellent	Fair	Poor	Fair
Control of sample	Fair	Excellent	Good	Excellent
Speed of data collection	Poor	Excellent	Good	Excellent
Response rate	Poor	Poor	Good	Good
Cost	Good	Fair	Poor	Excellent

Observation can have a number of shortcomings. Individuals in difficult cultures may react differently if their behavior is being observed. Also, the observer may need to be familiar with all the different languages spoken at the study site.

International technology provides new sources for observation-based information, such as point-of-sale (POS) store scanner data, which can offer outlets high quality, instant, as well as longitudinal, information on the movement of goods. such resources are amply available in the United States, Canada, and counties of the Europe Union. Increasingly, they are available in Asia and in emerging markets of Latin America. This information is used for tracking,as well as for managerial decision making.

(2) Quantitative Research 量化调研

Quantitative Research methods are more structured, involving either descriptive research approaches, such as survey research, or causal research approaches, such as experiments.

1) Content Analysis 内容分析法

Content analysis, an example of descriptive research, is a quantitative analysis that entails counting the number of times pre-selected words, themes, symbols, or pictures appear in a given medium such as printed materials or any medium with verbal or visual content. Content analysis is particularly useful in international marketing research, helping international marketing practitioners understand the complex multicultural environments in which they compete. At the same time, content analysis makes them aware of the subtle qualitative differences—such as taste, traditional, and symbolism—that are especially useful in market segmentation.

2) Survey Research 问卷式调研

Survey research, another example of descriptive research, typically involves the administration of personal, telephone, mail, or Internet questionnaires. The use of the questionnaires assumes that respondents are both willing and capable to respond to the questions. A cheap survey method involves the use of mail questionnaires; however, this method is fraught with obstacles in many developing countries. And, in most developing countries, there is a high level of illiteracy, which renders impossible the use of mail surveys. Nevertheless, this method is most popular in international marketing research, especially because it can be effectively used in cross-national comparisons.

3) Experimental Research 实验性调研

Experimental Research has the highest validity and reliability of all types of research. This research looks at cause-and-effect relationships, eliminating or controlling other extraneous factors that may be responsible for the results, and eliminating competing explanations for the observed findings. It requires the use of matched groups of subjects who are subjected to different treatments to ascertain whether the observed response differences are statistically significant.

11.4.5 Collecting, Analysing, and Interpreting the Information 信息的收集、分析和整理

In the final stage of the marketing research process, the researcher or research team is ready to collect the primary data. This expensive undertaking can be eventful. Researchers are frequently faced with respondents who have never had any experience participating in surveys. Non-response (inability or, more frequently, refused to participate in the study) can be a particularly serious problem, as previously seen. Even lateral processes that do not involve data collection, such as briefing the field force (training the interviewers) and evaluating the fieldwork quality, can be particularly difficult if the marketing researcher is not a national because communications may be encumbered by language and cultural differences. Ideally, local researchers should be in charge of implementing the data collection process because they are aware of the particulars of the environment that may have an impact on the data collection.

Finally, it is important that marketing managers not base all their decisions on the data collected because even proper planning of the data collection effort does not exclude the possibility of shortcomings in the study. For example, after one market research firm indicated that there was a substantial market for a specific product, a Swiss pharmaceutical firm built an 58 million manufacturing firm in Southeast Asia. The researchers, however, overlooked an important aspect of that market. the black market controlled by government officials. The added competition of the black market led to lower earnings for the company.

11.5 Decision Support System for Global Marketing 全球营销的决策支持系统

该系统是一个计算机程序,用于处理所搜集到的海外目标市场的数据和信息。该程序的设计考虑了三个信息源:母国市场、东道国市场和国际市场。

A decision support system is defined as "a coordinated collection of data, systems, tools, and techniques, complemented by supporting software and hardware designed for the gathering and interpretation of business and environmental data". In a global environment, the environmental data takes into account home country and host-country developments as well as development in other global markets that may affect operations.

Ideally, a global marketing decision support system should be:

① Computerized—Having a computerized support system is not possible in the case of many parts of global market, including those of developing countries, due to the increase in the capacity of personal computers to perform more complex tasks.

② Interactive—Managers can use online instructions to generate reports on the spot, without assistance from a programmer, who now may need to be present in the country of operations only periodically for system updating and training. This, of course, reduces the number of expatriates necessary at the operations site and the overall costs to the company.

③ Flexible—Managers can assess and integrate data from a variety of sources and manipulate the data in various ways (producing averages and totals, sorting the data, etc.). The system should allow managers to access information about firm operations in similar markets where the firm may be present and competitors' operations in the respective market where such information is available.

④ Discovery-Oriented—Such systems should produce diagnostics that reveal trends and identity problems.

In a global environment, there are different, country-specific information systems. Integrating the different approaches may lead to operational difficulties; managers must continuously take into consideration such as differences as they interface with the system.

A number of areas lend themselves well to Marketing Decision Support Systems (MDSS). In later Section "Sales Forecasting", we discuss different possible applications for such systems.

11.5.1 Sales Forecasting 销售业绩预测

This section will discuss the different methods of sales forecasting techniques. The more complex these techniques are, the more their efficiency can be improved in an MDSS environment. Nevertheless, input obtained from using the simpler methods (sales force composite estimates, jury of executive opinion, and the Delphi method) can be used to cross-validate the estimates given by the more sophisticated forecasting techniques (time series and econometrics models).

11.5.2 Sales Force Composite Estimates 根据销售人员报告预估

Forecasts from sales force composite estimates are based on the personal observations and "hunches" of the local sales force. These people are in the closest contact with the international consumer, and they are likely to find out about consumer desires and overall changing market trends.

11.5.3 Jury of Expert Opinion 专家估算

Forecasts from the jury of expert opinion are based on the opinions of different experts about future demand. The experts' opinions are then combined, and an aggregate demand estimation is offered. Because experts could come form both home and host country, as well as countries where other companies or the company in question, may face similar problems, obtaining a consensus perspective or aggregate forecast may be more difficult to achieve. At the same time, the awareness of the different possible outcomes or individual perspectives may prove invaluable in gaining insight on demand, particularly for a market new to the company.

11.5.4 The Delphi Method 德尔菲法

The Delphi Method entails asking a number of experts to estimate market performance, aggregating the results, and sharing this information with the experts. This process is repeated several times until a consensus is reached. Clearly, such an approach would be most cumbersome when dealing with a global company. First, in addition to impositions on executive's time, the company also must incur expenses related to the logistics of bringing together experts from different countries. Second, should the company attempt to use the Delphi method by mailing forecasting surveys, there is always the risk that international mail may impose, in addition to the high likelihood of noncompliance by executives, who may perceive such an exercise as an imposition on their time. Typically, these types of studies are performed at yearly or quarterly meetings of international managers.

11.5.5 Time Series and Econometric Models 时间序列与计量模型

Time series models use data of past performance to predict market demand. Typically, these models give more weight to recent developments. These methods assume that the future will be similar to the past. Econometric models, on the other hand, take into account different deterministic factors that affect market demand-factors that may or may not rely on past performance trends.

An example of an application of econometric models to global marketing is provided by the application of an autoregressive moving average (ARMAX) to predict consumer demand for beer in the Netherlands. The variables used as predictors of the demand for beer were temperature, price, consumer expenditures, and company advertising expenditures. The study concluded that advertising expenditures are not good predictors for beer demand; the authors suspected that the reason is a saturated market where all competitors advertise extensively and where additional advertising efforts may go unnoticed.

Table 11.4 Types of Samples

Probability Sample	
Simple random sample	Every member of the poulation has a known and equal chance of selection
Stratified random sample	The poultion is devided into mutually exclusive groups (such as age groups), and random samples are drawn from each group
Cluster (area) sample	The population is divided into mutually exclusive groups (such as blocks), and the resarcher draws a sample of the groups to interview
Nonprobability Sample	
Convenience sample	The researcher selects the easiest population members from which to obtain information
Judgment sample	The researcher uses his or her judgment to select population members who are good prospects for accurate information
Quota sample	The researcher finds and interviews a prescribed number of people in each of several categories

Time series and econometric models are dependent on the availability of historical data, data that are mainly available in developed countries but not in developing countries. For these markets, then, it is appropriate to estimate demand by analogy, nothing responses of markets with similar relevant characteristics, levels of economic development, cultural characteristics, and so forth.

11.5.6 Analogy Methods 类比法

The analogy method is an estimation method that relies on developments and findings in markets with similar levels of economic development, markets where the product is in the same development stage, or markets with similar cultural characteristics, or it may be based on sales of a related product in the key market of study. For example, to estimate anticipated adoption rate of cell phones in Latvia, it may be appropriate to identify the proportion of new adopters in a more advanced country in widely available, but which shares a similar history and similar geopolitics with Latvia. This is an example of country performance analogy.

To estimate the adoption rate of Internet service in Sri Lanka, it may be appropriate to evaluate the adoption rate of computers in this country. This is an example of product performance analogy.

Typically, in the country performance analogy, adjustments are made based on development level, cultural differences, trade barriers, competition, and so on. In the product performance analogy, adjustments are made for consumer traits such as purchase power, consumer innovation rate, and competitive environment.

11.5.7 POS Sales Based Projections 网点 POS 机销售记录预测

Point-of-sale-based projections are made with the help of store scanners, which are increasingly used by research suppliers, particularly in the United States (ACNielsen and Information Resources, among others), to assess market share and other relevant market dimensions.

Conclusion 结语

International market research is a prerequisite for the formulation and implementation of international market strategies. Therefore, as long as successful multinational marketing companies, the in-depth market research experience and methods are worthy of our research and study. International market research is different from the domestic market, and there may be obstacles in language, information availability, and cost. Therefore, in addition to paying attention to international market intelligence in a timely manner, mastering practical research methods is of great significance to successful market research. At the same time, it should be noted that because of the dynamic changes in the market environment, even authoritative forecasts in the past may have insufficient timeliness. Therefore, successful international marketing relies more on nuanced market observation and a keen market sense.

The Chapter's Referential Questions 本章参考题

(1) Suppose that you have been hired to evaluate the purchase behavior of adolescents in Latvia. What types of research studies could you conduct?
假设你受雇做一个关于拉托维亚青少年购买行为的调研与评价,你将采用哪种调研方法?

(2) What are some of the limitations of secondary data available to international marketing researchers?
对于国际营销调研人员,在收集二手数据方面存在哪些限制?

(3) Describe the challenges that researchers experience when designing and administering questionnaires in countries that are dissimilar from their own.
谈谈国际营销调研人员在外国市场设计和实施问卷调研时会遇到哪些挑战。

(4) Describe the international sales forecasting methods that marketing managers can use to better monitor and more efficiently react to information in the foreign business environment.
简述营销经理在应用销售额预测法时,如何能够控制并有效应对海外市场获得的信息。

(5) How to apply the method of POS Sales Based Projections?
如何运用网点 POS 机销售记录进行销售预测?

(6) How many methods can be applied for doing Sales Forecasting?
有哪些方法可以被应用于销售业绩预测?

(7) What is the function of market survey for KFC to select and decide its new Locations?
KFC 在开店之前所做的市场调查对其选址有何作用?

(8) What is the function of the Decision Support System for Global Marketing?
谈谈全球营销决策支持系统的功能和用途。

Further Reading 拓展阅读

Part 4

International Marketing Strategy Analysis

国际市场营销战略分析

Chapter 12　International Market Segmentation, Target Market Selection, Market Positioning (STP)

Chapter 13　International Market Entry Strategy

Chapter 14　International Market Competition Strategy

There are three chapters in this part. Firstly, Learn the STP theory, and then learn the international market entry strategy and competitive strategy. The contents of these three chapters belong to the strategic level, which not only requires a solid foundation for the previous market analysis part, but also sets a global framework for the learning of the follwing part of the strategy (tactics). Therefore, the strength of the strategic ability determines the effect of the strategy implementation. The study of this part will lay a good foundation for the study of the fifth part of the international market tactics.

本部分有三章的学习内容。首先学习 STP 理论，然后学习国际市场进入战略和竞争战略。这三章内容都属于战略层面，既需要前面市场分析部分的扎实基础，又要为后面策略部分的学习设定全局构架，因而，战略能力的强弱决定了策略实施的效果。通过这一部分的学习，为第五部分国际市场策略部分的学习打下良好的基础。

Chapter 12

International Market Segmentation, Target Market Selection, Market Positioning (STP)
国际市场细分、目标市场选择、市场定位

Learning Objectives
本章学习目标

(1) Concepts and methods of international market segmentation.
国际市场细分的概念和方法。

(2) International target market selection strategies and models.
国际目标市场选择策略和模式。

(3) The concepts and methods of international market positioning.
国际市场定位的概念和方法。

Key Words
关键词

Segmentation; Targeting; Positioning; Segmentation Variables; Cultural Groupings; Target Market

A company that decides to do business in a large market will realize that it is not possible to serve all customers in this market under normal circumstances. There are too many customers and their purchase requirements vary. In order to compete with ubiquitous competitors, companies need to identify the market segments that they can serve effectively.

Case Studies 12.1

—Philip Kotler

12.1 International Market Segmentation(S) 国际市场细分

STP 理论中的 S、T、P 分别是 Segmenting、Targeting、Positioning 三个英文单词

的缩写，即市场细分、目标市场和市场定位的意思。市场细分(Market Segmentation)的概念是美国营销学家温德尔·史密斯(Wendell Smith) 在1956年最早提出的，此后，美国营销学家菲利普·科特勒进一步发展和完善了温德尔·史密斯的理论并最终形成了成熟的STP理论[市场细分(Segmentation)、目标市场选择(Targeting)和市场定位(Positioning)]。它是战略营销的核心内容。

The concept of market segmentation has triggered the imagination of many international marketers during the last decade. It is a strategy which enables the company to maximize the results of a given marketing effort by exploiting clearly identified strength in relation to a submarket which is either inadequately satisfied by other manufacturers or where the company is particularly well placed to do an effective job.

12.1.1 The Meaning of International Market Segmentation 国际市场细分的意义

International market segmentation: The enterprise divides the entire international market into several sub-markets with different needs according to certain segmentation standards. The consumers in any sub-markets have the same or similar demand characteristics, The enterprise can select one or more of them as its international target markets.

Every marketer recognizes that it is most possible to satisfy the specific needs and requirements of every consumer. It is necessary to deal with groups of consumers or clusters of individuals who manifest similarities in consumption habits, social behavior, and economic characteristics or in some other distinguishable criterion. The extreme logical choices for the marketer are either to focus the attention on a wisely selected subgroup or submarket or to aim to differentiate the marketing programmer so as to satisfy the largest number of heterogeneous members of the total market.

Market segmentation can be defined as the strategy whereby the company partitions the market into submarkets (segments) likely to manifest similar responses to marketing inputs; the aim is to maximize the penetration of such segments rather than spread the effort thinly over the total market.

Market aggregation where the company treats the total market as one undifferentiated mass and whilst acknowledging that many social, cultural and economic differences are in existence, chooses to ignore such differences and standardize the marketing effort.

It is the objective of the first part of this chapter to discuss market segmentation in general terms. The second part will explore how this concept can be usefully applied to international marketing activities.

(1) Alternative Base for Segmenting Markets 市场细分的选择基础

Few areas of planning have evoked as much scope for creative thinking as the exploration of methods of market segmentation. The marketer who is able to identify a novel way for segmenting markets for his product or service may often escape the strong and harmful competition. Indeed, segmentation can be an extremely effective way of rejuvenating declining products or giving them a new lease of life. Furthermore, it may enable a relatively small company to hold its own in an industry in which it has to compete against giant companies.

There are many conventional ways for segmenting markets. The aim here is to concentrate on those bases of segmentation which have international relevance and applicability.

(2) Socioeconomic and Demographic Factors 社会经济与人口因素

Age, sex, family size, income, occupation, family life cycle, race, religion, social class, etc, are all such variable factors.

The system for segmenting markets has to encapsulate a number of socioeconomic parameters into one package. Thus when we talk about segments, we should be aware of that members of each segment possess certain income, occupation and social status characteristics. It enables the average marketer to divide the market into categories which are well understood and well monitored. Thus we can easily establish not only who consumes what but also who reads a specific magazine, who is the audience for a certain TV programmer—and all this in accordance with a classification which is standard amongst all marketers and their supportive service.

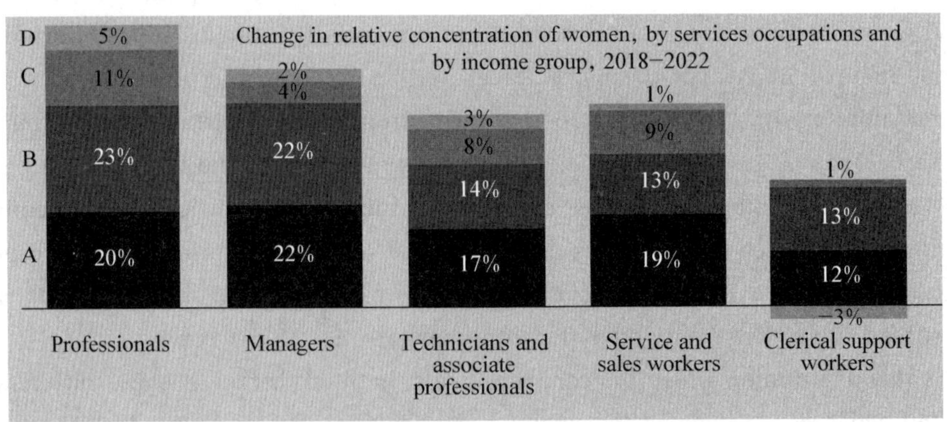

Source: WTO calculations based on ILO (2019).

Figure 12.1 The Number of Women in High-skilled Jobs is Increasing

The number of women in high-skilled jobs is increasing. Figure 12.2 shows the average number of social media accounts per internet user by age group. Millennials

and Generation Z constitute, on average, have more than 9 social media accounts. They also represent more than 50% of the users of major social media platforms and spend, on average, more than two and a half hours per day on social media, compared to one hour for Baby Boomers.

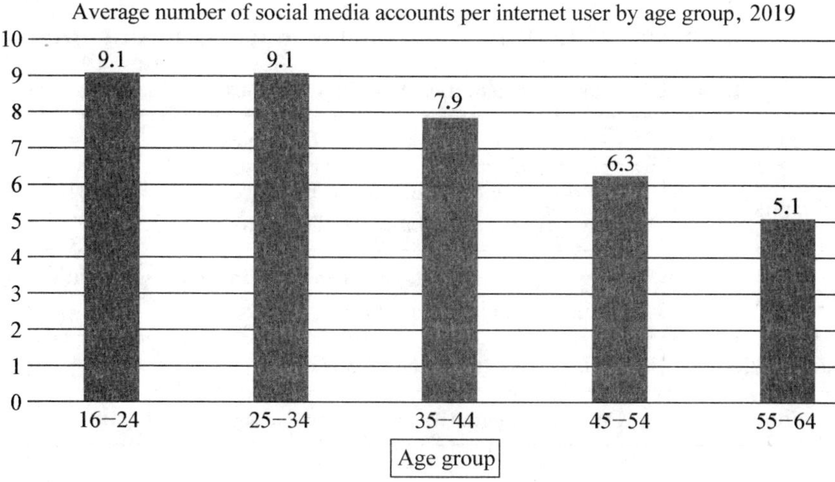

Source: www.statista.com.

Figure 12.2 The New Generation and Generation Z are the Most Active Users of Social Media Accounts

(3) Cultural Groupings 文化群体

This method for segmenting markets is particularly important in international marketing. Cultural influences are to a great extent determinant of the way the consumer behaves and the kind of consumption pattern which they develop. Cultural factors determine the kind of food that people eat, the type of homes they aspire to have, the style of design they favor and so on, fashion is thus linked to culture and so are general attitudes.

Grouping markets in accordance with their cultural differentiation can be very helpful to the international marketer. It may in certain circumstances be more useful than dividing markets in accordance with political or geographical borders. To take a simple example: in cultural term the French part of Switzerland has probably more in common with France than with the German speaking part of Switzerland. In terms of market segmentation, one is fully justified to cluster the French speaking part of Switzerland with France. This may be totally unworkable on political grounds or in monetary/fiscal terms but it is certainly logical on a cultural basis.

(4) Geographic Factors 地理因素

Most marketers recognize geographic variations within their market. On the domestic marketing scene, one encounters companies who distinguish in their marketing strategy between city customers and rural customers. Other companies may distinguish between various parts of the country and choose to devote more time and effort to those customers who happen to be located within easy access to the company's main office and installations. In fact, companies that organize their selling activity on a geographic basis have tacitly segmented the marker by this variable.

The segmentation by a geographic, or any other variable, in compunction with some other dimension can be illustrated very simply in diagrammatic form Table 12.1.

Table 12.1 Major Segmentation Variables for Consumer Markets

Segmentation Variable	Examples
Geographic	Nations, regions, states, counties, cities, neighborhoods, population density (urban, suburban, rural), climate
Demographic	Age, life-cycle stage, gender, income, occupation, education, religion, ethnicity, generation
Psychographic	Social class, lifestyle, personality
Behavioral	Occasions, benefits, user status, usage rate, loyalty status

(5) Consumer Behavioral Patterns 消费者行为结构

Under this heading a large number of variables can be considered as suitable bases for segmenting markets. It must be emphasized that no attempt is being made here to list all the available alternatives; the aim is purely to list a number of useful ways in which markets and consumers can be segmented.

1) Usage Rate 使用率

Heavy users of any product class, whether it is a consumer type product or an industrial product, represent a significant segment. The law normally applies to most cases, namely 15%～20% of all buyers ordinarily are expected to consume over half of the total purchases. The light users consume relatively little. The non-users may appear a useless segment but in practice they may prove a very profitable segment to a company that manages to identify the real reason as to why the non-user avoiding the product because he/she feels that the calorie content is too high. Such a person will become a user as soon as a Cola appear on the market which is sugar-free and hence non-fattening. In other words, if the information indicates that this is the cause for non-use of Cola, the choice of the "slimming" segment may prove a highly profitable one. A few companies in the UK have launched a whole series of dietetic foods such as sugar-free biscuits and chocolate. This is an interesting way to segment the market especially for companies that wish to escape from the rigors of competition which prevail in the branded biscuit and chocolate business.

2) Consumers' Motive 消费者动机

A market can be segregated by the motives that propel the customers to the buying

act. A host of motives operate in a person's buying decision process. These motives differ between one buyer and another, between one nation and another and between one culture and another. It's impossible to extrapolate motives from one market to another without in-depth study.

Motives are extremely important in understanding the marketing ecology of different markets and hence in determining the segments available for the most profitable exploitation. We saw earlier that sewing machines are purchased in different parts of the world for either satisfaction of physiological need as a motive, or as a hobby satisfaction motives, or as a status symbol, a purely emotive reason.

3) The Adoption Process 接受过程

The "adoption process" can offer a highly creative basis for segmenting markets. People respond at a difference to the stimulus of new products or concepts. Behaviorally a number of individual buyers tend to respond favorable to any kind of innovation-as soon as they perceive a new product they desire it. These are the kind of people who would purchase a digital watch the minute it is launched. At the other extreme one encounters the so-called "laggards". These are the kind of individuals who resist change and in marketing terms they only respond to a product when it has been on the market for a long time, sometimes when the product has in fact reached the end of its life cycle.

Between these two extremes one finds other adoption characteristics of varying intensity. Five adoption segments normally exist and can be summarized in Table 12.2.

Table 12.2 Adoption Categories and Segregation

Adoption Category	Possible Size(%)	Typical Characteristics
Innovations	2.5	Venturesome; prepared to experiment; higher social status; higher income group; urban
Early Adopters	13.5	Same as the "innovators" but less venturesome
Early majority	34	Display less leadership than previous two; avoid risk; rural rather than urban types; active in community life
Late Majority	34	Conservative; imitators; extra cautious; dislike change; older; lower income group; less prestigious occupations; more oriented to local contacts
Laggards	16	"Isolate"; stubbornly resist change; unimaginative

(4) Other Bases for Segmentation 细分的其他因素

As stated earlier, with creativity one can consider a large number of novel segmentation possibilities. Examples:

① Segmentation by attitudes, taste or predispositions.

② Personality traits.

③ Channels, patronage or store location.(Where do people buy?)

④ Sensitivity to pricing or advertising policies.

⑤ Original equipment or own label merchandise.

12.1.2 Conditions for Making Segmentation 市场细分的条件

It is normally suggested that before one can determine whether a segmentation strategy. is worthwhile one must fulfill three fundamental conditions.

(1) The Size of Each Segment 市场规模

Under consideration the size of each segment must be measurable. Smoke it must make sure that sufficient data are available about the segment in question or, alternatively, that an appropriate measurement methodology sexists. To select a segmentation policy in circumstances which make measurement impossible or too costly may defeat the whole purpose of such a strategy, the optimization of resources.

In international marketing this condition is of paramount importance in so far as there is little point selecting a specific segmentation policy if the measurability of the segments under consideration is problematic. A manufacturer of drills tried to market his products to the "do-it-yourself" segment in world markets. He knew the size of this segment in European markets but found it impossible to measure the size of this segment in most countries outside Europe. Measurement of the cement would have cost a fortune-far in excess of the eventual hoped for rewards.

(2) Yielding Adequate Returns 可盈利性

As a corollary of everything that was said hitherto the signal and to selected must be such that if you can yield adequate returns. In other words must be substantial enough to be profitable. This is simply a basic question of common sense. The trouble is that marketers that have been bitten by the segmentation bug, often tend to indulge in excessive segmentation; this in turn may mean that segments selected, although creative to the extreme, are too small to earn an adequate return on the efforts involved.

(3) The Segment Must Be Accessible 可进入性

Finally, the marketer must make sure that a segment chosen can be reached in an effective manner; it must be accessible. The institutional bodies that facilitate the marketing process must be in existence. Channels of distribution must exist in the marketplace; promotional media must be available; the type of selling that one would propose to use must be acceptable. It would be senseless to select a segment which calls

for an efficient retail distribution where such a system just does not exist. Similarly, the marketer who chooses a segment that depends entirely on television advertising medium is not available or not likely to become available for some time.

12.1.3 Applying Market Segmentation to Global Market 对全球市场进行细分

In the domestic context, most marketers realize that the choice of marketing strategy largely depends on whether segmentation decisions have been taken. Broadly speaking, three marketing strategies are available to the domestic marketer: undifferentiated marketing, differentiated marketing, and concentrated marketing.

In the case of undifferentiated marketing the company places on the market one product and seeks to draw as many consumers as possible with one uniformed and standardized marketing mix. It ignores the existence of specific segments with special needs and demands. In the case of differentiated marketing, the company modifies the product and the supportive mix ingredients to appeal to a number of submarkets. Through such a differentiation the company hopes to satisfy a larger number of segments and their specific needs and desires. In the third situation concentrated marketing, the company isolates one or more segments for special treatment and concentrates the total effort on these limited submarkets.

All three strategies are equally applicable to the world market. The only difference is the overall market and the dimensions of each segment. At one end of the spectrum one encounters the company that decides sales to derive most of its sales from the domestic markets and tends to regard sales abroad as grist to the mill' only. Such a company adopts an undifferentiated or standardized approach. It is fully realized that it could achieve a greater penetration of its markets through differentiation, but it opts for the more cost-effective strategy viz. standardization.

12.2 International Target Market Selection(T) 国际目标市场选择

确定目标市场，就是在市场细分的基础上，企业根据自身优势，从细分市场中选择一个或者若干个子市场作为自己的目标市场，并针对目标市场的特点展开营销活动，以期在满足顾客需求的同时，实现企业经营目标。

12.2.1 Factors Affecting the Choice of International Target Markets 影响国际目标市场选择的因素

① Market size and growth potential.

② Market attraction.

③ Corporate goals and resources.

④ Market homogeneity.

⑤ Competitor's marketing strategy.

12.2.2 Selection Strategy of International Target Market 国际目标市场的选择策略

(1) No Difference Target Market Selection Strategy 无差异目标市场选择策略

Non-differentiated marketing means that the company treats the overall market as a large target market, does not subdivide it, and treats the overall market with one product and a unified marketing mix. The biggest advantage of this strategy is that it can save costs, and the biggest disadvantage is low customer satisfaction. The scope of application is limited, such as globally integrated industries or powerful companies.

(2) Differential Target Market Selection Strategy 差异化目标市场选择策略

The differentiated marketing strategy is that on the basis of market segmentation, the company selects several market segments as the target market according to its own resources and strength, and formulates different marketing plans for this purpose. The biggest advantage of this strategy is that it can meet the needs of different customer groups in a targeted manner and improve the competitiveness of products; at the same time, it can also establish a good market image and attract more buyers. The biggest disadvantage is the substantial increase in cost.

(3) Concentrated Target Market Selection Strategy 集中目标市场选择策略

Concentrated marketing strategy means that on the basis of market segmentation, companies focus their targets on one or a few small international market segments, and formulate marketing plans for this part of the market. The advantage of this strategy lies in professional operation, which can well meet the needs of specific customers, occupy a higher market share in the market, have a higher reputation, concentrate resources, save costs, and enable enterprises to achieve economies of scale. The scope of application is small and medium-sized enterprises with weak resources.

12.2.3 The Choice Model of the International Target Market 国际目标市场的选择模式

① Market concentration model.

② Product specialization model.

③ Market specialization model.

④ Choose a professional model.

⑤ Comprehensive market model.

12.3 International Market Positioning(P) 国际目标市场定位

国际市场定位就是根据国际市场的需要和公司自身的情况，创造出与众不同的个性，将公司的产品与竞争对手的产品区分开来，从而使产品在目标市场中确定其适当的位置，以满足目标消费者。实际上，除了给自己的产品在国际市场塑造一个明确的位置空间，关键在于在消费者心里形成稳定而且明确的产品认知。

12.3.1 Definition 定义

According to the needs of the international market and the conditions of the company itself, the company creates a distinctive personality that distinguishes the products of the company from those of the competitors, so that the product can determine its proper position in the target market to meet the target consumers.

The essence of international market positioning is to gain a competitive advantage in the target market, determine the appropriate position of the product in the customer's mind and be impressed in order to attract more customers.

12.3.2 Methods of Positioning in the International Market 国际市场定位的方法

① International product origin positioning.
② International product category positioning.
③ International product feature positioning.
④ International product usage positioning.
⑤ International product usage time positioning.
⑥ International product grade positioning.

12.3.3 International Market Positioning Strategy 国际市场定位策略

① Avoid strong positioning.
② Head-on positioning.
③ Innovative positioning.
④ Re-locate.

12.3.4 International Market Positioning Steps 国际市场定位步骤

① Analyze competitive advantages and grasp the status.

② Select the initial positioning of the competitive advantage.

③ Demonstrate a clear positioning of competitive advantage.

As shown in Figure 12.3, the horizontal axis represents performance, and the vertical axis represents price. In this way, all products can theoretically find their own accurate coordinates on this graph. Such coordinates are conducive to determining the location of enterprises and products, and are beneficial to Consumer's choice. It should be noted that, like market segmentation, market positioning is also dynamically changing. With market competition, some products or companies withdraw from the market, and some products even reposition.

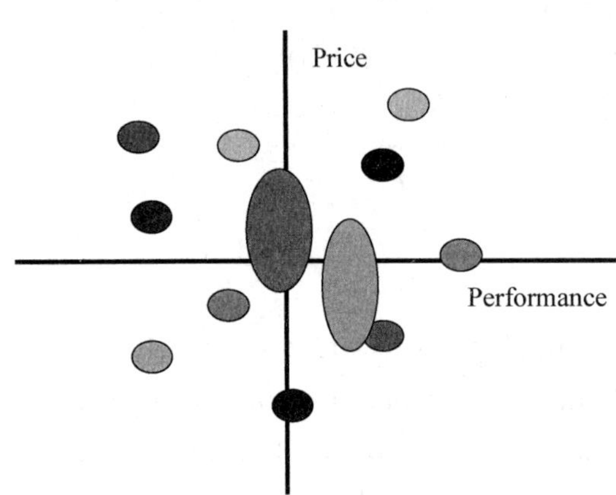

Figure 12.3 International Product Positioning Analysis Graph

Conclusion 结语

Market segmentation, target market selection, and market positioning are closely related to each other. Market segmentation is the prerequisite and basis. Only through market segmentation can we know which segmented market can become the company's target market. In the target market, any company and product must clarify its position in the market, which is conducive to the company itself, but also conducive to consumer choice. STP belongs to the strategic level and is the core of modern marketing. It is the result of scientific and accurate market surveys and is also a prerequisite for formulating market entry strategies and market competition strategies.

The Chapter's Referential Questions 本章参考题

(1) Describe the importance of market segmentation.
谈谈市场细分的重要性。

(2) What factors should you consider when doing market segmentation?

在实施市场细分时需要考虑哪些因素？

(3) Describe how to apply market segmentation to the global market.
简述在全球市场怎样运用市场细分策略。

(4) When considering about Consumer Behavioral Patterns, what variable parameters should be analyzed?
在考虑消费者行为结构时，需要分析哪些变量因素？

(5) List some examples for global market segmentation by using the geographic factors.
举出使用地理因素进行全球市场细分的例子。

(6) For China's High Speed Railway System entering overseas market, what types of market segmentation and positioning method should be adopted?
我国高铁打入国际市场，应该采取哪种细分模式和定位战略？

(7) What is the STP strategy in international marketing theory?
什么是国际市场营销的 STP 理论？

(8) Give an example to illustrate the respective target markets and market positioning of China's top private brands in the international rankings.
举例说明中国目前国际排名最靠前的民营品牌各自的目标市场和市场定位。

Further Reading
拓展阅读

【Chapter 13】

International Market Entry Strategy 国际市场进入战略

Learning Objectives 本章学习目标

(1) Offensive and defense objectives of multinational corporations.
跨国公司的攻防目标。
(2) Main modes of international market entry.
国际市场进入主要模式。
(3) Risk identification of entering international market.
进入国际市场风险识别。

Key Words 关键词

Offensive Target；Defensive Goals；Entry Mode；Exporting；Contract；Management Contract；BOT；OEM；Risk Identification；WEF；CROIC-IWEP；COFACE

13.1 The Global Economic Integration and the Offensive and Defensive Goals of Multinational Companies 全球经济一体化与跨国公司的攻防目标

Case Studies 13.1

13.1.1 The Main Reason for the Formation of the Global Network 全球网络形成的主要原因

More and more large companies have transferred geographical and national boundaries to become true multionationals. For most other domestic companies, the question is no longer existed. Should we go international? Instead, the questions relate to when, how, and where should the companies enter the international marketplace. The past 30 years have seen the reality of a truly world market unfold. In today's world, the global economy is becoming almost totally integrated. Primary reasons for previously separated, individual markets evolving to a network of interdependent economies include:

① The growing influence and economic development of lesser developed countries. In years to come, the real battleground for the two trade powers, the United States and Japan, will take place in the developing world. Containing 80% of the world's population and with growth rates nearly double those of industrial nations, these countries have emerged as the "fourth engine in the world economy" following the United States, Europe, China and Japan.

② The integration of world financial markets. For example, changes in currency exchange rates between the Chinese RMB and the US Dollar greatly influence issues relating to import and export activities for all countries.

③ Increased deficiencies in transportation and telecommunication and date communication networks. To illustrate, consider the cases of Eastern Europe, China, and Russia. In these areas, technological advances have allowed the emergence of stock exchanges on which brokers throughout the world can trade.

④ The opening of new markets. For example, the political and economic reforms in China have the country to the opening of a market that for decades was closed to western countries.

13.1.2 Offensive Target of Multinational Corporations 跨国公司的进攻目标

Multinational Companies invest in foreign countries for the same basic reasons they invest in own country. These reasons vary from company to company but all under the categories of achieving offensive or defensive goals. Offensive goals are to:

① increase long-term growth and profit prospects;

② maximize total sales revenue;

③ take advantage of economies of scale;

④ improve overall market position.

As many markets reach saturation, such as Japan and Germany, companies of these countries look to foreign markets as outlets for surplus production capacity, sources of new customers, increased profit margins, and improved returns on investment. For example, the ability to expand the number of locations of McDonald's restaurants in the United States is becoming severely limited. Yet, on any given day, only 0.5 percent of the world's population visits McDonald's. This fact illustrates the vast potential markets still open to the company. Indeed, in the recent past of the 50 most profitable McDonald's outlets, 25 were located in Hong Kong. For PepsiCo, the results are similar, and its restaurant division operates 7,400 Kentucky Fried Chicken, Pizza Hut outlets abroad, deriving over ＄5.6 billion in sales from these foreign locations.

13.1.3 Defensive Target of Multinational Corporations 跨国公司的防御目标

Multinational Companies also are investing in other countries to achieve defensive targets mainly desiring to:

① Compete with foreign companies on their turf instead of at their homeland;

② Have access to technological innovations that are developed in other countries;

③ Take advantage of significant difference in operating costs between countries;

④ Taking advantage of competitors' global moves;

⑤ Not be locked out of future markets by arriving too late.

In many ways, marketing globally is the same as marketing at home. Regardless of which part of the world the company sells in, the marketing program must still be built around a sound product or service that is properly priced, promoted, and distributed to a carefully analyzed target market. In other words, the marketing manager has the same controllable decision variables in both domestic and non-domestic markets.

Although the development of a marketing program may be the same in either domestic or non-domestic markets, special problems may be involved in the implementation of marketing programs in non-domestic markets. These problems often arise because of the environmental differences that exist among various countries that marketing managers may be unfamiliar with.

13.2 Problems with Entering Foreign Markets 进入外国市场会遇到的问题

While numerous problems could be cited, attention here will be focused on those companies most often face when entering foreign markets.

13.2.1 Cultural Differences 文化差异

The cultural environment has been studied in the previous chapters. Regarding cultural differences, students who are interested can continue to scan the code to learn.

13.2.2 Political Uncertainty 政治的不稳定性

Governments are unstable in many countries, and social unrest and even armed conflict must sometime be reckoned with. Other nations are newly emerging and anxious to seek their independence. These similar problems can greatly hinder a company seeking to establish its position in foreign markets. For example, companies scaled hack their investment plans in Russia due to the following reasons:

① A business environment plagued by mobsters;

② Political situation is heavily corrupted;

③ An economy troubled by runaway inflation and a pretty soft ruble.

This is not to say investment in Russia is not a wise choice. Rather, in such situations, caution must be utilized and companies must have a keen understanding of the risks involved in undertaking sizable investments.

13.2.3 Import Restriction 进口限制

Tariffs, import quotas, and other types to import Restrictions hinder global business. These are usually established to promote self-sufficiency and can be a huge roadblock for the multinational Firm. For example, a number of countries and regions, including South Korea, Taiwan China, Thailand and Japan, have placed import restrictions on a variety of goods produced in US, including telecommunications equipment, rice wood products, automobiles, and produce. In other cases, governments may not impose restrictions that are commonly adhered to in the United States. For example, Chrysler pulled out of a proposed investment deal in China, worth billions of dollars, because the Chinese government refused to protect its right to limit access to technological information.

13.2.4 Exchange Controls and Ownership Restriction 外汇管制和控股权限制

Some nations establish limits on the amount of earned and invested funds that can be withdrawn from it. These exchange controls are usually established by nations those are experiencing balance of payment problems. In addition, many nations have a requirement that local nationals hold the majority ownership of a company operating there. These and other types of currency and ownership regulations are important considerations in the decision to expand into a foreign market. For example, up until 1990, foreign holdings in business ventures in India were limited to a maximum of 40 percent. Once this ban was lifted later on numerous global companies such as Sony, Whirlpool, JVC, Panasonic, Kellogg's, Levi Strauss, Pizza Hut, and Domino's rushed to invest in this market.

13.2.5 Economic Conditions 经济环境

As noted earlier, nations' economies are becoming increasingly intertwined, and business cycles tend to follow similar patterns. However, there are differences, mainly due to political upheaval or social changes, and these may be significant. In determining whether to invest or not, marketers need to perform in-depth analyses of a country's stage of economic development, the buying power of its populace, and the strength of its currency. For example, when the NAFTA was signed, may American companies rushed to invest in Mexico, building production facilities and retail outlets. These companies assumed that the signing of the agreement would stabilize Mexico's economy. In the long term, these investments may pay off. However, many companies lost millions of dollars there due to the devaluation of the peso. Indeed, the crash of the peso cause the retailer giant Wal-Mart to scale back a $1 billion investment project to open stores throughout Mexico.

13.3 International Market Entry Mode 国际市场进入模式

进入国际市场大体可以分为三种模式:出口进入、合同进入和投资进入。出口包括直接出口和间接出口;合同进入包括许可贸易、特许经营、合同制造、管理合同;投资进入包括创办合资企业和独资企业两种,同时,投资也可分为直接投资和间接投资两种形式。

13.3.1 Exporting 出口

Exporting occurs when a company produce the product outside the final destination and then ships it there for sale purpose. It is the easiest and most common approach for a company making its first international move. Exporting has two distinct advantages. First, it avoids the cost of establishing manufacturing operations in the host country; second, it may help a company achieve experience in the market. By manufacturing the product in a centralized location and exporting it to other national markets, the company may be able to realize substantial scale economies from its global sales volume. This method is what allowed Sony to dominate the global TV market. The major disadvantages related to exporting include:

① The sometimes higher cost associated with the process;

② The necessity of the exporting company to pay import duties or face trade barriers;

③ The delegation of marketing responsibility for the product to foreign agents who may or may not be liable.

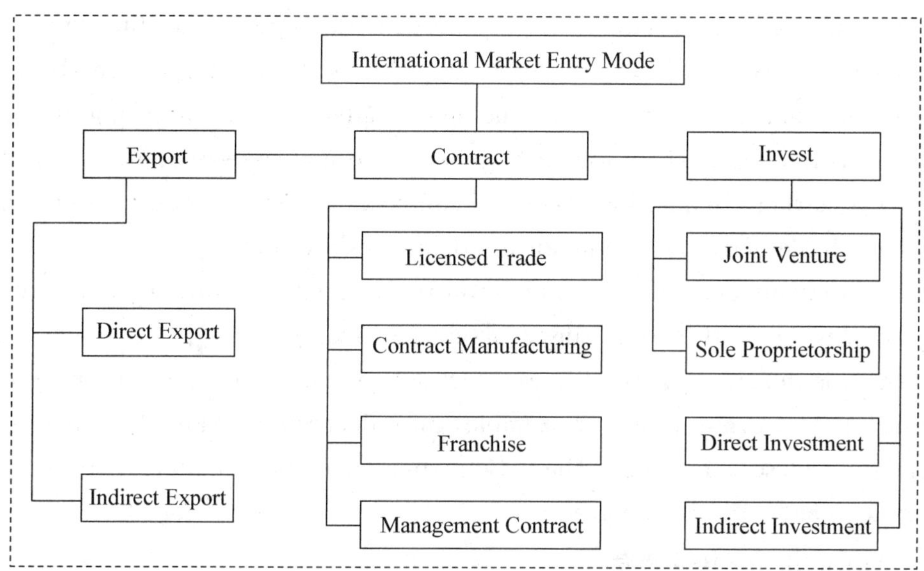

Figure 13.1 Classification of International Market Entry Modes

Direct export refers to the way companies sell products directly to overseas middlemen or end users. The main advantages of direct export are as follows: export companies can reduce or even eliminate dependence on export intermediaries; export companies can accumulate international experience and train international talents; export companies can improve their image in the international market; export companies can grasp first-hand information on the international market. The shortcomings of direct exports are: poor flexibility; higher costs; lack of economies of scale for enterprises with smaller export scales.

Indirect exports are products that go out through the purchase or agency of domestic foreign trade companies or foreign companies' institutions in the country. Since the indirect export method does not require foreign investment and additional organization, its main advantages are low cost, low risk, and simplicity. However, indirect foul language also has its shortcomings, which are manifested as: companies cannot understand and control overseas markets; they are not conducive to accumulating international marketing experience; they are not conducive to establishing their international market image (brand); they are highly dependent on middlemen.

13.3.2 Contract
合同进入

(1) Licensing 许可证

Companies can grant patent rights, trademark rights, and the right to use technological processes to foreign companies. This is the most common strategy for small and medium-sized companies. The major advantage to licensing is that the company does not have to bear the development costs and risks associated with opening lip a foreign market, In addition, licensing can be an attractive option in unfamiliar or politically volatile markets. The major disadvantages are that:

① the company does not have tight control over manufacturing, marketing, and strategy that is required for realizing economics of scale;

② there is the risk that the licensed technology may be capitalized on by foreign companies. RCA Corporation, for example, once licensed its color TV technology to a number of Japanese companies. These Companies quickly assimilated the technology and used it to enter the U.S. market.

(2) Franchising 特许经营

Franchising is similar to licensing but tends to involve longer-term commitments. Also, franchising is commonly employed by service as opposed to manufacturing companies. In a franchising agreement, the franchiser sells limited rights to use its brand name in return for a lump-sum and share of the Franchisee's future profits. In contrast to licensing agreements, the franchisee agrees to abide by strict operating procedures. Advantages and disadvantages associated with franchising are primarily the same as with licensing except to a lesser degree.In many cases, franchising offers an effective mix of centralized and decentralized decision making.

(3) Contract Manufacturing 合同制造

Contract manufacturing refers to a form of cooperation in which a company signs a contract with a foreign manufacturer, and the manufacturer produces products, while the company is responsible for product sales.

Contract manufacturing enables companies to enter the international market as soon as possible, and its risk is minimal. It is conducive to the establishment of partnerships between enterprises and foreign manufacturers or the purchase of all its property rights in the future.

Several modes of contract manufacturing include: CM (Contract Manufacture)、CDM (Contract Design Manufacture)、ODM (Original Design Manufacture)、OBM (Original Brand Manufacture)、OEM (Original Equipment Manufacture).

(4) Management Contract 管理合同

It means that an international enterprise with management advantages appoints other managers to a certain enterprise in another country through contract arrangements to undertake operations and management tasks, and obtain a certain management fee. The management contract is actually a kind of international management technology trade. This kind of contractual management right can be used to manage all the business activities of a certain enterprise, or it can only manage a certain part of the enterprise's activities or certain functions, such as production or marketing.

Regardless of whether the scope of management is large or small, the responsible management international enterprise cannot enjoy ownership. What it receives is only the management fee stipulated in the contract. The management fee can be a fixed amount, which can be divided according to sales, or it can be in a fixed amount, plus dividends.

BOT (Build-Operate-Transfer) means build-operate-transfer. It is a way for private enterprises to participate in infrastructure construction and provide public services to the society. It is one of the more popular PPP (Public-Private Partnership) models.

China generally refers to it as "concession rights", which refers to the signing of a concession agreement between a government department and a private enterprise (project company) for an infrastructure project, granting the contracting party's private enterprise (including foreign enterprises) to undertake the investment in the project, Financing, construction and maintenance, within the concession period stipulated in the agreement, permit it to finance the construction and operation of specific public infrastructure, and allow it to repay loans by charging users or selling products to recover investment and make profits. The government has the right to supervise and control this infrastructure. After the concession period expires, the private enterprise of the contracting party transfers the infrastructure to the government department free or paid.

13.3.3 Investment 投资进入

The United Nations Conference on Trade and Development (UNCTAD) recently released the *World Investment Report 2020* (hereinafter referred to as the "Report"), which predicts that in 2020, global foreign direct investment (FDI) flows will drop by nearly 40% from the 1.54 trillion U.S. dollars in 2019, this will make global FDI less than US $ 1 trillion for the first time since 2005. Following the sharp decline in 2017 and 2018, global FDI flows rose slightly by 3% in 2019, reaching US $ 1.54 trillion. Asia is still the world's largest recipient of foreign direct investment. In 2019, more than 30% of the world's foreign capital flowed into the region.

The major disadvantages associated with joint ventures are that: a company may risk giving up control of proprietary knowledge to its partner, and the company may lose the light control over a foreign subsidiary needed to engage in coordinated global attacks against rivals.

The establishment of a wholly-owned enterprise in overseas investment is the highest stage of the enterprise's process of entering the international market. In terms of ownership and control, this kind of wholly foreign-owned enterprise is a subsidiary wholly controlled by the parent company, and the enterprise accepts all the responsibilities for production and marketing in the foreign market. The advantages of sole proprietorship: relatively few internal contradictions and conflicts; conducive to the protection of technical and commercial secrets; exclusive marketing results. Disadvantages of sole proprietorship: a lot of investment; it may encounter greater political and economic risks.

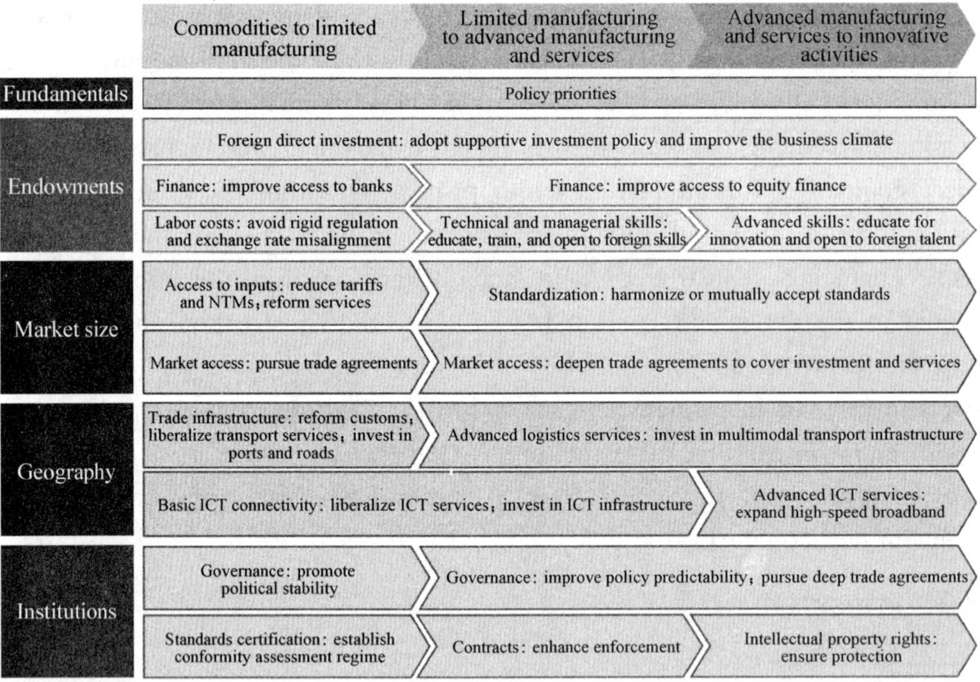

Figure 13.2 Transitioning to More Sophisticated Participation in GVCs: Some Examples of National Policy

National policies can and should be tailored to the specific circumstances of countries and to specific forms of participation in GVCs. Attracting FDI is important at all stages of participation. It requires openness, investor protection, stability, a favorable business climate, and in some cases, investment promotion. Some countries, such as those in Southeast Asia that have benefited from foreign investment in goods, still restrict foreign investment in services.

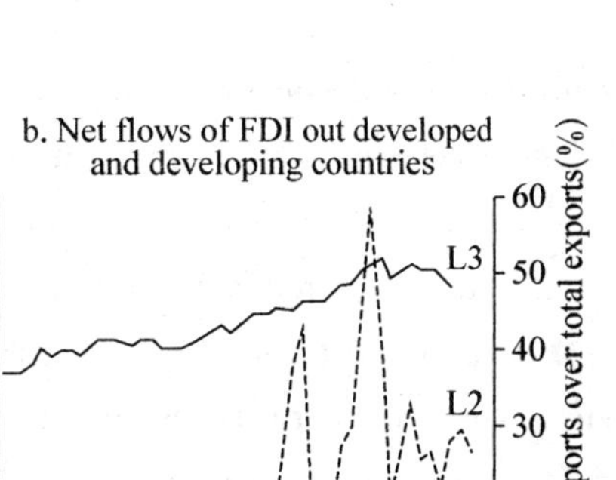

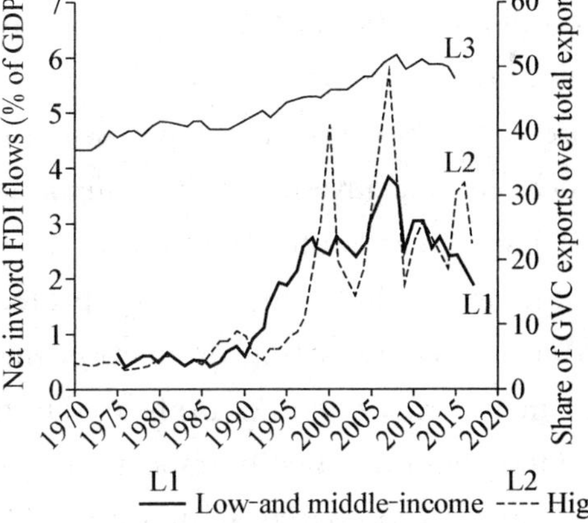

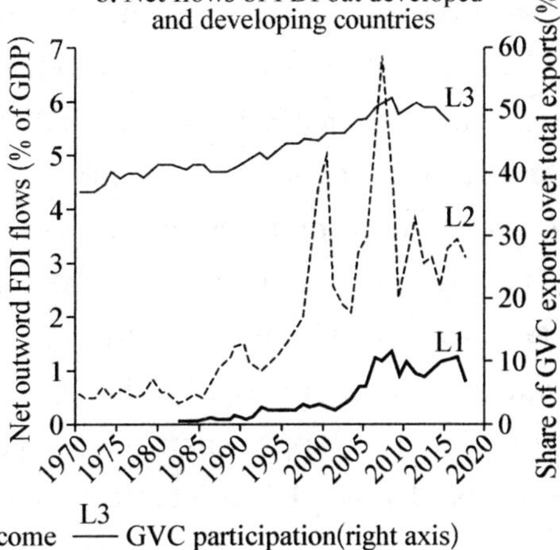

Source: WDR 2020 team, using data from the World Bank's WDI database.

Figure 13.3 Foreign Direct Investment Accompanied the Fragmentation of Production from 1970 to 2018①

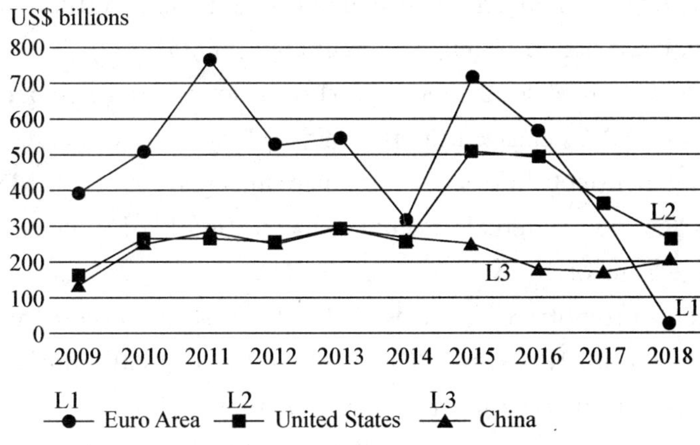

Source: World Bank Open Data.

Figure 13.4 Foreign Direct Investment Net Inflows②

① Note: Panel a reports the net inflows of investment to the reporting economy from foreign investors divided by GDP, and panel b reports the net outflows of investment from the reporting economy to the rest of the world divided by GDP. To avoid composition effects, the definitions of income groups are time-invariant and based on the World Bank's 2018 country classification. The GVC participation measure reflects the share of countries' exports that flows through at least two borders. It is computed as the share of GVC exports in total international exports. GVC exports include transactions in which a country's exports embody value added that it previously imported from abroad (backward GVC participation), as well as transactions in which a country's exports are not fully absorbed in the importing country and instead are embodied in the importing country's exports to third countries (forward GVC participation). FDI = foreign direct investment.

② Note: https: //data.worldbank.org/indicator/BX.KLT.DINV.CD.WD? end = 2018&locations = CN-XC-US&start = 2009&view = chart, accessed 15 December 2019.

For multinational corporations (MNCs), what are the most important determinants of efficiency-seeking foreign direct investment (FDI)* ?

Compared with investors with other motivations, efficiency-seeking firms, which connect countries directly to GVCs, find the following factors more important:

● Characteristics of host countries. Most are important, especially low-cost labor and inputs, which 66% of firms involved in efficiency-seeking investment find important or critically important, compared with only 39% of investors with other motivations.

● Investment policy factors. These factors include investment protection guarantees, owning all equity, hiring expatriate staff, importing production inputs, ease of obtaining approvals, bilateral investment treaties, and preferential trade agreements (PTAs). PTAs were found to be important or critically important by 65% of firms involved in efficiency-seeking investment, compared with only 45% of investors with other motivations.

● Incentives. 63% of efficiency-seeking investors rate incentives as important or critically important, in contrast with 43% of investors with other motivations. These firms rated eight different incentive instruments more highly than other investors, with an average difference of about 13 percentage points.

● Capacity and skills of local suppliers. This factor was rated important or critically important by 77% of MNCs engaged in efficiency-seeking FDI, compared with 70 percent of investors with other motivations. To promote linkages, 55% of MNCs involved in efficiency-seeking FDI have internal "talent scouts" to find local suppliers, compared with only 45% of investors involved in other types of FDI.

● Investment promotion agencies (IPAs). Fifty-two percent of efficiency-seeking investors identify IPA services as important or critically important, compared with 37% of investors involved in other types of FDI.

(Source: World Development Report 2020.)

*: This overview of locational determinants of FDI is based on findings from the World Bank's 2017 Global Investment Competitiveness survey on investor perceptions and preferences (World Bank 2018).

13.4 Risk Identification of International Market Entry 国际市场进入的风险识别

本部分介绍三个权威机构的风险评价指标：世界经济论坛、中国社会科学院世界经济与政治研究所、COFACE。通过这三个风险识别体系的学习，对我们了解和把握国际市场进入和参与国家竞争是非常有帮助的。

As of the end of 2018, more than 27,000 Chinese domestic investors had established 43,000 foreign direct investment enterprises in 188 countries (regions) around the world, and more than 80% of the world's countries (regions) had Chinese investment. Doing a good job of risk early warning, then accurately identifying risks, and effectively responding to corresponding risks is an important prerequisite for Chinese companies to increase the success rate of overseas investment.

13.4.1 World Economic Forum 世界经济论坛①

The latest edition of the World Economic Forum's 2020 international risk assessment indicator system is mainly based on five major aspects, namely economy, economic environment, geopolitics, society and technology. This chapter briefly mentions the main information about the World Economic Forum. We will focus on the analysis in the next chapter.

13.4.2 Institute of World Economics and Politics(IWEP), Chinese Academy of Social Sciences(CASS) 中国社会科学院世界政治与经济研究所②

On the afternoon of June 29, 2020, the team of the International Investment Research Office of the Institute of World Economics and Politics of the Chinese Academy of Social Sciences released the "Country-risk Rating of Overseas Investment from China". The evaluation index is based on the country. The evaluation index system introduced in this section mainly includes five first-level indicators: economy, solvency, social resilience, political risk, and Relations to China, including 42 subdivision indicators. For a detailed introduction of the indicator system, please read Table 13.1~13.7.

13.4.3 COFACE 科法斯

A modern and agile company with the most finely meshed international network, Coface is a reference in credit insurance and risk management.With over 70 years of experience as an industry leader, and a team of 4,100 experts serving around 50,000

---

① 世界经济论坛(World Economic Forum, WEF);因在瑞士达沃斯首次举办,又被称为"达沃斯论坛",是以研究和探讨世界经济领域存在的问题、促进国际经济合作与交流为宗旨的非官方国际性机构,总部设在瑞士日内瓦。

② 中国社会科学院世界政治与经济研究所主要从事全球宏观经济、国际金融、国际贸易、国际投资、经济发展、国际政治、国际战略、国际政治经济学、全球治理和世界能源等领域的研究,是中国经济政策、国际经济政策和中国外交政策等领域最有影响力的智库之一。研究所出版《世界经济与政治》《世界经济》《国际经济评论》与 *China & World Economy* 等重要学术期刊,以及《世界经济年鉴》《世界经济形势》黄皮书、《全球政治与安全形势》黄皮书、《中国海外投资国家风险评级报告》等重要年度报告。2016 年被中国外交部指定为二十国集团智库峰会(T20)中方首席牵头智库。

companies, Coface experts work to the beat of the global economy. Their ambition is to become the most agile, global trade credit insurance partner in the industry.

(1) Different Industrial Risks in Different Countries 各国不同产业的风险

As can be seen from Figure 13.5, the risk assessment results for the second quarter of 2020 show that the American market is in the textile-clothing and ICT fields, the metals, automotive, and textile-clothing fields in Western Europe, the transport in Central and Eastern Europe, Latin America, the Middle East and Turkey in Construction and metals, and the Asia-Pacific region have relatively high risks in the automotive, construction and other fields.

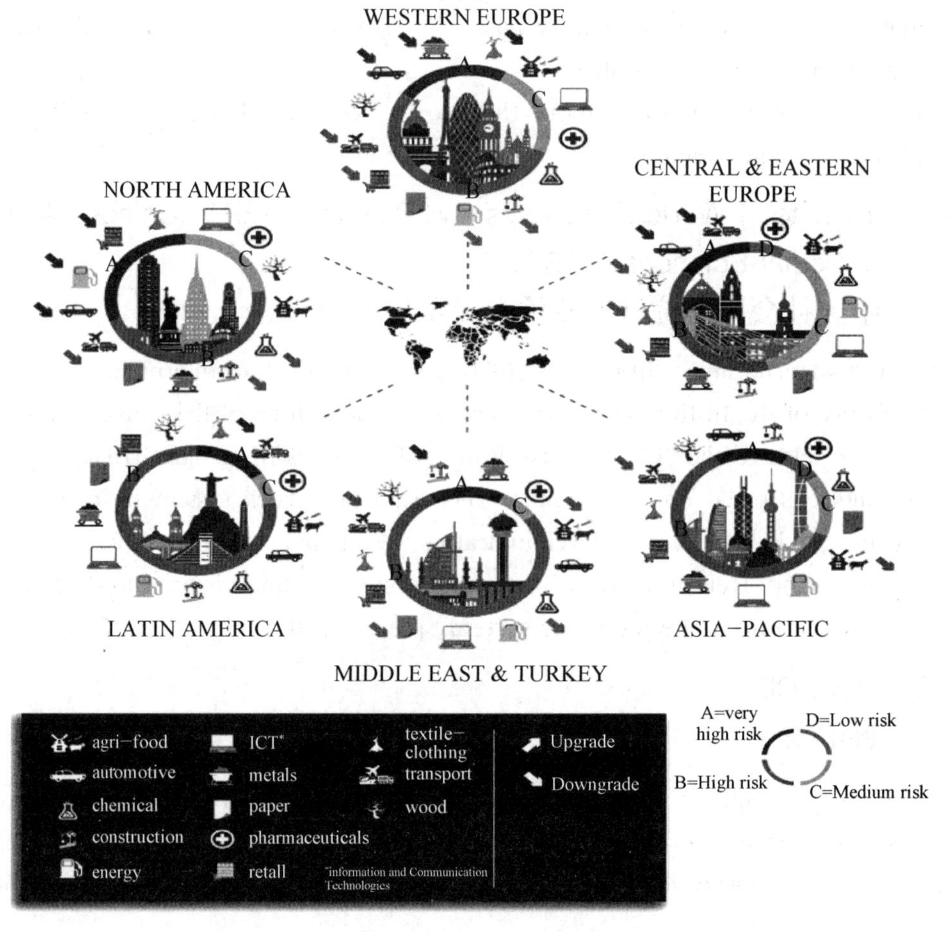

Source: Coface for trade.

Figure 13.5 Sector Risk Assements 2nd quarter 2020

(2) Business Default Risk 业务违约风险

Referring to the business default risk evaluation results in June 2020, business default risk of D and E is very high, namely Afghanistan, Laos, Myanmar, Paklstan, North Korea, Timor Leste, Albania, Armenia, Bosnia and Herzegovina, Kyrgzstan,

Tajikistan, Ukraine(Figure,见章末拓展阅读资源).

(3) Country Risk Assessment and Business Environment Assessment 国家风险评估和商业环境评估

Table 见章末拓展阅读资源 is the risk assessment system and regional calculation results. Please scan the QR code to understand and study.

Conclusion 结语

Entering the international market is the next step of the full market research and STP strategy. Entering the international market means facing greater and more complex challenges. The choice of which mode to use to enter the international market depends not only on the company's own conditions. The international environment and target market environment should also be considered. In addition, risk assessment of international market is essential. When we do these tasks well, the improvement of the competitiveness of enterprises in the international market is the next step of the research work, which will be studied in next chapter.

The Chapter's Referential Questions 本章参考题

(1) Why should companies enter the global market?
为什么企业能够走进全球市场?

(2) Can you give some examples of cultural differences in your region compared to other places?
就你所在的区域与其他区域比较,你能举出一些关于文化差异的事例吗?

(3) What are the advantages for companies doing direct ownership in overseas market?
企业以直接控股形式进入海外市场具有哪些优势?

(4) In what ways can enterprises enter overseas markets?
企业可以以哪些形式进入海外市场?

(5) What are the disadvantages for companies to enter the overseas market in the way of Joint ventures?
企业以合资形式进入海外市场具有哪些劣势?

Further Reading 拓展阅读

Chapter 14

International Market Competition Strategy
国际市场竞争战略

Learning Objectives
本章学习目标

(1) Generic Competitive Strategies.
一般竞争战略。
(2) Three dimensions of international market competitiveness.
国际市场竞争力的三个维度。
(3) Measures of competitiveness.
竞争力的测度。

Key Words
关键词

Generic Competitive Strategies; Cost leadership Strategy; Differentiation Strategy; Centralization Strategy; National Competitiveness; US NEWS; WEF; IMD; Urban Competitiveness; GaWC; GUCP; Industrial Competitiveness; Diamond model; RCA; TC

14.1 Generic Competitive Strategies 基本竞争战略

Case Studies 14.1

基本竞争战略是由美国哈佛商学院著名的战略管理学家迈克尔·波特提出。基本竞争战略有三种:成本领先战略、差异化战略、集中战略。企业必须从这三种战略中选择一种,作为其主导战略。要么把成本控制到比竞争者更低的程度;要么在企业产品和服务中形成与众不同的特色,让顾客感觉到你提供了比其他竞争者更多的价值;要么企业致力于服务于某一特定的市场细分、某一特定的产品种类或某一特定的地理范围。这三种战略架构上差异很大，成功地实施它们需要不同的资源和技能，由于企业文化混乱、组织安排缺失、激励机制冲突，夹在中间的企业还可能因此而遭受更大的损失。

14.1.1 Overall Cost Leadership 成本领先战略

Cost leadership strategy, also known as low-cost strategy, refers to a strategy for enterprises to reduce costs through effective ways, so that the total cost of enterprises is lower than that of competitors, even the lowest cost in the same industry, so as to obtain competitive advantage.

(1) Applicable Conditions and Organizational Requirements of Cost Leadership Strategy 成本领先战略的适用条件与组织要求

① The price competition among existing competitive enterprises is very fierce;

② The products of the industry in which the enterprise is located are basically standardized or homogeneous;

③ There are few ways to realize product differentiation;

④ Most customers use products in the same way;

⑤ The conversion cost of consumers is very low;

⑥ Consumers have greater bargaining power in price reduction.

(2) Risk of Adopting Cost Leadership Strategy 采用成本领先战略的风险

① Excessive price reduction leads to lower profit margin;

② New entrants may catch up;

③ Loss of ability to foresee market changes;

④ Technological change reduces the utility of enterprise resources;

⑤ Vulnerable to the external environment.

14.1.2 Differentiation 差异化战略

The so-called differentiation strategy refers to a strategy adopted to make the enterprise's products clearly different from the competitor's products and form distinctive characteristics. The core of this strategy is to obtain some uniqueness that is valuable to customers.

(1) Applicable Conditions and Organizational Requirements of Differentiation Strategy 差异化战略的适用条件与组织要求

① There are many ways to create differences between enterprises and competitors' products, and this difference is considered valuable by customers;

② Customer demand and use requirements for products are diverse, that is, customer demand is different;

③ Few competitors adopt similar differentiation approaches, that is, they can really ensure that the enterprise is "differentiated";

④ Technological change is fast, and the competition in the market mainly focuses on the continuous introduction of new product features.

(2) Risks of Adopting Differentiation Strategy 采用差异化战略的风险

① Some customers may be lost. If the competitor adopting the cost leading strategy depresses the product price and makes the product price gap between it and the manufacturer implementing the differentiation strategy very large, in this case, in order to save a lot of costs, users give up the product features, services or image owned by the manufacturer that obtains the difference and choose high-quality and low-cost products instead;

② The factor of product difference required by users decreases. When users become more and more sophisticated and have no clear understanding of the characteristics and differences of products, they may ignore the differences;

③ A lot of imitation reduces the perceived difference. Especially when the product develops to maturity, manufacturers with technical strength can easily reduce the differences between products through realistic imitation.

14.1.3 Focus 集中化战略

Centralization strategy, also known as focus strategy, refers to a strategy in which the business activities of an enterprise or business unit focus on a specific buyer group, a part of a product line or a regional market. The core of this strategy is to target a specific user group, a subdivided product line or a subdivided market. Specifically, centralization strategy can be divided into product line centralization strategy, customer centralization strategy, regional centralization strategy and low share centralization strategy.

(1) Applicable Conditions and Organizational Requirements of Centralization Strategy 集中化战略的适用条件与组织要求

① Have completely different user groups, which may have different needs or use products in different ways;

② In the same target market segment, other competitors do not intend to implement the focus strategy;

③ The resources of enterprises do not allow them to pursue a wide range of market segments;

④ There are great differences in the scale, growth rate and profitability of each

segment in the industry, which makes some segments more attractive than others.

(2) Risks of Adopting a Centralized Strategy 采用集中化战略的风险

① Since all the strength and resources of the enterprise are invested in a product or service or a specific market, when customer preferences change, technology innovation or new substitutes appear, it will be found that the demand for products or services in this part of the market will decline, and the enterprise will be greatly impacted;

② Competitors have entered the target market selected by the enterprise and adopted a more centralized strategy better than the enterprise;

③ Product sales may become smaller, product requirements are constantly updated, resulting in an increase in production costs, which weakens the cost advantage of enterprises adopting centralized strategy.

14.2 National Competitiveness 国家竞争力

14.2.1 WEF 世界经济论坛

At present, the ranking of national competitiveness by the world economic forum is more popular internationally. Refer to the ranking of national competitiveness by the world economic forum in 2019.

Table 14.1 National Competitiveness Ranking Index System

Framework	Pillars	Number of indicators included
Enabling Environment	Institutions	26
	Infrastructure	12
	ICT adoption	5
	Macroeconomic stability	2
Human Capital	Health	1
	Skills	9
Markets	Product market	7
	Labour market	12
	Financial system	9
	Market size	2

Continued

Framework	Pillars	Number of indicators included
Innovation Ecosystem	Business dynamism	8
	Innovation capability	10
Totals	12	103

The 2019 report evaluation framework includes 103 indicators under 12 pillars to analyze the competitiveness of 141 economies. Each index adopts a 0～100 point scoring system to show the gap between the economy and the ideal state.

Singapore ranks first in competitiveness, with a comprehensive score of 84.8. In addition, there are 12 economies with a comprehensive score of 80 or above, 24 economies with a score of 70 (inclusive) to 80, 39 economies with a score of 60 (inclusive) to 70, 38 economies with a score of 50 (inclusive) to 60, 22 economies with a score of 40 (inclusive) to 50 and 6 economies with a score of less than 40. The economy with the lowest comprehensive score is Chad, with only 35.1 points.

The average score of 141 economies is 61, which is nearly 40 points away from the full score.

The report believes that such a global competitiveness gap is particularly worrying against the background that the global economy may face recession. The changing geopolitical situation and increasing trade friction have exacerbated the uncertainty of economic development and may lead to economic recession.

From a regional perspective, the Asia Pacific region has become the most competitive region, ahead of Europe and North America. Singapore is a leader in the Asia Pacific region in terms of economic development. The United States is the leader in Europe and North America. Although it has dropped one place, it is still an innovation power. The global competitiveness of Latin America and the Caribbean, the Middle East and North Africa, South Asia and sub Saharan Africa is weak.

Klaus Schwab, founder and executive chairman of the world economic forum, believes that innovation has become a key factor in competitiveness in the new economy. Countries that focus on infrastructure, building human skills, research and development and supporting the backward are more successful than those that focus only on traditional growth factors.

Comparing the performance of the two major economies of China and the United States, it can be found that there is still an obvious gap between China and the United States on the whole. Among the indicators (Figure 14.1～14.2), the United States has five indicators in the top five, while China has only one indicator in the top five. It shows that China's market has surpassed the United States in scale, but the United

States still has absolute advantages in labor market, financial system, business dynamism and innovation capability.

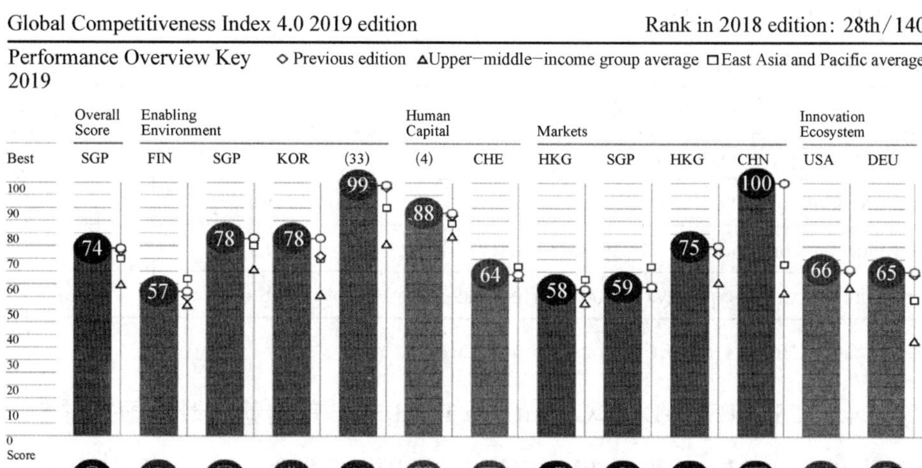

Figure 14.1 Ranking of China's Competitiveness in 2019

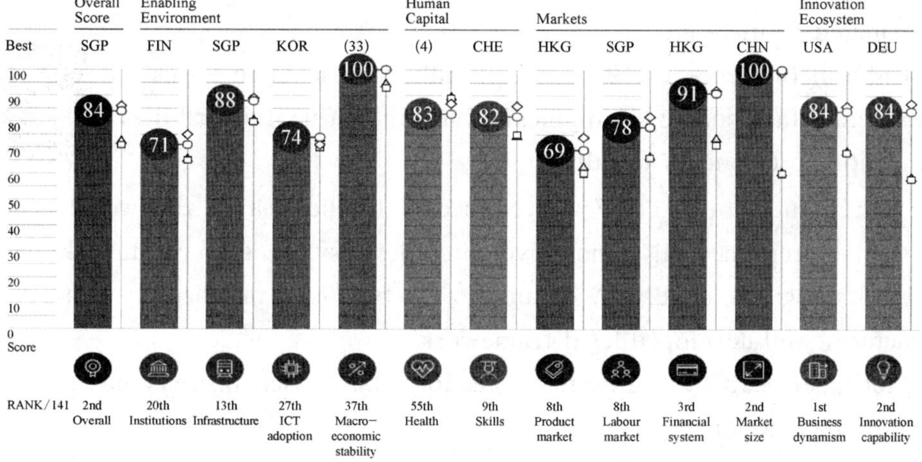

Figure 14.2 Ranking of American Competitiveness in 2019

Table 14.2 Comparison of Main Data between China and the United States

Performance	China	United States
Population millions GDP	1,395.40	327.40
per capita (US$)	9,608.40	62,605.60
10-year average annual GDP growth (%)	6.7	2

Continued

Performance	China	United States
GDP (PPP) (%) world GDP	18.69	15.16
5-year average FDI inward flow (%) GDP	1.2	1.8
Environmental footprint gha/capita	1.1	10.9
Renewable energy consumption share (%)	12.4	8.7
Unemployment rate (%)	4.4	3.9
Global Gender Gap Index 0~1 (gender parity)	0.7	0.7
Income Gini 0 (perfect equality) －100 (perfect inequality)	38.6	41.50

Source: The Global Competitiveness Report 2019.

(2)14.4.1 US NEWS-Best Countries Rankings 美国新闻最佳国家排名

The study and model used to score and rank countries were developed by BAV Group and The Wharton School of the University of Pennsylvania, specifically professor David J. Reibstein, in consultation with U.S. News & World Report.

The evaluation is based on 9 indicators, and the weights of each part are as follows:

① Adventure (2%): friendly, fun, pleasant climate, scenic, sexy.

② Citizenship (15.88%): cares about human rights, cares about the environment, gender equality, progressive, religious freedom, respects property rights, trustworthy, well-distributed political power.

③ Cultural Influence (12.96%): culturally significant in terms of entertainment, fashionable, happiness, has an influential culture, modernization, prestigious, trendy.

④ Entrepreneurship (17.87%): connected to the rest of the world, educated population, entrepreneurial, innovative, provides easy access to capital, skilled labor force, technological expertise, transparent business practices, well-developed infrastructure, well-developed legal framework.

⑤ Heritage (1.13%): culturally accessible, has a rich history, has great food, many cultural attractions.

⑥ Movers (14.36%): different, distinctive, dynamic, unique.

⑦ Open for Business (11.08%): bureaucratic, cheap manufacturing costs, corrupt, favorable tax environment, transparent government practices.

⑧ Power (7.95%): a leader, economically influential, politically influential, strong international alliances, and a strong military.

⑨ Quality of Life (16.77%): a good job market, affordable, economically stable, family friendly, income equality, politically stable, safe, well-developed public education system and health system.

(3) IMD[①] 全球竞争力报告

The competitiveness ranking in 2020 is mainly evaluated by four criteria: economic performance, government efficiency, business efficiency and infrastructure. Singapore has maintained its position as the world's most competitive economy for the second consecutive year.

Among the Asian economies, the ranking of other economies declined except Singapore, Taiwan of China from 16th to 11th, and South Korea from 28th to 23rd. Hongkong China, fell from 2nd to 5th, China slipped from fourteenth to twentieth, and Japan fell from thirtieth to thirty-fourth. In addition, the United States also slipped from third to tenth. The report points out that the trade war between China and United States has hit the economies of the two countries and reversed their competitive growth.

Table 14.3 Global Competitiveness Ranking 2020 (IMD)

2020	Country or Region	2019	Change	
1	Singapore	1	0	—
2	Denmark	8	6	↑
3	Switzerland	4	1	↑
4	Netherlands	6	2	↑
5	China Hong Kong	2	−3	↓
6	Sweden	9	3	↑
7	Norway	11	4	↑
8	Canada	13	5	↑
9	UAE	5	−4	↓
10	United States	3	−7	↓
11	Taiwan, China	16	5	↑
12	Ireland	7	−5	↓
13	Finland	15	2	↑
14	Qatar	10	−4	↓
15	Luxembourg	12	−3	↓
16	Austria	19	3	↑

① 从 1990 年开始，IMD(洛桑国际管理发展学院)每年对全世界主要国家和地区的竞争力，以及该国家和地区内的企业竞争力，进行分析和排名。目前，IMD 分析样本包括 61 个国家和地区。IMD 评测的指标主要分为经济绩效、政府效率、企业效率、基础设施四大类指标，其中又细分出 323 个指标。

Continued

2020	Country or Region	2019	Change	
17	Germany	17	0	—
18	Australia	18	0	—
19	United Kingdom	23	4	↑
20	China	14	-6	↓

Source: IMD.

14.3 Urban Competitiveness 城市竞争力

14.3.1 GaWC[①]

GaWC 将世界城市分为四个大的等级——Alpha(一线城市)、Beta(二线城市)、Gamma(三线城市)、Sufficiency(自给自足城市,也可以理解为四线城市),每个大的等级中又区分出多个带加减号(+/-)的次等级。

The GaWC ranks the world's cities using the distribution of the six "advanced producer services organizations" in the world's largest cities as an indicator. This includes: banking, insurance, legal environment, consulting management, advertising and accounting, focusing on the city's leading role and driving force in global activities. The GaWC's measure of world cities does not include direct GDP or manufacturing output. In other words, the more international institutions in these industries are distributed and ranked in cities, the higher the city's score, and the more it is regarded by the GaWC as an influential world city.

In the latest ranking in 2019, China's first tier cities include Hong Kong China, Beijing, Shanghai, Taipei China, Guangzhou and Shenzhen. GaWC researchers said that compared with the cities in the Yangtze River Delta except Shanghai, the cities in the Pearl River Delta have higher global connectivity. According to the latest monitoring and analysis of the agency, Guangzhou has emerged as China's fourth largest financial center right after Hong Kong, Shanghai and Beijing.

① GaWC 是一个以欧美学者组成的学术机构,发布的排名相对比较客观,是世界城市体系研究领域最为重要和权威的报告之一。GaWC 的全球城市分级排名是世界上对一、二、三、四线城市最权威的排名。

14.3.2 Ranking List of Urban Commercial Charm
城市商业魅力排行榜

第一财经和新一线城市研究所根据大数据得出的排名(2020),城市商业魅力排行榜主要参考的是城市的商业资源集聚度、城市枢纽性、城市人活跃度、生活方式多样性、未来可塑性。

Table 14.4 Ranking List of Urban Commercial Charm

Number	Project	Weight
1	Concentration degree of commercial resources	0.22
2	Urban hub	0.2
3	Urban population activity	0.18
4	Lifestyle diversity	0.18
5	Future plasticity	0.22

At present, there are four first tier cities in China, namely Beijing 174.45, Shanghai 157.10, Guangzhou 123.22 and Shenzhen 118.33. These four cities are also first tier cities in the world with very developed economy. In addition to the first tier cities, there are 15 new first tier cities in China. The ranking of the 15 new first tier cities in 2020 is: Chengdu 100, Chongqing 88.74, Hangzhou 87.41, Wuhan 80.36, Xi'an 79.90, Tianjin 73.65, Suzhou 71.92, Nanjing 71.05, Zhengzhou 63.92, Changsha 62.76, Dongguan 60.64, Shenyang 53.67, Qingdao 52.28, Hefei 51.99 and Foshan 50.93.

14.3.3 GUCP①
中国社会科学院城市与竞争力研究中心

GUCP successively released the top 200 global urban economic competitiveness and the top 200 global urban sustainable competitiveness in 2019. These rankings can clearly see the world rankings of cities in various countries and provide an effective reference for urban analysis.

On September 24, 2019, during the 74th United Nations General Assembly, the "Global Urban Competitiveness Report Conference" organized by UN Habitat was held at the United Nations headquarters in New York. The global urban

① 中国社会科学院城市与竞争力研究中心是2010年4月26日成立的一个有关城市与竞争力的院级非实体研究中心。先后承担了中央交办课题、国家重大社科基金招标课题、联合国、世界银行、欧盟、中组部、科技部、商务部、北京市、广州、成都市等国际组织、国家部委、地方政府委托的课题。到目前已发表11次《中国城市竞争力报告》(年度报告),3次《全球城市竞争报告》(双年度报告),3次《中国住房发展报告》(年度)、1次《中国国家竞争力报告》(双年度),为中国近20个省市政府进行案例、战略和对策研究。城市竞争力蓝皮书等已成为社科院重要的学术品牌,在国内外产生十分广泛的影响,也为中央及地方政府的相关决策提供参考。

competitiveness report 2018—2019-global industrial chain: shaping a networked Urban Planet (hereinafter referred to as the report), jointly completed by the Chinese Academy of Social Sciences and UN Habitat, was released at the meeting. This report is the third part of the annual report on global urban competitiveness. It was first released at the United Nations headquarters during the United Nations General Assembly to discuss important theoretical and practical issues in global urban development. The report shows that Asia's sustainable competitiveness continues to improve and Chinese cities continue to rise.

Looking at the world from the perspective of cities, the report found that an intelligent, global and networked Urban Planet has begun to take shape in the past 40 years. The collective rise of Chinese cities is the most important event of global cities in the past 40 years.

Economic competitiveness refers to the city's current ability to create value and obtain economic rent. From the perspective of display, economic density index and economic increment index are used. Sustainable competitiveness refers to the long-term sustainable ability of a city to better and more continuously meet the complex and critical social welfare of urban residents by improving its economic, social, environmental and technological advantages. The report mainly selects eight indicators for evaluation: economic vitality, environmental quality, social inclusion, scientific and technological innovation, global linkages, government management, human capital potential and infrastructure.

14.4 Industrial Competitiveness 产业竞争力

产业竞争力,亦称产业国际竞争力,指某国或某一地区的某个特定产业相对于他国或地区同一产业在生产效率、满足市场需求、持续获利等方面所体现的竞争能力。竞争力实质上是一个比较的概念,因此,产业竞争力内涵涉及两个基本方面的问题:一个是比较的内容,一个是比较的范围。产业竞争力比较的范围是国家或地区,产业竞争力是一个区域的概念。因此,产业竞争力分析应突出影响区域经济发展的各种因素,包括产业集聚、产业转移、区位优势等。

14.4.1 Diamond Model Theory 钻石模型理论

After in-depth research on the competitiveness of many countries and industries, Porter believes that industrial competitiveness is formed by the joint action of four main factors: production factors, domestic market demand, related and supporting industries, enterprise strategy, enterprise structure and horizontal competition, as well as two auxiliary factors such as government behavior and opportunities. Among them, the first four factors are the main influencing factors of industrial competitiveness, which constitute the main framework of the "Diamond Model". The four factors affect each other to form a whole, which jointly determines the level of industrial competitiveness.

14.4.2 Revealed Comparative Advantage Index RCA 指数

The so-called explicit comparative advantage index refers to the ratio of the share of a country's exports of a certain commodity in its total export value to the share of such commodity exports in the total world exports, which is expressed by the formula:

$$RCA_{ij} = (X_{ij}/X_{tj}) \div (X_iW/X_tW)$$

Where X_{ij} represents the export value of country j's export product I, and X_{tj} represents the total export value of country j; X_iW represents the export value of world export product I, and X_t Wrepresents the world total export value.

Generally speaking, RCA value close to 1 indicates neutral relative comparative advantage, and there is no relative advantage or disadvantage; If the RCA value is greater than 1, it means that the export proportion of the commodity in the country is greater than that in the world, then the product of the country has a comparative advantage in the international market and has a certain international competitiveness; If the RCA value is less than 1, it means that it has no comparative advantage in the international market and its international competitiveness is relatively weak.

14.4.3 Trade Competitiveness TC 指数

Trade competitiveness index, namely TC (trade competitiveness) index, is one of the commonly used measurement indicators in the analysis of international competitiveness. It indicates the proportion of the balance of a country's import and export trade in the total import and export trade, that is, TC index = (export volume − import volume) ÷ (export volume + import volume). As a relative value to the total trade volume, the index excludes the impact of fluctuations in macro factors such as economic expansion and inflation, that is, no matter what the absolute volume of import and export is, the index is between −1 and 1.

The closer the value is to 0, the closer the competitiveness is to the average level; When the index is −1, it means that the industry only imports but not exports. The closer it is to −1, the weaker its competitiveness is; When the index is 1, it means that the industry only exports but not imports. The closer it is to 1, the greater the competitiveness.

We have been discussing competitiveness from a macro perspective, but from the perspective of marketing, enterprises are the main body of market competition.When it comes to enterprises competing in the market, generally speaking, enterprises play four roles in the market, namely market leader, market challenger, follower and market nicher. Their strategies in market competition are different due to their different positions. Refer to Table 14.5 for details.

Table 14.5 Strategies for Market Leaders, Challengers, Followers, and Nichers

Market Leader Strategies	Market Challenger Strategies	Market Follower Strategies	Market Nicher Strategies
Expand total market	Full frontal attack	Follow closely	By customer, market, quality-price, service
Protect market share	Indirect attack	Follow at a distance	Multiple niching
Expand market share			

In addition to the above indicators related to the measurement of industrial competitiveness, there are many methods, including econometric means, to measure and explain competitiveness. This textbook does not do much explanation here. Students can continue to learn relevant knowledge such as industrial economy and urban economy.

Conclusion 结语

Competitive strategy is the inevitable choice for each organization to obtain competitive advantage through a series of operations and technologies. This chapter starts from the general competitive strategy and focuses on the relevant knowledge of competitive strategy from the dimensions of national competitiveness, urban competitiveness and industrial competitiveness. There is an old Chinese saying "planning in a tent and winning thousands of miles away", which explains the significant role of strategy. Whether the strategy formulation is scientific or not determines the fate and success or failure of the organization. This chapter is in the end of strategic part, we will begin to learn the marketing tactics in next part.

The Chapter's Referential Questions 本章参考题

(1) What are the applicable conditions and risks of cost leadership?
成本领先战略的适用条件和风险在哪里?

(2) Referring to the national competitiveness index system of the world economic forum, which aspects should China's market competitiveness improve the most breakthrough?
参考世界经济论坛的国家竞争力指标体系,中国市场的竞争力提升最应该从哪几个方面突破?

(3) In the context of the "One Belt and One Road" initiative, how can Chinese companies take advantage of the competition and participate in it?
在"一带一路"倡议下,中国企业如何发挥竞争优势参与到"一带一路"建设中去?

Further Reading
拓展阅读

Part 5

International Marketing Mix Strategy(4PS)

国际市场营销 4P 组合策略

Chapter 15　International Product Strategy

Chapter 16　International Pricing Strategy

Chapter 17　International Distribution Channel Strategy

Chapter 18　International Promotion Strategy

There are four chapters in this part, including product, pricing, distribution, and promotion, which complement each other and constitute a marketing mix system. International marketing strategy (tactics) is the concrete implementation of international marketing strategy, and it is also a full manifestation of international marketing skills. A systematic mastery of this part of the knowledge will help formulate a competitive marketing plan for future international marketing activities.

本部分有四章的学习内容，分别从产品、定价、分销、促销四个章节学习，它们之间是相辅相成的，共同构成营销组合体系。国际营销策略是国际营销战略的具体实施，也是国际市场营销技能的充分体现。系统掌握这一部分的知识，有助于为今后从事国际市场营销活动制定有竞争力的的营销方案。

|Chapter 15|

International Product Strategy 国际产品策略

Learning Objectives 本章学习目标

(1) International brand.
国际品牌。

(2) Product life cycle theory.
产品生命周期理论。

(3) Product development and innovation.
产品开发与创新。

Key Words 关键词

International Brand; AMA; Boston Matrix; Product Life Cycle Theory; New Product

雷蒙德·弗农(Raymond Vernon) 1931 出生,早期曾致力于区位经济学的研究,后转入对信息和专业化服务的研究,于 1966 年发表《产品周期中的国际投资和国际贸易》一文,提出了著名的"产品生命周期理论"。

3M 公司的"15%法则":允许员工 15%的工作时间"违反纪律"——去做有关产品创新的事。"如果你不想犯错误,那么什么也别干。"

15.1 International Brand Strategy 国际品牌

Case Studies 15.1

品牌作为企业的无形资产，具有动态的市场价值，因此，国际化品牌必然特别重视品牌建设，品牌价值的攀升是企业全方位努力的结果，品牌有助于企业、城市、国家竞争力提升。塑造国际品牌不仅是企业的目标，也体现政府的意志和消费者意愿。

The American Marketing Association (AMA) defines the brand as: A brand is a name, a term, a symbol, or a pattern design, or a different combination of them, to identify a product or service that distinguishes it from the competitor's products and services. Brand includes brand name and logo, appearance (packaging, structure, shape features) and so on.

Figure 15.1 Some Car Brands

Table 15.1 BRANDZ TOP 100 Most Valuable Global Brands 2020

2020 Ranking	Brand	Category	Brand Value (100 million USD)	Value Change	2019 Ranking
1	Amazon	Retail	4,158.55	32%	1
2	Apple	Technology	3,522.06	14%	2

2020 Ranking	Brand	Category	Brand Value (100 million USD)	Value Change	2019 Ranking
3	Microsoft	Technology	3,265.44	30%	4
4	Google	Technology	3,236.01	5%	3
5	Visa	Payment	1,868.09	5%	5
6	Alibaba	Retail	1,525.25	16%	7
7	Tencent	Technology	1,509.78	15%	8
8	Facebook	Technology	1,471.9	-7%	6
9	McDonald's	Fast Food	1,293.21	-1%	9
10	MasterCard	Payment	1,081.29	18%	12

Source: https://www.prnasia.com/story/284058-1.shtml.

WPP and Kantar jointly released the "BrandZ Top 100 Most Valuable Global Brands 2020" ranking. In 2020, a record 17 Chinese brands entered the BrandZ Global Top 100 list, an increase of two from 2019. China has also become the country with the second largest number of brands on the list. The first is the United States, which has 51 brands on the list, and the third is Germany, which has eight brands on the list. The total value of Chinese brands on the list has increased by 16%, almost three times the global growth rate.

Table 15.2 Chinese Brands in the Top 100 of Most Valuable Global Brands 2020

2020 Ranking	2019 Ranking	Brand	Category	Brand Value (100 million USD)	Value Change
6	7	阿里巴巴	零售	1,525.25	16%
7	8	腾讯	科技	1,509.78	15%
18	35	茅台	酒	537.55	58%
31	29	中国工商银行	地区性银行	381.49	-1%
36	27	中国移动	电信运营商	345.83	-12%
38	40	平安	保险	338.1	15%
45	47	华为	科技	294.12	9%
52	66	京东	零售	254.94	24%
54	78	美团	生活方式	239.11	27%
58	59	中国建设银行	地区性银行	210.89	-7%
64	71	滴滴出行	交通出行	200.41	0%
68	89	海尔	物联网生态	187.13	15%

Continued

2020 Ranking	2019 Ranking	Brand	Category	Brand Value (100 million USD)	Value Change
69	82	中国农业银行	地区性银行	186.39	2%
79	无	抖音	娱乐	168.78	N/A
81	74	小米	科技	166.44	-16%
91	63	百度	科技	148.4	-29%
97	无	中国银行	地区性银行	136.86	N/A

15.2 Product Portfolio—Boston Matrix 产品组合——波士顿矩阵

Boston matrix was first founded in 1970 by Bruce Henderson, a famous American management scientist and founder of Boston Consulting Company. We name them as Boston Consulting Group approach (BCG).

① Stars. Stars are high-growth, high-share businesses or products. They often need heavy Investments to finance their rapid growth. Eventually, their growth will slowdown, and they will turn into cash cows.

② Cash cows. Cash cows are low-growth, high-share business or products.These established and successfful SBUs need less investment to hold their market share.Thus, they produce a lot of the cash that the company uses to pay its bills and support other SBUs that need investment.

③ Question marks. Question marks are low-share business units in high growth markets.They require a lot of cash to hold their share, let alone increase it. Management has to think hard about which question marks it should try to build into stars and which should be phased out.

④ Dogs. Dogs are low-growth, low-share businesses and products. They may generate enough cash to maintain themselves but do not promise to be large sources of cash.

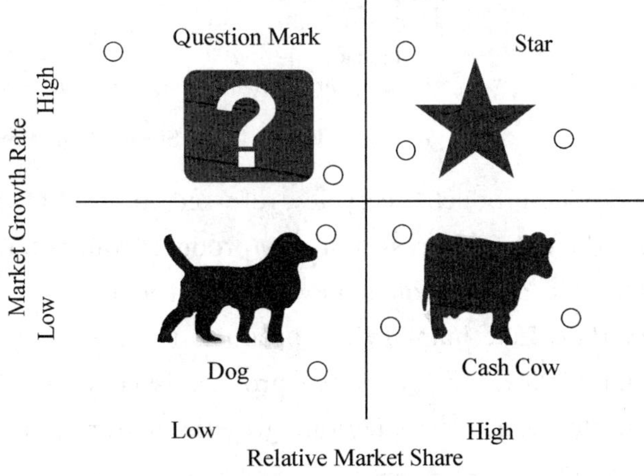

Figure 15.2 The BCG Growth-Share Matrix

The 10 circles in the growth-share matrix represent the company's 10 current SBUs①. The company has two stars, two cash cows, three question marks, and three dogs. The areas of the circles are proportional to the SBU's dollar sales. This company is in fair shape, although not in good shape. It wans to invest in the more promising question marks to make them stars and maintain the stars so that they will become cash cows as their market mature. Fortunately, it has two good-sized cash cows. Income from these cash cows will help finance the company's question marks, stars, and dogs. The company should take some decisive action concerning its dogs and its question marks.

15.3 Product Life Cycle Theory 产品生命周期理论

产品生命周期理论是美国哈佛大学教授雷蒙德·弗农 1966 年在其《产品周期中的国际投资与国际贸易》一文中首次提出的。产品生命周期(Product Life Cycle),简称 PLC。

PLC is the product of the market life, that is, a new product from the beginning to enter the market to the market out of the whole process.

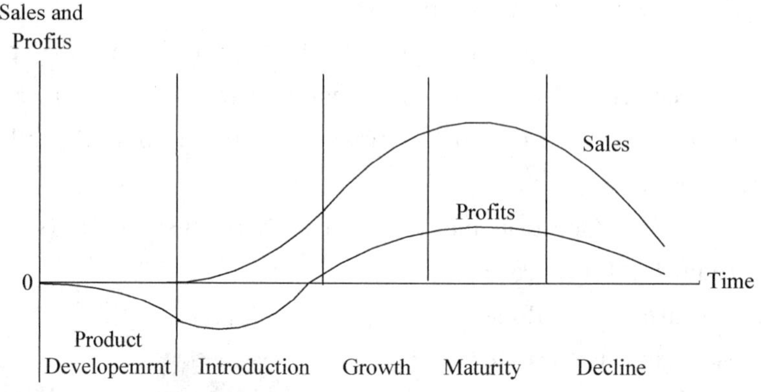

Figure 15.3 Stages of the Product Life Cycle

The product life cycle, referred to as PLC, is the market life of a product, that is, the entire process of a new product from entering the market to being eliminated by the market. Vernon believes that product life refers to the life of marketing in the market. Like human life, products undergo a cycle of formation, growth, maturity, and decline. As far as the product is concerned, it means going through a stage of development, introduction, growth, maturity, and decline. In countries with different

① The company must decide how much it will invest in each product or business (SBU). For each SBU, It must decide wether to build, hold, harvest, or divest.

technological levels, the time and process of occurrence of this cycle are different. There is a large gap and time difference during the period.

A typical product life cycle can generally be divided into four stages, namely the introduction period (or introduction period), the growth period, the maturity period and the decline period.

Table 15.3 Summary of Product Life-Cycle Characteristics, Objectives, and Strategies

Characteristics	Introduction	Growth	Maturity	Decline
Sales	Low sales	Rapidly rising sales	Peak sales	Declining sales
Costs	High cost per customer	Average cost per customer	Low cost per customer	Low cost per customer
Profits	Negative	Rising profits	High profits	Declining profits
Customers	Innovators	Early adopters	Middle majority	Laggards
Competitors	Few	Growing number	Stable number beginning to decline	Declining number
Marketing objectives	Create product awareness and trial	Maximize market share	Maximize profit while defending market share	Reduce expenditure and milk the brand

Strategies

Product	Offer a basic product	Offer product extensions, service, and warranty	Diversify brand and models	Phase out weak items
Price	Use cost-plus	Price to penetrate market	Price to match or beat competitors	Cut price
Distribution	Build selective distribution	Build intensive distribution	Build more intensive distribution	Go selective: phase out unprofitable outlets
Advertising	Build product awareness among early adopters and dealers	Build awareness and interest in the mass market	Stress brand differences and benefits	Reduce to level needed to retain hard-core loyals
Sales Promotion	Use heavy sales promotion to entice trial	Reduce to take advantage of heavy consumer demand	Increase to encourage brand switching	Reduce to minimal level

It is this time difference that is manifested as the technological gap between different countries, which reflects the difference in the competitive position of the same product in different countries' markets determines the changes in international trade and investment. In order to facilitate the distinction, Vernon divides these countries into innovative countries (usually the most developed countries), generally developed countries, and developing countries.

Product life cycle theory has very important application value. Combining this theory, we can judge which industries or enterprises and products in a country have developed to which stage, and therefore, we can formulate corresponding strategies. For example, China's current solar energy, 5G, traditional Chinese medicine manufacturing, automobile industry, supermarkets, Huawei, Haier Group, China Petroleum and so on.

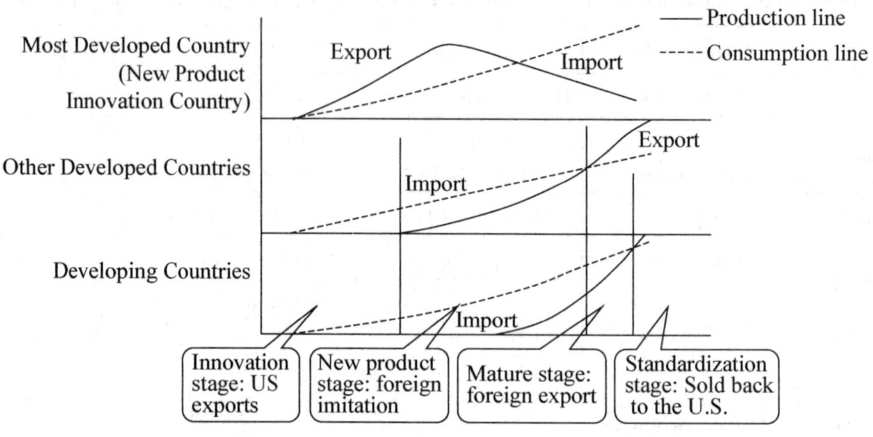

Figure 15.4 International Product Life Cycle Stages

15.4 The Product Life Cycle in International Marketing 国际市场营销中的产品生命周期

15.4.1 General Principles 一般性原则

The product life cycle concept is well known to most marketers. Its impact on the company's marketing efforts that differ from company to company and from product to product. A manufacturer of pharmaceutical products has to pay very serious attention to this concept and plan in advance the various strategies that he proposes to adopt at each stage of the life cycle. On the other hand, a house builder need not concern himself too much with the meaning of this theory, because in practice, each house he builds is a product, once erected and sold, the transaction is finished (with the exception of the after-sales service commitment) and the ravages of the life cycle hardly apply; any change in taste or habits can be easily translated into the next product without substantial planning and investment. Nonetheless the concept is a useful one; it alerts the marketer to the fact that market dynamism affects not only the appearance and functionality of a product but also the effectiveness of the supportive marketing mix ingredients at each stage of a product's life. This is the aspect which is often overlooked by those who tend to describe the value of the product life concept as an impractical one.

Briefly, the product life cycle concept can be summarized thus: every product has a life span of a limited duration. Some products live for many years, others have a short life. If the sales of the product are plotted over a period of time the result will be a curve as shown in Figure 15.5.

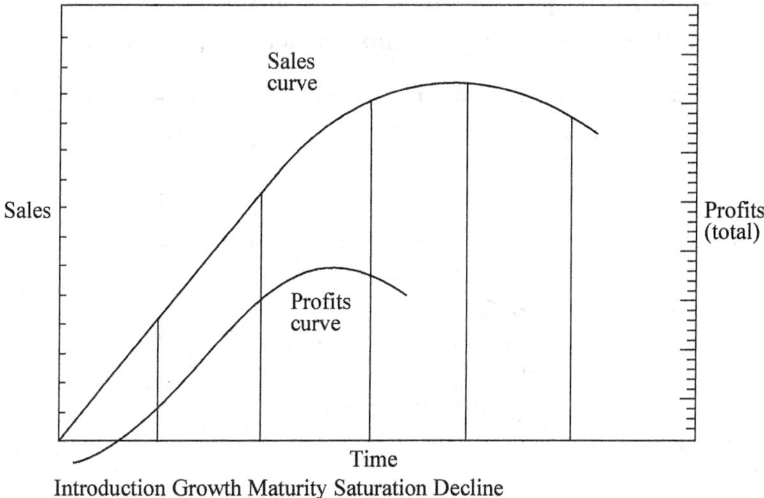

Figure 15.5 Product Life Cycle Pattern, Typical Sales and Profit Curves

The curve, or life cycle is normally divided into five distinct periods-introduction, growth, maturity, saturation and decline. Whilst the shape of the curve will more or less the same for most products, the time duration and the rapidity of change from stage to stage will vary enormously among products. The life cycle of the hula-hoop only lasted a few months; the life-cycle of the ballpoint pen has lasted many years although during those years the product has undergone fundamental marketing changes.

The significant point to remember in this connection is the fact that in most instances, the product's profits tend to follow a predictable pattern through the life cycle. Profits are either absent during the growth stage and reach a peak during the maturity stage. During the saturation stage they normally manifest signs of erosion and all but disappear during the decline stage. If we plot the profit performance on Figure: 15.5 (the scale shown on the right-hand side) it would become apparent that in typical circumstances, peak profitability is reached before peak sales. The marketer who is aware of this situation seeks to overcome the problem by either differentiating the product thus giving it a fresh lease of life or by introducing new products in order to safeguard the company's overall profitability. When a car manufacturer introduces a "face-lift" to a well-established model that he seeks to "cheat old age" through differentiation. When he launches a new model, he introduces a totally new product with a distinct life cycle curve in order to generate a new profit pattern which runs in parallel with the decaying product and eventually takes over the task of sustaining the company's performance. This can be demonstrated in Figure 15.6 and Figure 15.7. The first shows how an endeavor is made through differentiation to give the product extra life where in normal circumstances it would enter the saturation stage. Figure 15.7 illustrates how a succession of products with their distinct life cycles helps the company to maintain a steady profit performance. The point to remember is that quite the difference between these two strategies is not as clear in practice as in theory.

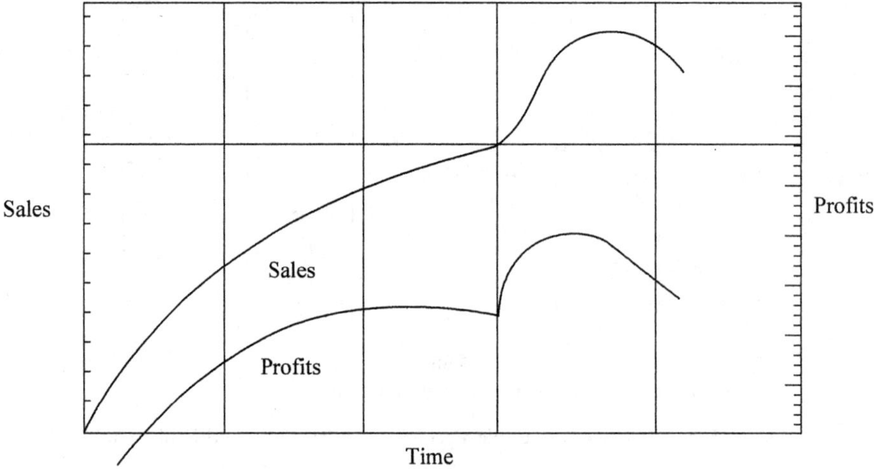

Figure 15.6 The Effect of Differentiation on the Product Life Cycle, Sales and Profit Curves

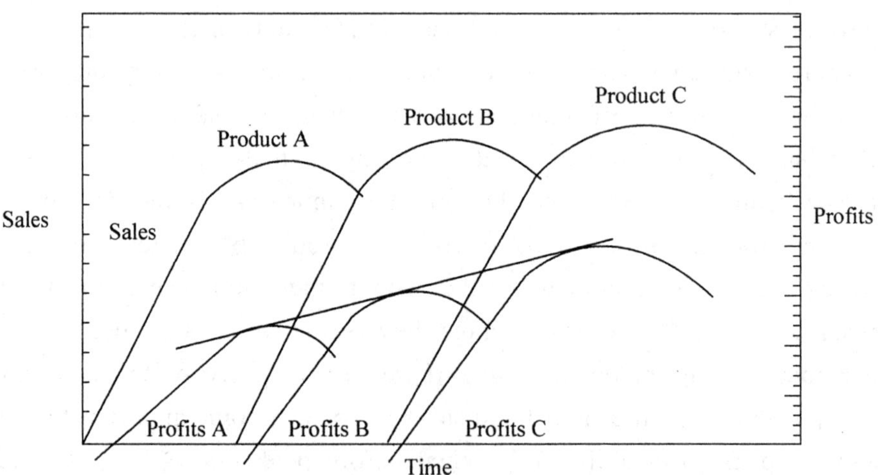

Figure 15.7 New Product Policy and Its Effect on Profit Performance

In this connection, it is vitally important to remember that growth in sales and profitability is not necessarily a sign of long—term success. A product may well earn outstanding profits for one, two or more years but may still represent a poor investment. A marketer must never overlook this aspect of the life cycle theory. A product is only successful in strategic terms when it is capable of earning sufficient returns during its total life cycle in relation to the investment made in it. In other words, a product must be capable, first and foremost, to earn sufficient funds to recover the full investment that the company has incurred in it. It is only at the point of investment recovery that the question of returns and profits arises. Furthermore, when we talk in terms of investment we must include not only the cost of design, manufacturing and inventory but also the full cost of pre-launch marketing projects such as market research, promotion, sampling, physical distribution, etc. It often happens that a company needs to drop a product because of its to poor performance but is reluctant to do so because the investment in that product has not yet been fully recovered. Maintaining such a "sick" product in the range is tantamount to throwing good money after bad. It is therefore essential for marketing managers to monitor not only sales and profits but also the investment recovery as the product life cycle progresses.

The position is shown in Figure 15. 8. It shows the relationship between investment, sales and direct costs. The profit on this diagram is the gap between the sales curve and cost curve. As a generalization one will normally find that if the investment in a product has not been recovered by the time the product has reached the saturation stage, it is unlikely to ever show a satisfactory return on investment over the life of the product. Of course this angle must not be overlooked when evaluation the future of aging products.

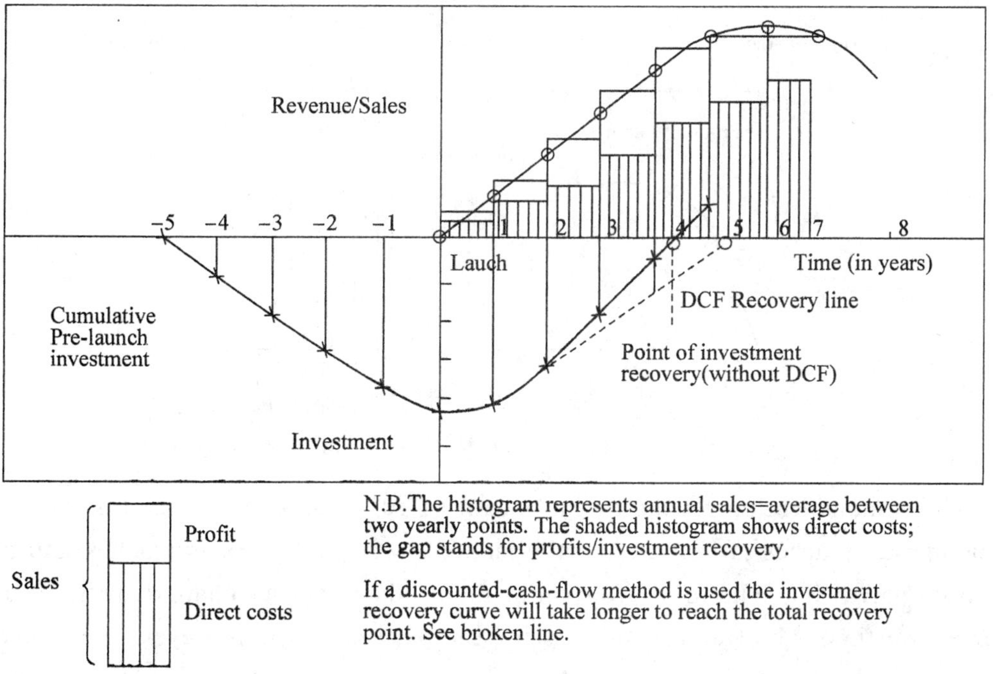

Figure 15.8 The Investment Recovery Process and Product Life Cycle

15.4.2 International Implications
国际影响

The product life cycle concept has a significant relevance to international marketing. Historically, most companies tended to operate in their domestic markets as and long as such markets offered adequate commercial rewards. As soon as signs of sales and profit erosion started to manifest themselves, the company would seek to fill the growing gap trough exports. This in turn means that one could discern differing life cycle patters in different parts of the world. Figure 15.9 illustrates this point. This diagram shows how a product that has reached the decline stage in the domestic market is at the growth stage in country A, at the introduction stage in country B, whilst in country C it is still unknown. The fifth chart in this diagram shows the gap that one would expect to detect between the two extreme situations (excluding course these countries where the product has not been launched at all).

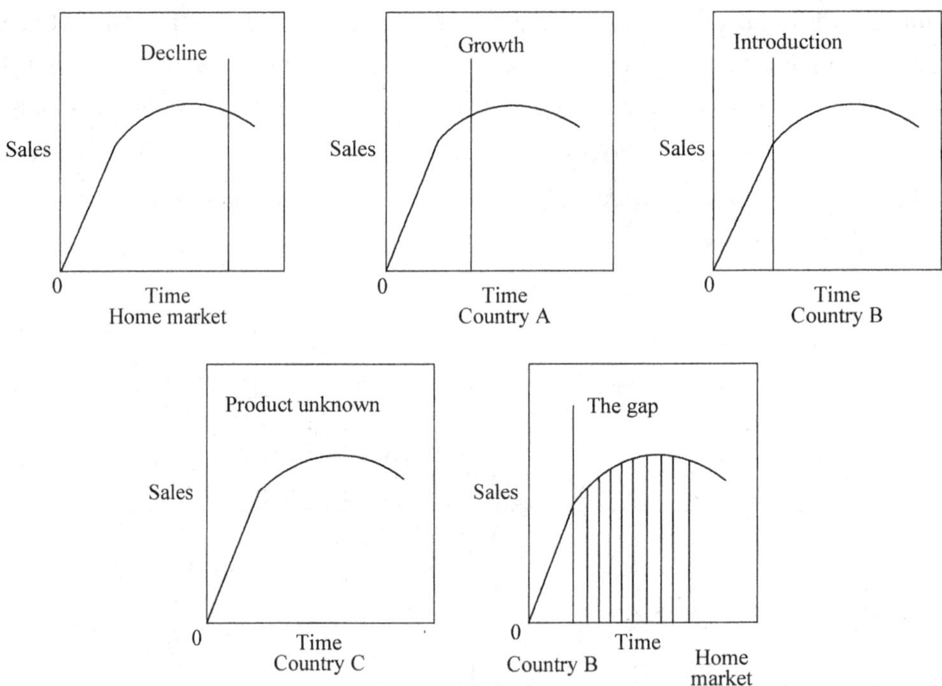

Figure 15.9 Variations in Life Cycle Performance in Different Countries

The communication revolution has meant that the gap between the time when the home market reaches saturation and the last of the export markets reaches saturation has been narrowing. The total life span of the product over all its markets has become shorter overtime. The trend in fact, is for the pattern of the life cycle in a domestic market to become identical to the pattern in other markets. The change illustrated in Figure 15.10 is the underlying philosophy that has made international marketing so different from the previous process of "selling abroad". This is one of the main reasons why the marketer of today must focus on international markets simultaneously, with the view of planning a global launch. Failure to do so may in many instances mean that good opportunities will be lost.

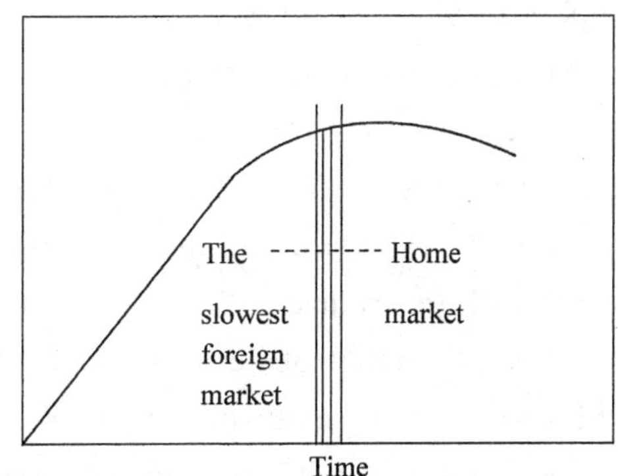

Figure 15.10 The Narrowing Gap between Product Life Cycle Extremities

In summary, a full understanding of the product life cycle is an essential concept for the international marketer. It not only allows him to monitor the progression of his products through their various stages of development, thus determining marketing strategies, but also enables him to plan for a rapid investment recovery effort. This latter point is becoming an elementary and important strategy in the sort of markets that one has to operate nowadays.

15.5 New Product Development 新品开发

Generally speaking, major stages in New-Product Development includes the following aspects: Idea Generation, Idea Screening, Concept Development and Testing, Marketing Strategy Development, Business Analysis, Production Development, Testing Market, Commercialization. So where is the competition from? Figure 15.11 gives you the answer.

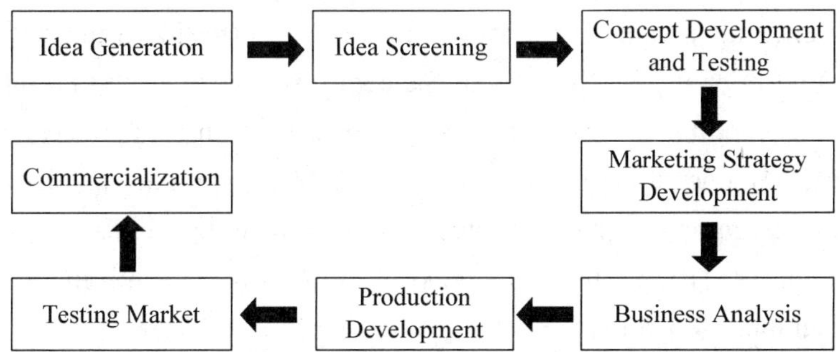

Figure 15.11 Major Stages in New-Product Development

It can be seen from the figure below that, in fact, the competition between enterprises is not about products being produced and sold on shelves. In fact, since the product developers or decision makers of enterprises have ideas for new products, competition has already begun.

New products in the traditional sense refer to products made from scratch. In fact, the concept of new products is larger, including four forms, as follows:

① Brand-new products: new principles, new technologies, new materials, and new processes to realize brand-new functions are the transformation of technological inventions into products.

② Replacement of new products: On the basis of the original products, some new technologies, new materials, new components and new processes are adopted to achieve significant performance improvement.

③ Improved new products: products that have been improved in terms of performance, structure, function, style, color, variety and other aspects of existing products.

④ Imitation of new products: The enterprise imitates the performance and technology of products that already exist on the market, and produces its own new products.

Therefore, the development of new products of an enterprise should combine its own technical conditions and strengths, and select appropriate new product development forms and partners on the premise of comprehensive market research.

15.6 Considerations Determining International Product Policy 国际产品策略的思考

为国际市场提供产品绝不能掉以轻心,一个小失误可能会导致损失惨重。因此,在企业进行国际市场开发的初级阶段,就应该及早认真设计产品策略。

It is apparent that product decisions relating to international markets must not be taken lightly. Errors can creep in without the company realizing the full implications. The difficulties that may occur can be very costly. To try to unravel a mess is much more expensive than taking one's time in planning a sound and systematic product policy at the initial stages of the company 's development as an international company.

The main considerations that must be kept in mind in determining a sound product policy can be summarized thus:

15.6.1 Corporate Objectives 企业目标

This point is fundamental; a company that seeks to maximize profits regardless of international market penetration goals is more likely to strive towards product standardization. By the very nature of such a strategy it is likely to generate, certainly in the shorter term, a better profit performance. however, this consideration must be looked at in juxtaposition to other and often equally important aspects to be discussed hereafter.

15.6.2 The Markets Needs 市场需求

Here we are concerned with the nature of the product itself and the special requirements of the marketplace. We come back to the question of information and the basic "input" needed in this connection is the marketing profile analysis which we discussed at some length in earlier chapters. A profile analysis relating to the product itself can be undertaken. The "product" is dissected into its major components viz. Functional attributes, design, packaging and branding. Depending on the individual circumstances, one can determine the exact nature and number of elements that one wants to research. The important point to remember is that this is the kind of "input" which facilitates the decision as to whether a standardization policy is on the cards or not. Attempting to take a decision of this nature without the information that the profile analysis can yield is asking for trouble.

In other words, one of the major considerations which the marketer must explore when determining his international product policy is the real needs of the markets. He must ask himself: are the needs of the individual markets so different from each other that standardization will limit the use of our product to uneconomic levels?

15.6.3 Company Resources 企业资源

Differentiation is a fairly expensive exercise. A company seeking to attain maximum level of satisfaction of foreign markets through a non-standardization policy must be aware of the fact that such a policy will absorb considerable investment in production resources, inventory, and of course, in the various ingredients of the marketing mix. It is quite easy to drift into a differentiation strategy without fully realizing the financial consequences.

15.6.4 The Nature of the Product 产品性质

Here the marketer must have a good look at the product itself and try to consider the following points:

① Is the life of the product likely to be short?

If the answer is yes, differentiation is probably owing to the investment recovery principle explained earlier.

In this respect past history of the company's other products can be very helpful in providing a clue as to the kind of life cycle performance that one can expect to encounter in the future. Although as a generalization, one can observe that there is a tendency toward a shortening of life cycle characteristics many companies will discover, on careful monitoring, that products do tend to behave in a fairly consistent way within a given industry.

② Is the product of universal appeal?

Some products, by their very nature, are capable of international acceptance without any differentiation. Japanese manufacturers of Hi-Fi equipment, for instance, have recognized that a well-designed piece of equipment which is capable of attaining a substantial penetration of world markets. It would be a strategy of immense waste to endeavor to re-design the product for every market. The interesting point to remember is that ever in the case of Japanese electronics, total standardization is not possible, insofar as wiring standards, safety rules and regulations are laid down by the laws of individual countries and need to be fully satisfied. Nonetheless, if a company starts from the basic strategy of wanting to standardize the product, it can ensure that deviations from a standard product are kept to the absolute minimum viz as demanded by the legal system of individual countries.

③ What level of service shall be required?

Products requiring considerable technical service and attention—either before or after delivery to the customer—usually prescribe a higher level of standardization. A computer manufacturer would find the technical justification for a standard product or range of products a decisive factor in his product planning and approach. An aircraft manufacturer will also strive towards avoiding any kind of differentiation—partly because of the importance of service and partly because of the universal appeal discussed earlier.

If a company manages to develop an internationally recognized brand or trademark for a particular product, this pressure will be detrimental to differentiation.

④ Is production easy or difficult?

It is impossible dissociate product policy from production realities. A product requiring complex manufacturing processes is unlipthy to support differentiation strategies than a product which can be manufactured with ease. This is of course an important consideration and in many cases production factors may outweigh the marketing benefits that differentiation may yield.

⑤ Are there any legal constraints?

Legal systems can have a major impact on the design of the product, its packaging the printed messages incorporated thereon. Thus, a packet of cigarettes sold in the UK must contain a warning about the health hazard of smoking. The same packet sold in Canada must contain a warning in two languages-English and French and the actual wording is different from the one prescribed in the UK. In other words, the legal systems of the two countries virtually impose a differentiation policy. The law is not interested in the inconvenience that such regulations may impose on marketing personnel. Such variations in legal requirements are particularly troublesome in relation to weights, measures and contents of food products. Such legal requirements must be adhered to most scrupulously. The only way that partial standardization can be achieved in such situations is through the incorporation of multi-lingual messages, each complying with the rules and regulations of the country of destination. However, it needs a very large label to be able to accommodate the legal requirements of eighty or more countries.

⑥ Are there any Country-of-Origin effect?

The COE (Country of Origin) effect can be defined as any influence of the country of manufacture, assembly or design on the positive or negative consumer perception of the product. A company competing in today's global market manufactures products on a global scale; when customers know the country of origin, the place of manufacture may affect the product or brand image. Once the market gains an experience with the product, it can overcome negative national stereotypes. In addition, national stereotypes or "national fairness" can be overcome through good marketing.

Conclusion 结语

Product strategy is the first of the 4P strategy. No matter how good the other conditions are, if there is no product to support it, it will be meaningless. On the basis of domestic marketing, if a company wants to manage an international brand, it needs to design, maintain and manage the brand, to learn from the experience of international outstanding brands. At the same time, product innovation should be persisted from beginning to end. Life cycle theory has very important reference value in practice. It is necessary to make full use of this theory to guide the practice of enterprise product strategy, and ultimately enhance the value of the enterprise in the international market through successful brand strategy.

The Chapter's Referential Questions 本章参考题

(1) Why is it said that the Product is the heart of the Marketing Mix?
为什么说产品是营销组合的核心?

(2) How could you consider the of life cycle product when making investments in foreign markets?
在企业对海外市场进行投资决策时,应该如何考虑产品的生命周期?

(3) What are the advantages and disadvantages of the standardization of products?
标准化产品设计有哪些优缺点?

(4) What are your major considerations when determining the international product policy?
在制定国际产品策略时,企业通常会有哪些主要因素需要考虑?

(5) What steps are usually taken when companies undertake the classical screening process for new products normally?
在设计新产品时,企业通常的传统做法有哪些步骤?

(6) List some examples for multinational companies doing standardization or differentiation for their product strategies.
列举在全球市场中跨国企业实施标准化和差异化产品策略的事例。

(7) Define a global brand. How important are the global brands?
定义一个全球品牌。全球品牌有多重要?

(8) Define Country-of-origin effect. How can a company overcome this effect?
定义原产国效应。公司如何克服这种影响?

Further Reading
拓展阅读

【Chapter 16】
International Pricing Strategy
国际定价策略

Learning Objectives
本章学习目标

(1) Pricing target.
定价目标。
(2) Factors affecting pricing.
影响定价的因素。
(3) New product pricing strategy.
新品定价策略。
(4) International transfer pricing.
国际转移定价。

Key Words
关键词

Trade Term; Psychological Pricing; Parallel Imports; Letter of Credit; Pricing Strategies; Cost-oriented Pricing; Demand-Oriented Pricing; Competitive Oriented Pricing; Skimming Pricing; Moderate Pricing; Penetration Pricing; Transfer Pricing

Case Studies 16.1

The price strategy in international marketing is the most active factor in the entire marketing mix, with a strong competitive and multi-factor comprehensive. How does an international marketing campaign of a business performance largely depends on whether the price is reasonable.

16.1 The International Market Pricing Target Analysis 国际市场定价目标分析

Pricing target refers to the expected marketing effect that the enterprise hopes to achieve through price means. Pricing objectives can generally be expressed in five aspects: maintaining operation as the pricing objective; maximizing current profits as the pricing objective; increasing market share as the pricing objective; leading product quality as the pricing objective; taking product or company image as the pricing objective.

When the business is not doing well, or because of fierce market competition, sudden changes in customer needs and preferences, etc., resulting in poor product sales, a large backlog, poor capital turnover, or even bankruptcy, the company can only do so. The product is set at a low price in order to quickly clear the inventory and recover the funds. But this kind of goal can only be a short-term goal when the enterprise is facing difficulties, and the long-term goal must be developed, otherwise the enterprise will eventually go bankrupt.

The goal of quality-leading pricing is to achieve the goal of ultimately obtaining greater returns by pursuing a leading position in quality in the target market. Use high profit margins to make up for the high production costs and R & D expenses associated with leading quality.

16.2 Factors Affecting the Pricing of International Market 国际市场定价影响因素

From the perspective of economics, the main factors affecting prices are costs, market demand, competition conditions and the government's price control policies. In addition, it also includes the impact of some natural factors or uncontrollable factors on prices.

In addition to these theoretical factors, environmental factors and transaction form factors also have a very important impact on pricing. At the same time, different pricing methods will also result in different prices.

16.2.1 Environment Related Challenges to Pricing 环境因素对定价的挑战

Pricing decisions are affected by all the external elements in a company's international environment. An international company must react effectively to changes in the competitive environment, in the political and legal environment, and in the economic and financial environment. Table 16.1 addresses examples of different challenges in the international firm's environment that affect the firm's pricing decisions.

Table 16.1 Environmental Factors Affecting Pricing Decisions

The Competitive Environment	Gray market/parallel imports as a competitive threat; Dumping as a competitive threat
The Political and Legal Environment	Transfer pricing; The price of protectionism
The Economic and Financial Environment	Inflationary pressures on price; Fluctuating exchange rates; Shortage of hard currency and countertrade

(1) The Local Competitive Environment 当地的竞争环境

International and local competitions often pose serious concerns to multinational firms. Competitor's offerings, as well as the price sensitivity of customers, influence the pricing decisions of the firm. Also, if it is costly for consumers to switch from one product to another, firms have to price their offering low enough to get customers to switch to their brands. On the other hand, if the firm is operating where barriers to entry, such as non-tariff barriers, patents, or technological advantages are high, they can retain relatively high prices without fear of competition. Finally, if competition can keep product prices low by manufacturing in a low-labor-cost country, then the firm must face this challenge and maintain at a low price, potentially at a loss.

(2) Parallel Imports as a Competitive Threat 来自相同产品进口的威胁

A firm engaging in a differential pricing strategy could be vulnerable to competition from unauthorized channels. In fact, differential pricing (price discrimination) by the manufacturer has been identified as a main cause of parallel importing-diverting products purchased in a low-price market to other markets (parallel imports) by means of a distribution system unauthorized by the manufacturer, otherwise known as a gray market.

A manufacturer may charge different prices in different markets for the same product:

① To meet the needs of target consumers who have a limited purchasing power;

② To keep the product price competitive in markets that are actively targeted by competition;

③ Due to changes in the exchange rate in countries where the products are sold; the product is likely to be cheaper in the countries with the weakest currency;

④ Due to the fact that it offers discounts to wholesalers buying higher quantities;

⑤ Due to differences in wholesale prices in different markets: for example, wholesale prices for luxury goods are relatively high in the United States compared with wholesale prices in the rest of the world.

(3) Dumping as a Competitive Threat 来自竞争对手倾销的威胁

Firms also face challenges from companies dumping products in their target market. Dumping is an important factor affecting pricing decisions. A typical example of dumping involves a foreign company that enjoys high prices and high profits at home as a result of trade barriers against imports; the company uses those profits to sell at much lower prices in foreign markets to gain market share and improve profitability of competitors with open home markets. According to the WTO, dumping should be condemned if it threatens to cause injury to an established industry in a particular market and if it delays the establishment of a viable domestic industry.

(4) Parallel Imports and Dumping 平行进口和倾销

Due to the needs of marketing strategies (such as expanding market share and market share), the prices of goods produced by trademark owners sold to foreign distributors or foreign manufacturers licensed to use the trademark are relatively low. These products are usually imported in parallel. It will have a certain impact on the domestic market of trademark owners. Therefore, in order to protect the normal domestic market order, many countries have adopted different methods to prevent parallel imports of commodities.

As established by the WTO, after determining that price discrimination did indeed occur and that a particular local industry was injured by the dumping activity, governments are entitled to impose anti-dumping duties on the merchandise. Similar to these are countervailing duties, which are imposed on subsidized products imported into the country. Such subsidizing could, for example, take the form of government aid in the processes of production and distribution.

Enforcement of anti-dumping regulation is particularly intense when the economy is not faring well and when price competition is intense. In the recent past, the Department of Commerce of US and the International Trade Commission scrutinized numerous importers' pricing practices, using strict criteria to determine whether the importer had committed price discrimination and, if so, if it resulted in injury to a particular local industry. Electronics, textiles, and steel originating in countries from Japan and Russia to China and Mexico have been at the center of anti-dumping action in the past few decades. In the case of Mexico, the current U.S.administration has imposed prohibitive and unreasonable anti-dumping duties on imports of cement, in spite of the shortage of cement in the United States; instead, builders in the United States must rely on suppliers from Asia, who take on average 44 days to deliver the product at a U.S. port.

In spite of more-strict enforcement, companies continue to be affected by pricing actions of importers taking advantage of loopholes in the anti-dumping legislation. To avoid price discrimination charges, the importers modify their products slightly so as not to permit then to be directly compared with products sold in other countries at higher prices.

(5) The Local Political and Legal Environment 当地的政治与法律环境

Governments regulate prices charged by multinational firms. Regulations and restrictions exist with regard to many pricing decisions, ranging from dumping to setting limits on wholesalers' gross margins and on the product's retail price.

Multinational companies are also affected by local government subsidies to local manufacturers—in particular, to producers of agricultural products and to exporting firms. Subsidies lower the price charged in international marketers for products and challenge the competitive position of firms operating in the same industry. Finally, governments can also impose tariffs and other duties on products in certain industries, particularly if those industries are in infancy in the respective countries. Governments defend such action under the infant industry argument, which permits setting high tariffs on imports that challenge emerging local producers.

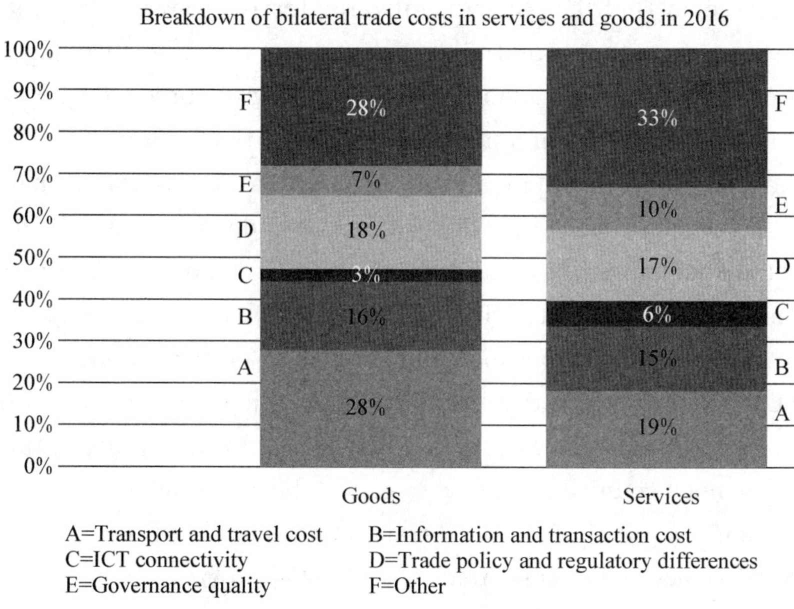

Source: WTO estimates.

Figure 16.1 Policy-related Factors Account for a Significant Part of Trade Costs①

① Note: Figure 16.1 shows to what extent various factors contribute to explaining the bilateral variance in goods and services trade costs. "Other" represents the part of bilateral variation in trade costs that remains unexplained in our analysis.

In general, governments use numerous strategies in their attempts to restrict the repatriation of profits by multinationals and to tax or to encourage the reinvestment of profits. One way that companies can bypass such restrictions is through the use of transfer pricing.

(6) The Local Economic and Financial Environment 当地的经济和金融环境

1) Inflationary Pressures on Price 通货膨胀压力与价格

An Inflationary environment has put much strong pressures on companies to lower prices; often, pricing competitively may mean that companies are not generating a profit. During inflationary periods, firms often find that they must decide between maintaining a competitive presence in a market and weathering the downside of the economic cycle or abandoning the market, which is a high-cost, high-risk proposition. Companies operating in Latin America in the 1980s and early 1990s often faced challenges posed by inflation. In the United States and Europe, inflationary fears emerged as a result of the rapid increase in gasoline prices in 2006 and 2007.

2) Fluctuating Exchange Rates 浮动汇率

Fluctuating exchange rates provide both challenges and opportunities for firms trading on the global stage. Companies that do not pay attention to fluctuations in exchange rates could find that their profits are greatly eroded during the time lapsed between contract negotiations and the actual product delivery. Including a percentage that covers exchange rate fluctuations when specifying the product price is one strategy companies use to address the unpredictability of such fluctuations.

Traditionally, firms facilitate all transactions in a strong, stable, hard currency—usually the US Dollar. Since the dollar's ups and downs in the 1970s and 1980s, however, other currencies have emerged as standards for exchanges. Increasingly, pricing decisions are facilitated by the advent of successful venues for regional integration, such as the European Union and the Southern Cone Common Market (MERCOSUR). Member countries have adopted a single currency, in the case of the European Union, or, in the case of MERCOSUR, they are attempting to peg the currency of member countries relative to each other. The advent of the Euro in the European Union has greatly facilitated transactions in the region.

3) Hard Currency and Counter-trade 硬通货与易货贸易

Developing countries face a significant shortage of hard currency reserves. Hard currency is currency that is accepted for payment by any international seller; soft currency is currency that is kept at a high artificial exchange rate, overvalued, and controlled by the national government. This situation, compounded by the inability to borrow from international banks or other sources such as the International Monetary Fund, has led developing countries to resort to counter-trade to remain active in international trade and to address the needs of local consumers. Moreover, as global markets are growing competitive, increasingly, the balance of power is shifting from sellers to buyers; in the process, buyers require sellers to engage in reciprocal purchases, known as counter-trade.

Often, counter-trade is conducted with the help of counter-trade brokers because it is rate that a perfect match can exist for product exchanges and because the exchanges are complex. Exchanges could range from paying sausages to rock stars for their performances, and bringing French high fashion to Russian consumers by selling quality Russian crystal to Saudi merchants.

Numerous companies specialize in brokering barter deals. Located in many financial centers, such as London and New York, as well as in countries that have transactions of brokering barter agreements, such as Sweden, these brokers can put together intricate exchanges. Among the major U.S. corporate barter firms doing large-volume business are the firms of Argent Trading, Active International, Media Resources International, and Tradewell, Inc.

(7) Trade Term 贸易术语

In international trade, because of the differences in trade terms, price differences are often understood as normal phenomena, such as FOB, CIF, CFR, and so on.

(8) Terms of Payment 付款方式

Buyers and sellers can agree on a number of methods of payment in international transactions:

① Cash in Advance.This is the most advantageous payment option for the sellers, but not for the buyer. It is used for sellers' markers primarily or for high-risk buyer environments.

② Open Account. This method entails delivering goods or services without a guarantee of payment; the buyer and seller had conducted transactions in the past, and there is an expectation of continues business for both parties. The Basic Open Account entails payment reasonably soon after the shipment arrives or within an agreed—on period. This method is risky for the seller, who must choose the buyer well.

③ Consignment with Open Account. Sellers can reduce risk with this type of Open Account because they still own the merchandise. However, the costs of recovering the goods are typically high in international transactions.

④ Documentary Collection. With this method, title and possession pass to the buyer when the documents attesting to the title and the shipping documents pass as well. These documents can be a bill of lading, a commercial invoice, an insurance certificate, or a certificate of origin. The payment document, known as a bill of exchange or draft, requiring the buyer to pay immediately (sight draft) or at a specified time (time draft), is seat through the sellers' bank to the buyers' bank after the goods have been shipped the time draft, the documents are released to the buyer, and the buyer can take possession of the goods.

⑤ Letter of Credit (L/C).With this method, the letter is drawn by the buyers' bank, which guarantees to pay the seller for the merchandise upon the presentation of documents stipulated in the letter that provide evidence of shipment, adherence to the purchase order, and even inspection, if so stipulated. The bank releases the funds when all the conditions of the transaction are met. Most L/Cs are irrevocable. In the sense that neither party can change it without the consent of the other party.

It should be mentioned that the risk of selling to international buyers, especially using cash in advance or on open account, can be alleviated by purchasing insurance using the different sources.

16.2.2 International Market Pricing Method 定价方法

(1) Cost-oriented Pricing 成本导向定价法

This method uses the cost of the product as the basis for pricing, and takes the market demand and competition conditions into full consideration.

(2) Demand-oriented Pricing 需求导向定价法

This method takes the consumer's perception of product value and the intensity of demand as the basis for pricing in foreign markets.

(3) Competitive Oriented Pricing 竞争导向定价法

This method is based on the prices of competing similar products in the international market to determine the price of one's own products. Companies can use this pricing method in the following situations: it is difficult to estimate the cost; they intend to get along with their peers in peace; and they cannot obtain market feedback of other pricing.

Auction pricing and bid pricing are competition-oriented pricing methods. These two pricing methods are two typical competition-oriented pricing methods. The auction price is the buyer's open bidding price, and the bidding price is the seller's sealed bid price.

16.3 International Pricing Decision Process 国际定价决策程序

Pricing decisions are determined by the location of production facilities and the companies' abilities to track costs.

Pricing is especially important in international marketing strategy decisions because of its effect on product positioning, market segmentation, demand management, and market share dynamics. The international pricing decision is complex. Variables internal to the firm, such as the location of production plants and factory utilization rates, as well as variables external to the firm, such as the economic climate, the price sensitivity of customers, and barriers to entry, must be evaluated before determining the final price of products and services. Pricing decisions are further affected by companies' experience in international markets, market share, exchange rates, tariffs, inflation, and government intervention in pricing.

16.3.1 Estimate the Value of Production Equipment and Facilities 估算生产设备和设施价值

Production facilities are important internal-within the firm's control-decision making factors in international pricing strategy. The location of production facilities determines the extent to which companies can control costs and price their products competitively. Multinationals usually can afford to shift production to take advantage of lower costs and exchange rates, whereas small to medium-sized enterprises are often limited to exporting as the only venue for product distribution. Companies often price themselves out of the market in certain countries, especially if they do not shift production to a low-labor-cost, low-tax country. As an example, Marc Controls purchases raw materials in Korea, China, and India to lower the price of its products and ships them to the United States for manufacturing; its products are competitively priced when sold on the German market, but they are considered overpriced in most of Asia.

Important aspects related to firms' production facilities are factory capacity utilization, internal cost structures, and the market contribution rate.

Factory capacity utilization. Firms with factories operating at full capacity are able to spread fixed costs over more units, and thus have more flexibility in their pricing strategies. On the other hand, firms with factories operating at less-than-full capacity have high costs to contend with and do not have much price flexibility.

Internal cost structures. Some firms have more advantageous cost structures than others. For example, firms with production facilities in countries that have an abundance of cheap labor have an advantage over firms with production facilities in countries that have no excess labor. Also, firms that exploit technological advantages have cost advantages that ultimately brings an impact on their pricing strategies.

Market contribution rate. This is the percentage of total firm profits from a particular product—this product will garner more attention than a less-lucrative product and thus affecting pricing decisions.

16.3.2 Ability to Keep Track of Costs 掌握成本要素

Product components are often manufactured in different countries. Usually, the final products are assembled in a particular country—which is usually not the company's home country—and then sold all over the word. It is consequently difficult for financial officers to keep track of product costs. However, with improvement in information technology and electronic data interchange (EDI) systems, which are increasingly coordinated throughout the supply chain, firms are better able to track product costs in emerging markets and even in lower-income countries.

16.3.3 Pricing 定价

Setting prices internationally tends to be intuition and experience driven and highly decentralized. The skill in pricing lies in exploiting differences in consumers willingness to pay for products and services; consequently, it is important for marketing managers to be familiar with the price elasticity of their products in a particular market.

Important determinants of the final price are currency fluctuations. Managers must decide what their reactions should be to currency fluctuations. Should they adjust their prices based on these fluctuations, or should they fix the prices on their home country currency or the currency in the country of production? Should they pass on price increases to customers or choose a lower profit? Due to the instability or currencies, many sales contracts have exchange rate fluctuations and exchange risk. Periodic examinations of exchange rate trends determine the adjustments necessary to align prices accordingly.

Additional important determinants of the final prices paid down the chain of distribution, in business-to-business transactions. In these transactions, buyers and sellers need to agree to the terms of sale on the terms of payment. The terms of sale determine what is and not included in the price quotation and when the seller takes possession of the goods. In a business-to-business environment, a buyer can correctly evaluate price deals on their face value only when fully taking into account the terms of sale and the terms of payment offered by the seller. Consequently, these considerations constitute important competitive tools when quoting prices. It is helpful to be aware not only of the prices that competitors set, but also the terms of sale and terms of payment quoted. Moreover, it is important to note that certain markets may have a preference for one type or category of quote over another, and that certain markets may not be well equipped to handle a higher level of risk, for instance.

The terms of sale are stated using Incoterms, the International Commercial Terms. As a general trend, marketers tend to be more inclined to quote more inclusive terms—the-terms.

Other important determinants of the final price are the terms of payment offered by the seller. Handling the payment is often one of the last items to be considered in the international transaction and, as a result, it is sometimes given less weight. The methods of payment are typically determined by the company's reasons for going international, the company's strategy in the respective market, and its expected return. The company needs to find out what forms of payment are preferred in a particular market and are acceptable for the buyer; this information will also shed light on the partner's financial strength.

In setting prices, companies need to examine existing conditions, the labor market and materials costs, the buying power of consumers, and the goal of the company with regard to the respective target market. The company may price products higher or lower in the home market; it could engage in aggressive export pricing, skimming, or penetration pricing; or it could use standardized pricing worldwide or local pricing. These strategies are described next.

16.4 Pricing Strategies in the International Market 国际市场定价策略

定价方法确定产品的基本价格。定价策略对产品价格进行修正。定价策略是指企业在充分考虑影响企业定价的内外部因素的基础上，为达到企业预定的定价目标而采取的价格策略。制定科学合理的定价策略，不但要求企业对成本进行核算、分析、控制和预测，而且要求企业根据市场结构、市场供求、消费者心理及竞争状况等因素做出判断与选择，价格策略选择是否恰当，是影响企业定价目标的重要因素。

Pricing strategies can be divided into seven forms: new product pricing, integer pricing, psychological pricing, discount pricing, geographic pricing, transfer pricing, and price adjustments. New product pricing strategies include three forms: skimming pricing, moderate pricing and penetration pricing. The following will focus on demonstrating several pricing strategies.

Table 16.2 **Product Mix Pricing**

Price Situation	Description
Product line pricing	Setting prices across an entire product line
Optional product pricing	Pricing optional or accessory products sold with the main product
Captive product pricing	Pricing products that must be used with the main product
By-product pricing	Pricing low-value by-products to get rid of or make money on them
product bundle pricing	Pricing bundles of products sold together

16.4.1 The Skimming Pricing Strategy 撇脂定价策略

Also known as the skimming pricing strategy, is a pricing strategy for new products. It refers to the investment period or growth period of the product life cycle, the use of consumers' desire for novelty and wonder, and in fact that fierce competition has not yet emerged. It is a pricing strategy that sets the price purposefully at a favorable opportunity in order to obtain as much profit as possible in the short term and recover the investment as soon as possible. Its name comes from skimming milk fat from fresh milk, which means extracting essence. The following conditions should be met to adopt this strategy:

① New products have enough buyers and are willing to accept higher prices.

② The difficulty of imitation of new products makes it difficult for competitors to enter the market quickly.

③ Compared with similar products and alternative products, new products have greater advantages and irreplaceable functions.

④ The profit gained by adopting a high-price strategy for a new product is sufficient to compensate for the loss caused by the reduction in demand caused by the high price.

At the end of the Second World War, the American Renault Company produced a pen. Taking advantage of the news boom of the world's first atomic bomb at that time, it took a fashionable name—ballpoint pen (now ballpoint pen) as a Christmas gift. Coupled with various mysteries through various propaganda, the value of the pen has doubled. Its cost was only 50 cents, but the price was as high as 20 US dollars then. When the mystery coat of this kind of commodity was constantly revealed and its value plummeted, the capitalists had already gone to manage newer commodities with their wallets that were about to break.

In 1990, when Sony first introduced high-definition color TV (HDTV) in the Japanese market, this high-tech product was valued at $43,000. This type of TV was positioned for customers who could afford high prices for high-tech. Over the next three years, Sony kept reducing prices to attract more customers. By 1993, Japanese customers could purchase a 28-inch high-definition color TV for only US$6,000. In 2001, Japanese customers could buy a 40-inch high-definition color TV for only US $2,000, and this price was affordable by most people. In this way, Sony obtained the maximum profit from different customer groups.

16.4.2 Penetration Pricing 渗透定价

The market penetration pricing strategy is to enter the market at a lower price, to accelerate growth in the short term, sacrificing high gross profit to obtain a larger sales volume and market share, so as to produce significant cost-economic benefits, and making costs and prices continuously reduced. Penetration price does not mean absolute cheapness, but relatively low price to its value.

In 1930s, the famous overseas Chinese Mr. Tan Kah Kee, who was hailed as the king of rubber shoes in the world, in the first few years of his rubber shoes, he penetrated the market with a price much lower than the cost, obtaining a large number of consumers, and quickly improved sales until when the rubber shoes became a famous brand, they gradually increased the price then, and finally made a great fortune.

Multinationals that have sales-based objectives, attempting to gain a large sales volume, are likely to use penetration pricing. Firms using this strategy price the product at first below the price of competitors to quickly penetrate the market at their competitors' expense. Compaq, which sells computers, was able to quickly capture the European market by using this strategy. In the Netherlands, for example, Compaq offered deals unmatched by any brand name competitor and coupled this pricing strategy with excellent warranties and support.

Alternatively, firms may have pricing objectives centered on generating a high profit and recovering product development cost. Competitors thus use a skimming strategy, piecing the product above that of competitors, when competition is minimal. In general, consumers responding to skimming strategies are more concerned with quality, uniqueness and status, rather than price.

16.4.3 International Transfer Pricing 转移定价

Transfer pricing is a pricing strategy used in intra-firm sales: the pricing of products in the process of conducting transactions between units of the same corporation that are within or beyond the national borders of the parent company is known as transfer pricing and regarded as a legitimate business opportunity by transnational corporations. Developing countries often bring the issue of transfer pricing to the attention of international trade bodies as a strategy that could help a multinational company under-report profits and decrease its tax burden in countries where it has foreign direct investment, thus evading taxation. Instead of pricing products at cost, products can be priced at market level, known as market-based transfer pricing, where the price reflects the price products sell for in a particular market; at cost, known as cost-based transfer pricing, where the cost reflects not the cost incurred by the company, but the estimated opportunity cost of the product; or products can be priced using a combination of the two strategies.

16.4.4 Standardized Pricing versus Local Pricing 标准定价和当地定价

Companies charge different prices for products in order to meet the needs of consumers, to account for their purchase power and to account for differences in distribution systems, market position, and tax systems; this type of pricing is known as local pricing. In different markers, certain pricing traditions are followed. For example, in luxury markets in the United States, products ate priced using even numbers-for example, $500 for a pair of Prada shoes. When those shoes go on sale, they are priced using odd pricing, such as $199. Alternatively, products in most discount outlets and in grocery stores are priced under odd pricing.

In Europe and Asia, odd/even pricing strategies are used increasingly, even though even pricing used to be preferred because it facilitated calculation. Strategies depend on the country, the currency, and even on the local price. To illustrate, in Japan, prices appear to be mostly even for non-luxury goods, as well as for luxury goods, and this might have to do with the currency—there are 133 yen to the dollar.

Similarly, products in China are mostly priced evenly, even though the currency there is on a closer parity to the dollar and the euro, at about 7 yuan to the dollar. Consumer research shows that consumers in high context, non-Western cultures were found to be less prone to the illusion of cheapness or gain created by odd price endings, and more likely offended by perceived attempts to "fool" them. Thus, Western firms need to be cautious when attempting to replicate odd ending practices in non-Western markets. Even pricing is thought to be a "safer" format for the Chinese or the Japanese.

Table 16.3 Price Adjustments

Strategy	Description
Discount and allowance pricing	Reducing prices to reward customer responses such as volume purchases, paying early, or promoting the product
Segmented pricing	Adjusting prices to allow for differences in customers, products, or locations
Psychological pricing	Adjusting prices for psychological effect
Promotional pricing	Temporarily reducing prices to spur short-run sales
Geographical pricing	Adjusting prices to account for the geographic location of customers
Dynamic pricing	Adjusting prices continually to meet the characteristics and needs of individual customers and situations
International pricing	Adjusting prices for international markets

On the other hand, and contrary to the pricing theory discussed earlier, in Taiwan China, odd prices appear to be predominant. Even in luxury markets, sales signs abound and information on price-cutting is everywhere.

Finally, odd prices are becoming popular in the European Union. At first, right after the adoption of the Euro, prices were pretty strange, with endings all over the place. European retailers wanted to prove to their consumers that they diligently transformed prices based on the original currency (Franc, Deutsche Mark, Lira) to the Euro. Subsequently, odd-pricing strategies became prevalent then.

Conclusion 结语

In recent years, non-price factors have become relatively more important in buyer choice behavior. However, price is still one of the most important factors that determine a company's market share and profitability. In the marketing mix, price is the only factor that can generate revenue, and other factors are represented as costs. Hermann Simon, Ambar G. Rao and Melvin F. Shakun, Robert J. Dolan and Abel P. Jeuland respectively proposed three pricing Model. In the contemporary international market, pricing strategy is the most active factor in marketing strategy. Learning pricing strategy will help to create greater wealth for the company in future marketing activities.

The Chapter's Referential Questions 本章参考题

(1) What is dumping? Why do international companies use dumping strategy when choosing target market?
什么是倾销?在选择目标市场时跨国企业为什么会使用倾销策略?

(2) What are the different motivations behind a company when setting prices higher or lower in the home country?
为什么企业在本国市场采用高价位(或者低价位)策略?是何用心?

(3) What are the factors affecting the international market pricing?
影响国际市场营销中的价格策略的因素都有哪些?

(4) What are gray markets? How do distributors using parallel imports affect a multinational firm's operations in the target market?
什么属于灰色市场?目标市场上平行进口会怎样影响跨国企业的经营活动?

(5) How should the penetration pricing strategies be applied in international marketing?
在国际市场营销中怎样运用价格渗透策略?

(6) Discussing about the position of the U.S. Government towards the international trade, especially when new administration came to power led by Barack Hussein Obama and Donald trump.
谈谈美国政府对于国际贸易的立场,尤其是以奥巴马、特朗普为首的政府上台以来。

Further Reading
拓展阅读

Chapter 17
International Distribution Channel Strategy
国际市场分销策略

Learning Objectives
本章学习目标

(1) The international marketing and distribution.
国际市场营销与分销。
(2) How to develop distribution channels.
如何开发分销渠道。
(3) How to manage the brokers.
如何对中间商进行管理。
(4) The development trend of cross-border e-commerce.
把握跨境电子商务发展趋势。

Key Words
关键词

E-commerce; Distribution Decisions; Selecting Channels; Distribution Arrangements; B-to-B; B-to-C; Cross-Border E-Commerce

Distribution decisions are pretty difficult in domestic marketing and more complicated in the international marketing. The problem of selecting the right channels is simply multiplied by as many countries as one wishes to serve. Yet it is essential for companies which market their products internationally to be able to find their way through the maze of channels that are available or can be developed in each market.

Case Studies 17.1

The variations that exist in institutional availability are very extensive indeed and no one person can ever hope to become aware of the details of the channel options in every country. Furthermore, environmental and legal constraints play an important role in the choices that can be made and the distribution strategies that can be explored.

It is important to remember that the best product in the world may prove a commercial disaster if the channels of distribution selected are incapable or unwilling to provide the "utility of place" and the "utility of time" which the local consumer expects. The expectation of the consumer is ultimately the criterion of effectiveness and therefore failling to satisfy consumers means a ineffective marketing effort.

17.1 Channels of Distribution in World Markets 全球市场中的分销渠道

不同的跨国企业在选择分销渠道方面有不同的做法。一个生产型企业非常可能在国外选点建厂而注重物流和后勤保障;而一个营销型企业会更注重分销渠道,并会根据分销渠道的格局建立生产线。

An international company can have a number of bases for channel decesions which channel. A manufacturing orientated company would have a number of plants located around the world and distribution decisions will probably stem from logistics rather than marketing considerations. On the other hand, a marketing orientated company will look at the problem differently; it will identify the best marketing opportunities, determine distribution patterns and then seek to recommend locations for manufacturing facilities which could best serve the marketing objectives.

The difference is fundamental insofar as the marketing orientated company may come to the conclusion that one manufacturing unit in one centrally-located place is perfectly adequate to be able to serve world markets. A production orientated company seldom wishes to recognize the validity of such an approach. To the production and technical staff such an approach is much too parochial and they refuse to acknowledge that in certain circumstances it may be much more profitable to build a company's international trade from one manufacturing base. There may, of course, exists very compelling legal and commercial reasons for establishing local manufacturing plants in various parts of the world. However, to the marketing orientated company, such decisions must be fully justified by marketing and commercial realities. In this connection, the way the Japanese industry has developed its penetration of world markets is good example of this approach.

It is useful to keep in mind the fact that a company that has been proliferated its production facilities in many countries is gradually ceasing to perform an international marketing task. For all intents and purposes such a company is approaching a situation where the company is becoming a collection of domestic units, operating under one corporate flag. In such an extreme situation, each member of the group has a normal domestic marketing task to perform, knowledge of international marketing ceases to be an essential quality of an effective management. The channels of distribution selected in each market in such circumstances, would be purely a domestic matter for the local management and in accordance with locally defined criteria of choice.

Our objective here is to deal with situations where marketers operating on an international scale has to lay down distribution policies in a number of countries. We are not concerned here with the problem of selecting channels within a single domestic market. Our aim to assist the marketer who has to select, or help others to select, distribution channels in a number of international markets of differing marketing ecologies.

It is quite difficult to describe in a schematic way all the permutations of channels of distribution that exist in world markets. However, as a general framework we can provide a useful starting point for exploring the kind of channels that one can expect to meet in world markets. Whilst the chart cannot be treated as comprehensive, any marketer who wants to study the distribution patterns of a country with which he is not familiar will find it a helpful checklist. On identifying the channels available to him, he can proceed to an evaluation of the advantages and disadvantages of each option and record his findings at the appropriate space provided.

The point to remember is that in most international distribution situations, goods cross borders and a machinery of sorts must be identified or developed for coping with physical movement of goods, including the transfer of title to intermediaries and/or consumers in foreign countries. This makes the selection of the right channel that much more complicated and mistakes pretty costly.

17.2 Main Considerations for Selecting Channels 选择分销渠道时应主要考虑的问题

分销渠道对于企业的影响是长期的,会对产品、价格和促销都产生影响。因此,选择分销渠道时要格外慎重。分销渠道决定了企业对于一个特定市场能否实施有效开发。

It must be kept in mind that channel decisions may have a long-term effect on the following aspects.

17.2.1 Every Ingredient of the Marketing Mix 营销组合中的所有成分

An early, albeit well intentioned, mistake may affect the company's position in a given market for many years. Alternatively, it may cost substantial amounts of money to extricate the company form undesirable commitments. Thus a British company that chose to distribute its decorative products through a chain of supermarkets in Switzerland, on an exclusive basis, discovered that it had very little control over the price of the product. The distributor, in this situation, opted to use the product in question as part of his loss leadership' price strategy, with the result that the retail price eroded to levels that could not be justified within the supplying company's pricing objectives and policies. Inevitably, the pressure on prices had to follow suit in other markets, where the supply was being made by manufacturer's own marketing subsidiaries.

17.2.2 To Control the Effective Exploitation of the Given Markets 对于特定市场有效开发的控制

Channel decisions normally involve the company in legal commitments of a long term nature. The cancellation of such arrangements can be highly problematic in certain instances. National legislation differs significantly from country to country as to what constitutes a just cause for the termination of distribution agreements, and as to the supplier's obligations in such case. An agreement, entered at a stage when the company is trying to introduce itself into foreign markets, may prove a serious obstacle at a future point when the company plans to launch a major penetrative strategy in the same market. Ignoring the pitfalls at the beginning can be very costly in the future.

The following considerations should be explored in some depth prior to taking channel decisions.

(1) The International Marketing Objectives 企业国际市场营销的目标

It is fundamental that one cannot determine a distribution policy until the international marketing objectives have been clearly defined. In extreme situations, the selection of channels is totally inappropriate in certain markets, insofar, as the markets in questions may be outside the company's objectives in relation to their size, development or longer term viability. Furthermore, the kind of objectives which have been defined for the company's international marketing effort will determine whether the channels to select should be long (indirect) or short (direct).

(2) Other Corporate Considerations 其他考虑事项

The choice of distribution in a multinational environment is often determined by the size of the company, the way it is organized and the managerial resources available to it. Given comparable market considerations, some companies are better equipped than others to have shorter channels or even opt for a direct distribution approach to the ultimate consumer or user. In this connection, the main considerations are:

1) Managerial Resources and Their Experience 管理人员及其经验

The management of distribution channels depends to a great extent on the experience those vests in the company's managers. A company that is entering international operations for the first time, normally lacks the expertise that is required to be able to choose and control short channels or the company's own local subsidiary. Obviously, companies with limited international marketing know-how would prefer to turn the job to middlemen. Even well-established companies often seek the help of middlemen in situations of involving new products or new segments calling for the acquisition of a new type of experience. It is therefore essential that a company identifies its strengths and weaknesses in this area; mistakes can be pretty costly.

2) Company's International Organization 企业的国际化程度

The way the international company is organized is also highly relevant. The company that has opted for a macro-pyramid structure is likely to look at each market with a cold and factual approach with the view of maximizing the opportunities of each market. Such a company will endeavor to identify the markets which are likely to yield 80% of the company's revenue and sales, both in the short and long term, and pour its managerial and financial resources into the best opportunities thus identified. This is seldom the case with companies adhering to the "umbrella structure". The fact that strategic authority has been delegated to the local management means that channels of distribution, and other important decisions alike, will be made at local level. In the "umbrella situation", it is inevitable that the financial success of the local market will prevail over the international marketing considerations. In extreme situation as discussed earlier, the local company becomes a purely domestic company which just happens to belong to an international company. In such a case, the meaning of international marketing and its value case to apply.

3) Company's Image 企业形象

A company must consider the effect that its distribution choice may have on its international image. This means, that among other factors, it must probe carefully into the questions of middlemen's respectability and the way in which the world at large would view the arrangement reached with a given channel of distribution. Any arrangement which is made with a middleman, whose image is dubious, can have a long-lasting and far-reaching impact on the company's image at a global level. Competitors will be quick to capitalize on such an error of judgments.

When making allocation decisions, the impact on neighbouring countries must be taken into account. A decision to sever the company's relationship with a local wholesaler, in order to set up one's own subsidiary, is bound to create a fear of repetition in neighboring markets, and nothing is more harmful to the middleman's performance than the feeling that his security of tenure is limited.

4) Distribution Arrangements in Each Market 市场中的营销渠道设置

A multi-product company may have existing distribution arrangements in many markets although the nature of the products is such that different channels are required for each product line. It is important that those responsible for selecting channels in a given country pay attention to other arrangements that already exist there. In other words, before one starts looking for totally new relationships, it would be wise to explore the usefulness of existing channels; they may prove better than one expects. They may be capable of further development. In any event a marketer must not generate unhappiness among existing channels, despite of the fact that he himself may never have to work with them. The international marketer must be sensitive to any achievements and goodwill that other parts of the company have attained in each market.

5) Timing 时间

The speed with which a company has to penetrate each market is a vital consideration when one is choosing channels of distribution. The need to act fast and achieve results may force the hand of the marketer to select channels which in the longer term may not be ideal. However, such a decision must be taken with one's eyes wide open as to the longer-term implications.

(3) Channels Availability 可利用的分销渠道

This is of course a major consideration. You cannot expect to select a specific type of channel in a given country if:

① Such a channel does not exist;

② It belongs to a competitor;

③ It is fully committed to other suppliers;

④ It does not wish to distribute your product.

It must be kept in mind that channels of distribution are independent and harnessing their help is not always an easy task. Furthermore, each country has developed different patterns of distribution, coupled with supportive institutions over years, and it is hazardous to assume that because the Netherlands possesses a specific type of distribution method, the same occurs in Belgium. This indeed is one of the difficulties and subtleties of international marketing, and this is why the marketing profile analysis is an invaluable tool.

(4) Financial Considerations 财务方面的考虑

Cost of different marketing channels. Before selecting channels of distribution, the international marketer must analyzed in detail the relative costs of different channels. Such a study must bring into consideration the fact that in the initial stages, costs are distorted by the start-up expenditure. These costs are in the main of a nonrecurring nature. Furthermore, the cost evaluation must be geared to the expected market performance that one can forecast for the various channels. In other words, the fact that through direct marketing one could achieve a cost ratio of 6% to sales can be meaningless if at 8% ratio, based on indirect distribution (viz. using middlemen), one can expect to achieve three times the volume of sales. It is the total business coupled with the final pay-off to the company that must be appraised.

In this connection the following elements must be investigated:

① The cost of staffing and training local personnel;

② The comparative administrative costs;

③ Possible expenditure resulting from moving personnel from head office to the local subsidiary;

④ Cost of canceling current arrangement with a local distributor;

⑤ Cost of incorporating a company and any additional costs involved in complying with the legal obligations of the market in question, having to have local directors, keeping books, etc.;

⑥ The cost of promotion to be incurred in direct distribution as against indirect distribution;

⑦ Cost of registering patents and/or trademarks;

⑧ The difference in cost of duty; in the case of a subsidiary importing there often exist complications;

⑨ Tax difference based on the nature of the revenue received;

⑩ Physical distribution costs including warehousing;

⑪ Start-up costs and the length of time needed for break-even.

The cash flow effectiveness of the channels under consideration.

To many international marketers, it is often vital to ensure that the channels selected for distributing the company's products are capable of generating a quick cash recovery. This in turn means that the company's cash resources must not be over-stretched through the inevitable level of credit that one has to grant to one's direct customers. In most instances, middlemen provide the cash cushion that a company with limited cash resources requires. Indeed, the provision of early cash recovery is one of the important tasks of a distribution channel. A company must balance its margin objective with the cash flow needed before deciding to choose short or long channel arrangements.

(5) Capital Factors 资本因素

Closely linked with the above consideration, the marketer must explore the financial and capital implications of choosing a channel of distribution to the exclusion of another one. Examples of this aspect are:

① Can one raise local capital easily?

② Is the local currency stable or convertible?

③ Can earnings be remitted out of the country and capital repatriated?

④ Are there any borrowing restrictions on foreign companies?

⑤ Is the local government likely to offer substantial capital support to a domestic film in order to protect the country's balance of payment?

(6) The Market and Its Characteristics 市场及其特征

The market itself, its state of development and special needs, constitute a very important "input" in determining the kind of distribution choice that should be made. Once again, the marketing profile analysis should prove a very valuable tool in identifying the appropriate elements in this respect. Relevant factors are:

① The medium and longer-term economic health of the country;

② The extent to which a channel selected may be vulnerable to political change;

③ The size of the market in term of personal disposable income, income distribution, etc.;

④ The potential growth for the company's products or similar ones;

⑤ Special trade arrangements such as cartels or trade associations;

⑥ The market's receptiveness to new and sophisticated products, specific habits of the consumer which preclude the possibility of by-passing traditional channels;

⑦ Marketing techniques which depend on third parties such as merchandising agencies.

(7) The Specific Needs of the Product 产品的具体需要

The product itself may have a major influence on the type of channels that the company can choose for achieving distribution goals. Points to remember are:

① A product calling for extensive pre-sale or after-sale service is normally best handled by the company's own distribution facilities provided of course it can be achieved economically;

② Bulky items can often justify direct marketing. Thus a company distributing tankers requires only one or two representatives in a whole region to perform an effective distribution effort.

③ Sophisticated products such as computers or electronic equipment installations are more likely to justify a direct distribution approach than fast moving consumer goods. The client normally expects an intimate knowledge of the intricacies of the product which is more likely to be available among the company's own employees.

④ The unit value of a product also influences channel decisions. Obviously, if the product has a high value, more funds can be derived from each unit sold thus permitting the luxury of short channels.

⑤ Perish-ability is another significant factor in international distribution development. The fact that product subject to physical and fashion perish-ability must be speeded through channels to the ultimate consumer often forces the manufacture to choose short channels. This is particularly common in the fruit and vegetable trade.

⑥ Products which are custom—made will probably be distributed direct to the ultimate consumer or user. Too much personal contact has to exist between the manufacturer and the buyer to allow for middlemen. Nonetheless, even in such situations, one often encounters active agents who collects an introductory commission for identifying and bringing opportunities to the notice of the manufacture.

In the previous few sections, we attempted to summarize number of important considerations that ought to be explored in some depth before channel decisions can be taken in relation to international markets. Most of these points are based on simple common sense. Unfortunately, when a marketer is faced with a myriad of markets, with conflicting needs and conditions, he tends to lose sight of what is the best course of action in a given set of circumstances. One cannot overemphasize the value of a carefully assembled marketing profile analysis. Other questions can be added in order to make the checklist more comprehensive and relevant to a particular marketing project. This method is extremely useful not only in ensuring that all relevant facts are assembled, but also in helping the marketer to view all markets in a rational and systematic way. With these two ingredients, he is more likely to take rational distribution decisions.

17.3 The Management of Middlemen 对于中间商的管理

企业对于中间商管理的重视程度应等同于企业内部的销售人员，无论这个中间商是企业子公司的雇员，还是作为独立法人同时服务于几家企业。应该重视对于分销企业的培训和管理。

Middlemen must be managed with the same care as one normally applies to a company's own sales force. Whether the intermediaries are the employees of the company's subsidiary or they are totally independent, there is a mutual interest between the supplying company and its channel's personnel. And it is important that the best principles of man management are applied to the management of personnel. working in the distribution process. Assuming that the channels selected were right in the first place one has to manage them in such a way as to:

① Create distributors loyalty;

② Ensure that distributors are adequately remunerated;

③ Train and develop distributors and their personnel;

④ Determine standards of performance;

⑤ Evaluate performance against standards;

⑥ Maintain an efficient communication system with every distributor.

17.3.1 Creating Distributor Loyalty 培养分销商的忠诚度

In order to achieve distributor loyalty, it is important that they do not feel at any stage that his relationship with suppliers is temporary. A company that is able to demonstrate that throughout its international activities, it has treated its distributor fairly and reasonably is more likely to earn the loyalty of its foreign agents and distributors.

The task of building distributor's loyalty should be shared with the public relations department; in the absence of such a department, the marketer should employ some of the principles of the public relations function. In this connection, one may find that house magazines have an important role to play. Similarly, organizing visits to factories for the best performers and their families tends to develop a feeling of belonging. Such a sentiment is the foundation of a happy and fruitful relationship with people who are not directly under the company's managerial jurisdiction. Other ways that have been found useful in an attempt to build loyalty among the company's foreign distributors can be summarized as follows:

① Provide prizes, medals, plaques, cash bonuses to excellent performers and generate sufficient publicity among the international community of distributors so that others will strive to join those honored in previous years.

② Arrange for senior personnel of the parent board to visit periodically distributors in their own country and on their home ground. It is important that such visitors are alerted to the cultural idiosyncrasies of each territory to be visited. Nothing is more harmful to a distributor relationship than a rumor that the chairman of the company visited a certain country and refrained from making contract with the local agent or distributor.

In certain instances, it may be very helpful to invite the son or daughter of the distributor to come to the company's head office or regional headquarters for a period of training.

The point to remember is that although the distributors tries to maximize his profit out of the company's products, he is a vital link in the route to success and his monetary reward, however high, must not be looked at by the company's own personnel with pusillanimous envy. It often happens that unnecessary friction develops between an agent and principal's staff for no better reason than the latter resent the level of success that the former has achieved. Good management in international marketing calls for the kind of generosity that enables a person to regard the personal success of a distributor as a pleasant evidence of the company's achievement in the specific market. This approach does indeed help in most cases to develop a long-lasting and genuine loyalty.

17.3.2 Remuneration of Distributors 分销商的薪酬

Middlemen must be rewarded in such a way that they are motivated to do an effective job. In those countries where channel traditions exist the level of remuneration is probably well accepted by each individual concerned. The difficulties begin in those markets where the product to be marketed is new and no precedents exist as to what constitutes an acceptable "package". The package normally consists of commission, contribution towards promotion, discounts for prompt payment, and other financial incentives. There is no hard and fast rule as to what constitutes a perfect level of remuneration in every situation. The point to remember is that a distributor can be as easily over-remunerated as under-remunerated. Those responsible for reaching a distribution arrangement with the foreign middleman must strike a happy medium between the two extremes, whilst maintaining at the same time equity vis-à-vis middlemen in other territories and the company's own objectives. Over-remuneration can of course generate the right incentive among the distributors, but is bound to affect the ultimate profit; under-remuneration may lead to minimal effort on the part of the middleman.

The biggest problem arises when a company enters the international marketing scene indulges in distribution/agency arrangements with different remuneration terms in each deal. Whilst this can work for a while, complications are sure to come. Middlemen whose level of remuneration is lower than others will react strongly when they discover such deviations and the results can be quite unpleasant. Trying to keep special arrangements confidential, seldom work insofar as the slightest clerical error may bring the house down. It is sufficient for a commission statement to be inserted in error in wrong envelope for the information to become public knowledge and a source of general aggravation.

Remuneration therefore must be worked out in detail and in accordance with a logical plan with the view of keeping all the middlemen happy. Ideally, one should aim to develop a standardized remuneration package, in the same way as one is always trying to work in accordance with a salary grading system; anomalies must be capable of an explanation should the situation arise.

17.3.3 Training Middlemen and Their Staff 对中间商及其员工的培训

The distributors and its staff need training and development as much as any company's personnel. It is very much in the interest of the supplying company to ensure that such training is actually undertaken, because in the final analysis competent personnel with perform a more effective job and that in turn will mean better sales in the market and hopefully better profits.

A well-planned program of training held either at the center or at some neutral venue can not only help distributors and their personnel to improve their effectiveness, but can contribute enormously to the feeling of loyalty that the company wishes to foster. Furthermore, it may serve as a communication forum where distributors form different countries can exchange views, and compare distribution methods and practices. Training programs could include:

① Knowledge of the company and its products.

② Knowledge of the specific products which the distributor handles should be developed in depth.

③ The above should include specific details about servicing complicated products.

④ Selling skills—these must of course be adapted by the trainer to the specific needs of each market. To that extent, a strong communication must exist between the trainer and local management.

⑤ Communication skills including report writing, and effective presentations.

17.3.4 Determining Standards of Performance 为中间商定制工作服务标准

Once again, distributors and agents have to be managed in the same way as one normally tries to manage one's own personnel, with the major exception that such middlemen do net actually work for the company and should therefore be treated with considerable tact and diplomacy. At the same time there is a great merit, even form the middleman's point of view, to know what amounts in the eyes of his principal to a good performance and what constitutes a poor result.

It is important, however, that standards of performance ascribed to each middleman are fair and based on a sound assessment of what is an attainable target in each market. Setting standards of performance which are neither realistic nor achievable can do more harm than good. A particularly useful approach is to have the supplying company and the distributor develops jointly standards for the latter's performance. Jointly agreed norms are always more palatable than are those imposed from above. Standards of performance should include:

① Sales volume objective;

② Market share in each market;

③ Inventory turnover ratio;

④ Number of accounts per area;

⑤ Growth objective;

⑥ Price stability objective;

⑦ Quality of publicity;

⑧ In the case of distributors who carry other lines the percentage of floor space allocated to the supplying company's products can be defined in standards terms;

⑨ General image of the middleman in the market place.

These are only a few standards that one normally encounters in international distribution. Others can be defined to meet the requirements of specific arrangements and locations. Standards must be meaningful in the sense that the middleman is able to understand what is expected of him. If they are too complicated or couched in jargon, the likelihood is that the distributor will wash his hands of the whole matter and ignore the standards set for him.

17.3.5 Evaluation Performance
对中间商的服务评价

Where standards of performance have been defined and communicated to distributors it is relatively easy to monitor achievement. Such an evaluation should be carried out at periodic interval and the results should be discussed with the distributors with the purpose of identifying weaknesses and dangerous trends. It must be made clear to distributors that such procedures are aimed at monitoring performance and if necessary form the basis of remedial measures. They are not just an instrument of bureaucracy and red tape. Distributors aboard are normally happy to go along with the former, they deeply resent the latter.

Many companies, especially if they have a large number of agents and distributors, use appraisal forms. It's important to emphasize that in each marketing area, one must identify the most important parameters to be achieved. What is applicable in pharmaceuticals is not necessarily applicable in the produce trade. Furthermore, there is no point including an evaluation dimension in the procedures unless it is relevant and measurable. Thus there is little point in including details of market share if neither the company nor the distributor possesses information about market share performance in a given market. Similarly, if the product is such that the price behaves in a commodity fashion and the distributor is unable to control price behavior, it is futile to include price details in the evaluation procedures. The evaluation method must be based on standards which are directly relevant to what constitutes good or bad performance and very little else. The items measured must be such that consistently poor returns may cost the distributor his right to handle the companies products in the future. Anything else is quite irrelevant and must be avoided in such procedures.

17.3.6 Maintaining an Efficient Communication 保持有效的沟通

Good communication between suppliers and its international distribution network is an essential condition for a successful marketing effort with middlemen scattered all over the world and with major language and cultural differences. Developing a sound communication system with one's international distributors is certainly one of the major tasks of the international marketer. This is equally true whether the company is small and is entering the international market for the first time or whether the company is a well-established multinational company with years of experience. Communication can be effectively maintained through:

① Ensuring that letters are promptly answered and such correspondence is carried out in very clear and sympathetic style;

② Information sheets and/or house magazines;

③ Periodical visits to each distributor. Such visits must be well planned with clearly defined objectives;

④ Invitations to distributors to visits head office and/or regional headquarters;

⑤ Occasional conferences held in a central point or at some resort where all distributors can get together and discuss major issues of mutual interest;

⑥ The establishment of a "distributor consultative council" as discussed earlier.

17.4 Cross-Border E-Commerce 跨境电子商务

跨境电子商务是指分属不同关境的交易主体,通过电子商务平台达成交易、进行支付结算,并通过跨境物流送达商品、完成交易的一种国际商业活动。近年来,随着互联网技术的快速发展,全球跨境电商行业发展迅速。

The share of services exports through branches and subsidiaries established in other economies is declining in leading developed traders. For example, in the European Union, this trend started in the financial sector after the 2008 - 2009 global financial crisis, alongside the structural transformation that the banking system underwent post-crisis. In 2017, the share of financial services exported by European Union-controlled affiliates was 6 percentage points lower than in 2005, matching development in the United States. At the same time, the United States' financial services exports through cross-border transactions almost tripled compared with 2005, reaching US $ 109.6 billion.

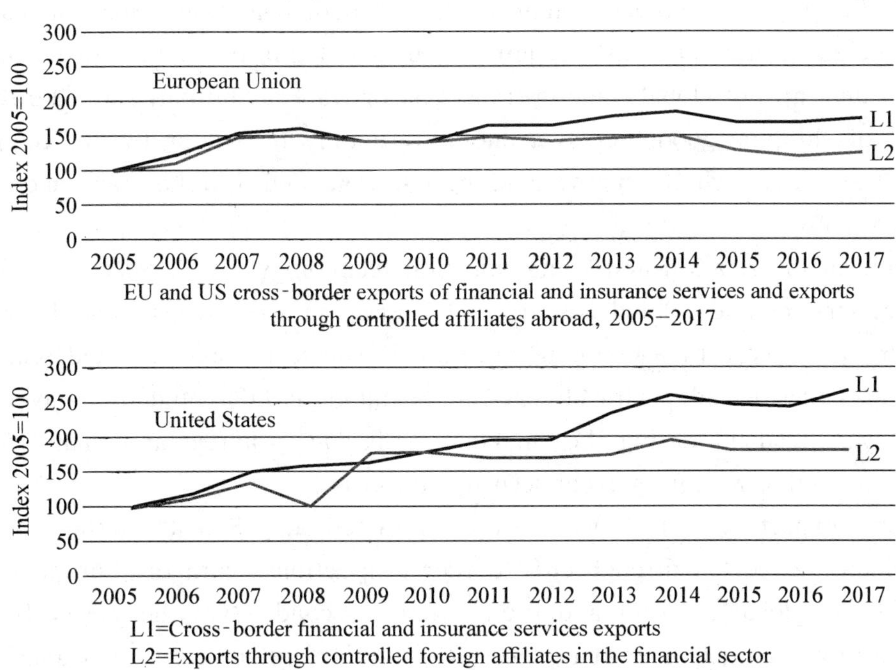

Source: World Trade Report 2019.

Figure 17.1 EU and US Cross-border Financial and Insurance Services Exports are Growing Faster than Exports Through Foreign-controlled Affiliates①

In distribution services, electronic payments, innovative software and evolving mobile technology are enabling consumers to order goods online from anywhere in the world. This has resulted in a boom of online cross-border sales with many wholesalers and retailers, especially in developed economies, closing physical stores and choosing to sell online, or blending physical presence with online ordering and delivery options. Distributors face fierce competition, especially on the web, and in order to satisfy consumers' expectations of fast delivery, they are supposed to be able to rely on transport operators.

Table 17.1 Online Marketing Domains

Targeted to consumers	Targeted to businesses
B-to-C (business-to-consumer)	B-to-B (business-to-business)
C-to-C (consumer-to-consumer)	C-to-B (consumer-to-business)

① Note: The European Union is calculated as the sum of the 28 EU member states and includes intra-EU trade.

Online marketing can be classifed by who initiates it and to whom it is targeted. As consumers, we're most familiar with B-to-C and C-to-C, but B-to-B is also flourishing.

Whether products are ordered online or through traditional means, the distribution of goods, including internationally, requires an efficient transport and logistics industry. In 2017, one-third of global trade in transport, or US$529 billion, related directly to the cost of shipping goods across economies, mainly by sea or by air. Supporting transport services such as cargo handling, storage and warehousing made up an additional 16%.

Trade in information and communication technology (ICT) services, including computer services and related activities (IT services) was estimated at US$1,756 billion in 2017, more than doubling since 2005. The sector has recorded remarkable growth in the last decade, with IT services expanding by 11% annually on average. IT services were resilient during the financial crisis due to a regular demand for new software as well as mounting cyber security concerns.

World exports of IT services were estimated at US$438 billion in 2017, predominantly exported through cross-border transactions, with the European Union as the largest global exporter and India ranking second. Over the years, India has become a prominent exporter of IT services, with the United States and Canada as the main importers. In 2017, India's exports exceeded US$52 billion, of which some 13% was exported through the deployment of IT professionals abroad.

With a young generation of full-time anchors and social media influences, advertising is shifting from traditional media, such as television, radio and newspapers digital channels. Data collected through social media platforms, search engines and websites enables the creation of automated and personalized advertisements which can reach potential customers from all over the world. As a result, firms worldwide are increasingly turning to online advertising for their goods and services. For example, since 2006, US exports of cross-border advertising services have almost quadrupled, while the share of exports through US affiliates established in other economies has fallen by more than 23 percentage points.

Trade in professional and management consulting services through cross-border transactions and the physical presence of professionals abroad expanded by 8 percent on average per year since 2005, to total US$308 billion, with the largest share, around 70%, held by developed economies.

17.4.1 Increased Investment in Cross-border Platforms 跨境平台的加大投资

Cross-border trading platforms led by Easy and Amazon have increased their investment in China in recent years, increasing the number of regional investment managers in China, and promoting their platforms by participating in various cross-border summits and forums. Therefore, Chinese enterprises have also entered these platforms to sell their products to overseas consumers, increase their sales and profits, and promote the rapid growth of the number and scale of export cross-border ecommerce sellers. However, with the increasing number of Chinese sellers, some sellers have also begun to use irregular competition methods, causing platforms such as Amazon to adjust their strategies and adopt stricter mechanisms of access than before.

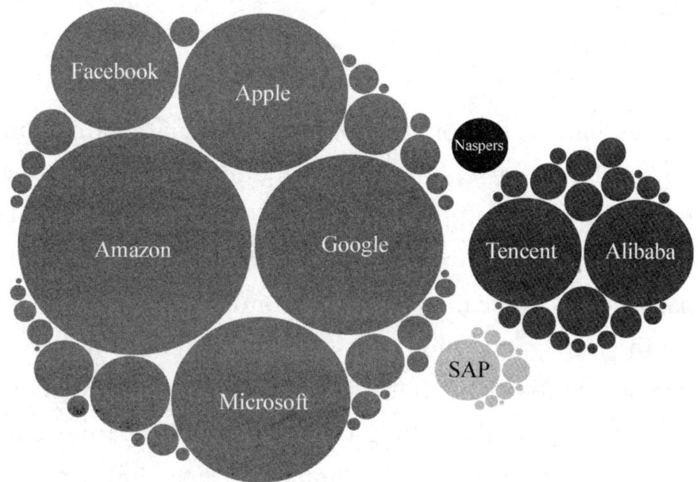

Source: Peter C. Evans, Global Platform Database, Platform Strategy Institute, 2019.

Figure 17.2 Large Platform Companies are Concentrated in North America and Asia①

17.4.2 Advantageous Position of Made in China 中国制造的优势地位

Most Chinese manufacturers are stronger than product research and development, but weaker than product marketing and promotion, so that some truly good products have not completely gone abroad. In fact, many foreign consumers are very eager for China's 3C products, clothing and accessories. The 2008 financial crisis gave Chinese products a good opportunity to "go global", although the global economic situation has improved in the future. However, most foreign consumers have already relied on products made in China, and the dominant position of China's manufacturing has been revealed to the fullest, which has also brought China's export cross-border e-commerce to a new level.

The main cross-border markets currently targeted by Chinese sellers are the

① Note: The figure shows the concentration of the world's 75 largest platform firms by region, with bigger circles representing firms with more market capitalization.

United States, the United Kingdom, Germany, France and other developed countries in Europe and the United States. Some emerging emerging markets are also involved in some sellers, such as Brazil, India, Russia, etc., and other markets such as the Middle East, Africa, and Southeast Asia. The transaction volume is also growing. The governments of these countries have gradually realized the benefits brought by cross-border e-commerce, and certain improvements and adjustments in customs, logistics, taxes and fees have been made.

Conclusion 结语

Most companies embarking on the path to internationalization go through a classical pattern of evolution in relation to distribution policies. They commence their overseas development by means of an export effort. They appoint agents or distributors in foreign countries and motivate them towards hard and effective selling. At a certain point, the company comes to realize that the contribution from a certain market is sufficiently high to justify a wholly-owned subsidiary company. The agent or distributor in such a country has to be bought out or dismissed and a subsidiary company established to handle the selling on behalf of the parent company. The full contribution belongs now to the parent company. Depending on the success of the subsidiary and the size of the market, one starts considering the establishment of manufacturing or assembly plants. At this stage, an intricate international structure comes into being and a fully-fledged multinational company is born.

Some companies opt for license agreements instead of building their own operating subsidiaries. With technologically advanced companies, this approach can prove highly rewarding, especially where the company seeks to maximize profits rather than sales.

This description oversimplifies the real situation inasmuch as the modern multinational often operates through a myriad of arrangements. In a number of markets, it will operate through subsidiaries. In other markets, it will work through agents. Yet, in other countries it may opt for license arrangements. A hybrid situation like this is fairly common and inevitably presents the international company with intricate managerial and controlling problems.

It is well known that channels are an important intangible asset of a company. Therefore, companies that attach importance to channel development can continue to expand their living space of business. Online channels are becoming increasingly important. In the future, online platform companies will dominate more global e-commerce activities.

The Chapter's Referential Questions 本章参考题

(1) Describe the possible major channel options in each market.
谈谈每一个特定市场中可能存在的的主要分销渠道。

(2) What are the main/minor considerations for selecting channels?
在选择分销渠道时，哪些是重要或者不重要的考虑因素？

(3) How could you manage Middlemen effectively and efficiently?
怎样才能对中间商进行有效、高效的管理？

(4) Comparing with domestic marketing, how much more complicated the distribution process could be in international marketing?
与国内市场分销相比，国际市场的分销有多复杂？

(5) How could a good communication between the company and its international distribution network be ensured?
在企业与分销渠道之间怎样保持有效沟通？

(6) How could the company evaluate middleman's performance?
企业怎样对中间商的服务进行评价？

(7) How could the company determine standards of performance for middleman?
企业如何为中间商制定工作服务标准？

(8) How could the company provide training for middleman?
企业如何为中间商制定培训计划？

Further Reading 拓展阅读

|Chapter 18|

International Promotion Strategy
国际促销策略

Learning Objectives
本章学习目标

(1) International promotional mix and international communication process.
国际促销组合和国际沟通过程。

(2) The forms and practices of advertising on a global scale.
全球范围内的广告形式和实践。

(3) The advertising strategy and budget, and some examples of international applications.
广告战略和预算,以及国际应用的实例。

(4) Considerations for international public relations.
国际公关的注意事项。

Key Words
关键词

International Promotional Mix; International Advertising; International Public Relations; International Exhibition; UNESCO

促销策略是指企业如何通过人员推销、广告、公共关系和营销推广等各种促销手段,向消费者传递产品信息,引起他们的注意和兴趣,激发他们的购买欲望和购买行为,以达到扩大销售的目的的活动。通过大众传播媒介在同一时间向大量消费者传递信息,主要包括广告、公共关系和营销推广等多种方式。此外,目录、通告、赠品、店标、陈列、示范、展销等也都属于促销策略范围。

Case Studies 18.1

As a means of promotion, advertising are omnipresent in all countries of the world. Promotion has become part of the world landscape, framing highways, lighting crowded down-towns, projecting glamour on walls of slums, and shading street cafes. It reaches consumers in both high-income and low-income countries, on their doorsteps, in mail or E-mail, and via blasting stereos or drumbeats: Promotion is daily life in the markets of Dar es Salaam, in the blazing Shanghai skyline at night, and on the famous avenues of wanton consumption in Buenos Aires and Manhattan.

A good promotion strategy can play a multi-faceted role, such as providing information; guiding to purchase desire and expanding product demand; highlighting product characteristics and establishing product image; maintaining market share, consolidating market position, and so on.

Worldwidely, sales promotion has been condemned as creating consumption desires for products that consumers cannot afford or do not need initially, and celebrated for its creativity and for setting new trends. See the following example on Dove's "Evolution" ad.

18.1 The International Promotion Mix 国际促销组合

国际市场促销组合的组成部分包括国际广告、对国际促销人员的培训和管理、公共关系、国际博览会以及大众传媒的运用等。

The components of the international promotional mix are international advertising, international sales force management, international sales promotion and public relations and publicity (Figure 18.1). Companies use the promotional mix to communicate with international consumers about their products and services. In the process of expanding internationally, companies are faced with numerous challenges to their plans for communicating with consumers. Many of the challenges are attributed to cultural differences. As described in previous chapters, "Cultural Influences on International Marketing", a good understanding of the norms, motivations, attitudes, interests, and opinions of the target market is crucial to the success in marketing and in communication with in different cultural context globally. Companies also must be prepared to handle the challenges presented by the local media, local advertising infrastructure, and the different layers of government regulating all aspects of communication with the target market.

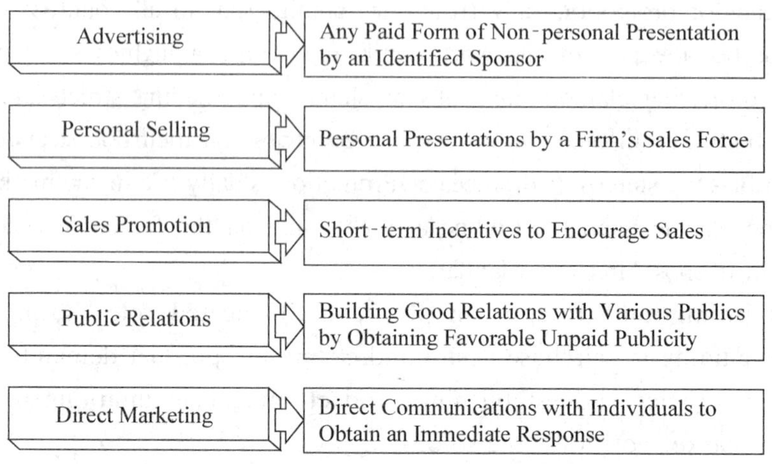

Figure 18.1　The International Promotion Mix

18.2　International Advertising 国际广告

18.2.1　International Business Advertising 国际商业广告

国际商业广告被定义为,一种通过公认的发送者在国际间开展的使用广播、电视、印刷品、交互式媒体的,有商业目的的,非人员沟通方式。国际商业广告正在日趋复杂化。

International advertising is becoming increasingly complex; more local and international companies are competing for consumers who are increasingly sophisticated and demanding. International advertising is defined as a non-personal communication by an identified sponsor across international borders, using broadcast, print, and/or interactive media.

(1) The Media Infrastructure 媒体基础设施

The media infrastructure provides different challenges in countries with different levels of economic development. And, even though the media structure is essentially the same in most industrialized countries, challenges still arise in terms of business practices: a medium might not be considered appropriate for advertising. For example, newspapers might not constitute the right medium for advertising a particular product in one country, whereas, in other countries, advertising a particular type of product or service might be restricted or prohibited in other media-for instance, television.

Media infrastructure challenges are discussed below. However, one additional caution is in order: it is not just the infrastructure that poses challenges in a target market, but also the status of promotion and the extent to which management considers promotion to be an important strategic tool.

Case Studies 18.2

1) Media Challenges 源于媒体的竞争

Some of the challenges that firm's encounters on the media front are availability, reliability, restrictions, and costs.

Table 18.2 Profiles of Major Media Types

Medium	Advantages	Limitations
Television	good mass-marketing coverage; low cost per exposure; combines sight, sound, and motion; appealing to the senses	high absolute costs; high clutter; fleeting exposure; less audience selectivity
The Internet	high selectivity; low cost; immediacy; interactive capabilities	potentially low impact; the audience controls exposure
Newspapers	flexibility; timeliness; good local market coverage; broad acceptability; high believability	short life; poor reproduction quality; small pass-along audience
Direct mail	high audience selectivity; flexibility; no ad competition within the same medium; allow personalization	relatively high cost per exposure; "junk mail" image
Magazines	high geographic and demographic selectivity; credibility and prestige; high-quality reproduction; long life and good pass-along readership	long ad purchase lead time; high cost; no guarantee of position
Radio	good local acceptance; high geographic and demographic selectivity; low cost	audio only; fleeting exposure; low attention ("the half-heard" medium); fragmented audiences
Outdoor	flexibility; highly repeated exposure; low cost; low message competition; good positional selectivity	little audience selectivity; creative limitations

To continue learning about international advertising information, please scan the QR code.

18.2.2 The Advertising Strategy—Standardization versus Localization 广告策略——标准化，还是当地化

One of the most important decisions for an enterprise designing an international promotional mix is whether to standardize and whether (globalize) its promotional strategy (standardization of the advertising strategy), to adapt their promotional mix to each country or market (adaptation of the advertising strategy), or to create local campaigns. Practitioners are divided on this issue. Sponsors, as well as advertising agencies, agree that using a standardized strategy worldwide presents substantial advantages. This is most obvious from a cost perspective: costs are reduced considerably, companies need not to duplicate creative efforts and undertake communication campaign in each market. In addition, as product life cycles shrink, companies are pressured to accelerate worldwide roll-out of new products; developing communication strategies for each market would delay launch. Moreover, world consumers are developing common product preferences and increasingly share similar frames of references with regard to products and consumption because they are exposed to the same sources of influence (broadcast and print media, in particular, as well as blockbuster films and tourists, among others).

Different among countries, however, might render standardization a challenge, or even impossible. The following are barriers to advertising standardization:

① The communication infrastructure is one barrier: a particular medium might be inappropriate or unavailable for advertising.

② International advertising agencies might not serve a particular market.

③ Consumer literacy level constitutes another major barrier: consumers might not be able to read the body copy or the advertisement, so the information conveyed to consumers should be visual.

④ Legal restrictions and industry self-regulation might also impede standardization: comparative advertising is not permitted in many countries, whereas, in others-Korea, for example-Confucianism forbids the public criticism of others.

⑤ Values and purchase motivations differ across countries and cultures, as illustrated in chapter 3, "Cultural Influences on International Marketing". Targeting consumers with a campaign that stresses the good life, exemplified by driving a luxury car and having a blonde on one's side, might be inappropriate in countries where consumers are living a subsistence existence and just as improper in highly civilized environments. Consumers form collectivist cultures will also question the values suggested by such ads. The decision of whether to standardize is most often contingent on the degree of cultural similarity between the sponsor and the target market: standardization of communication is recommended when similarity exists between senders and receivers in the communication process.

⑥ Attitudes toward the product or service country of origin create another barrier, especially in environments where is some level of hostility toward the United States and its economic and cultural dominance, it might be best to change an advertising campaign that stresses the product's country of origin.

⑦ The elements of the promotional mix-particularly advertising-are especially difficult to standardize because communication is in specific language and culture context.

18.2.3 Budgeting for International Advertising Campaigns 国际广告预算决策

Companies use the following approaches to advertise spending decisions.

(1) Objective-and-Task Method 目标决算法

Companies using the objective-and-task method first identify advertising goals in term of communication goals such as target audience reach, awareness, comprehension, or even purchase. As a next step, research is conducted to determine the cost of achieving respective goals. Finally, the necessary sum is allocated for the purpose.

This method is the most popular one used by multinational corporations in the process of deciding on their advertising budgets, because it takes into consideration the firms' strategies. A comprehensive international study suggests that this method is more frequently used by firms form Canada and Singapore and less frequently used by firms of Swedish and Argentinean.

(2) Percent-of-Sales Method 销售额比例决算法

The percent-of-sales method determines the total budget allocated to advertising based on past or projected sales. This method is difficult to adopt for firms entering new markets, which are more likely to benefit form budgeting methods such as competitive parity or objective-and-task. The problem with this method is that it causes advertising expenditures to decline as sales decline; at this point, the company should increase its advertising spending.

For firms that have been in a particular international market for some time, this method is used by almost half of the respondents in the study on transnational advertising practices. This study found that the percent-of sales method is most popular in Brazil and Hong Kong China and less popular in Germany.

(3) Historical Method 历史决算法

Firms using the historical method base their advertising budget on past expenditures, usually giving more weight to more recent expenditures. The percent-of-sales method uses the historical method as a first step, if the percentages allocated to advertising are based on past, rather than projected sales. This method is not recommended for firms that operate in environments with unstable economic, political, or competitive conditions.

(4) Competitive-Parity Method 竞争决算法

The competitive-parity method uses competitors' level of advertising spending as benchmarks for a firm's own advertising expenditure. This approach is not recommended for a firm entering a new market and whose brands are not known locally. Moreover, this method suggests that a firm's goals and strategies are identical with those of competitors, which, most likely is not the case.

(5) Executive-Judgment Method 管理者决算法

In the executive-judgment method, executive opinion is used in determining the advertising budget. A third of the responding firms queried in the study on transnational advertising practices reported relying on executive judgment.

(6) All-You-Can-Afford Method 孤注一掷决算法

Most small and medium sized enterprises entering a new market do not have the large budgets of multinational corporations. The all-you-can-afford method best suits the financial limitations of these firms. Unfortunately, this approach completely ignores strategic issues.

With the exception of the year 2001, advertising expenditures worldwide have increased since 2000. U.S. advertising spending used to account for more than half of world totals. However, it is no longer the case now. According to the *Advertising Age*, the largest top 100 media spenders boast $98.27 billion in global media spending. The top spender until 2006, is Procter & Gamble Co. with $8.19 billion, followed by Unilever, at $4.27 billion; General Motors Corp., at $4.17 billion; and Toyota Motor Company, at $2.8 billion. The top 100 spent $47.46 billion in the United States, or 48.2% of the total, followed by Europe, at $30.17 billion or 30.7%. Noteworthy is also China, where media spending has been growing at more than 35% per year, or 15.8% of total spending ($15.57 billion).

Don't forget—advertising is only part of a broader set of marketing and company decisions. Its job is to help communicate the brand's value proposition to target customers. Advertising must blend well with other promotion and marketing mix decisions.

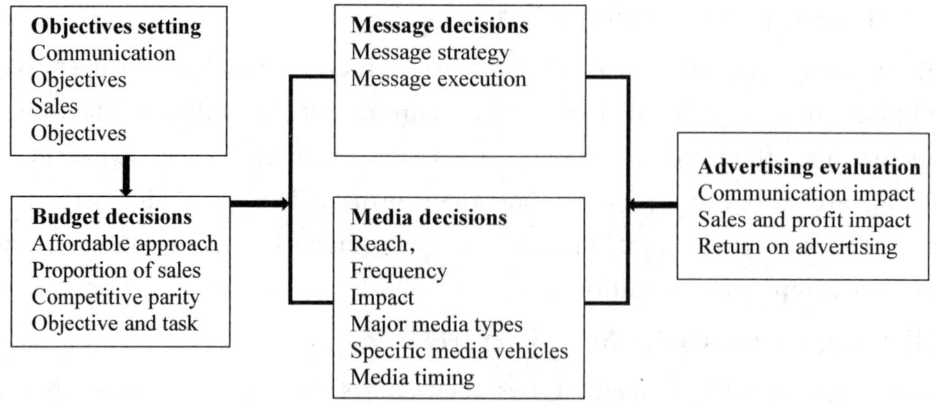

Figure 18.2 Major Advertising Decisions

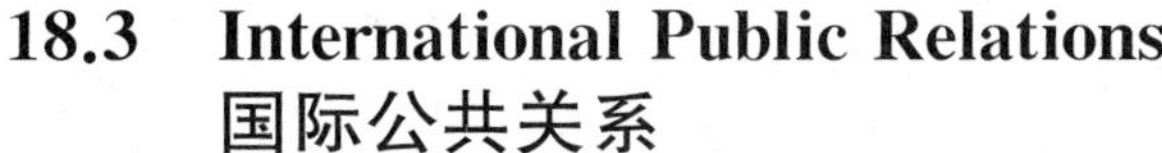

18.3 International Public Relations 国际公共关系

> 国际公关是指一组织针对本国以外公众所进行的公关活动或对国外有着显著影响的公关活动。在企业中，国际公共关系是指企业为增进公众的信任和支持，利用传播的手段以及各种形式的国际交往，树立企业的良好形象，协调企业与社会、企业与消费者，以及企业与其他同行关系的活动。公共关系的对象是公众，其目的是要增进企业与公众之间的相互了解与信任，创造企业良好的社会形象。

18.3.1 The Communication Significance of International Public Relations 国际公共关系的传播意义

① Develop international public relations and serve the opening up;

② Use cross-cultural communication methods to promote the internationalization of the organization's image.

18.3.2 Attention in International Public Relations 国际公共关系的注意事项

First of all, when conducting international public relations, we must follow the international conventions in international exchanges, local laws and regulations, and the general principles of my country's opening to the outside world.

Secondly, we must respect local culture and customs and strive to implement localization strategies.

Finally, it is important to note that different organizations should use different methods when conducting international public relations.

18.3.3 Basic Principles of International Public Relations 国际公共关系基本原则

① Have a global vision, value local characteristics, and abide by international conventions.

② Safeguard national interests, respect each other, equality and mutual benefit.

③ Understand the attitudes of foreign publics and related economic, political and social conditions, understand and be good at using news media that foreign publics frequently come into contact with.

④ Use cross-cultural communication methods to make their information conform to the language, culture, beliefs, and habits of the foreign public, so that they can be accepted, because the essence of international public relations is cross-cultural communication.

18.4 The International Communication Process 国际营销沟通过程

国际营销沟通过程是指,由于促销组合整体发挥的作用,信息由国际委托机构发出,通过沟通渠道,国际消费者最终接收到该信息。

The international communication process involves using the entire promotional mix to communicate with the final consumer. Regardless of the elements of the promotional mix involved, the communication essentially has the same format. The international sponsor (sender), usually represented by an advertising agency, encodes a message into words and images. The message is then translated into the language of the target market and transmitted through a channel of communication, or medium, to international consumers in the target market (receiver).

The medium may be a non-personal medium:

① A print medium, such as a newspaper, magazine, billboard, pamphlet, or a point of-purchase display.

② A broadcast medium, such as television and radio.

③ An interactive medium, such as a Web page or a computer terminal on the retailer's premises.

Alternatively, the channel may be a personal medium:

① A salesperson calling on a supplier or a door-to-door salesperson calling on consumers.

② A telemarketer calling on consumers(telemarketing).

③ A trade show, where one can address questions to an individual who is knowledgeable about the product.

The international consumer (receiver) receives the message and decodes it into meaning. Ideally, decoded information should be identical to the meaning of the encoded message. However, noise-all the potential interference in communication process, particularly noise attributed to cultural differencesmay impede communication. During the transmission and delivery processes of messages, noise may interfere with proper message reception. The sponsor (sender) collects and relies on information regarding the effectiveness of the message (feedback) to evaluate the success of the promotional campaign; such information may be provided by sales data or by advertising research evaluating message recall rates.

Each step of the international communication process presents challenges to the message sponsor beyond those encountered when marketing to home-country consumers. First, in encoding the message, the source determines whether the attitudes, interests, and motivations of consumers in the international target market are different from those in the home-country target market. Manufacturers of Peugeot bicycles in France selling their product in Belgium and the United States need to be aware that consumer motivations behind the purchase differ. In Belgium, the main purpose of using the Peugeot bicycle is transportation. Major cities have bicycle paths on the sidewalks, and pedestrians and automobiles are not allowed to block them; bicycle paths also have their own signals at intersections. In the countryside, paths, in parallel with the main roads or highways, are reserved for bicycles. A Belgian consumer who purchases a Peugeot bicycle wants a product that is reliable and can perform optimally, regardless of weather. Communication about the product, then, should stress its durability, reliability, and quality. In the United States, a Peugeot bicycle is used primarily for recreation. Communication about the product is more likely to be successful if it focuses on a weekend recreational activity and on performance.

When encoding messages, one must ensure that the messages are appropriately translated. In the process of translating the message, one should note that language and advertising strategy are closely related. For example, English requires less space in print and less airtime for broadcast advertising (this is one of the reasons it is widely used in advertising). Translated into German, Dutch or French, the title, text, and tag line require more space for a print advertisement and more airtime for a broadcast ad.

From the product name to the entire marketing communication, it must be monitored to ensure that the intended meanings are what's conveyed. There is an explosion of naming consultancies, set up as offshoots of advertising agencies, which develop product names that are intended to work worldwide; because consumers travel everywhere, it is important that brand names are consistent in any country where they are sold. From names such as Vauxhall's Nova automobile, meaning "no go" in Spanish, to airlines claiming that one will fly "naked" (as opposed to "on leather") in first class, companies have made many mistakes when communicating with international consumers.

Sending the message through the appropriate channel is often a challenge; the media infrastructure might be such that the most appropriate medium cannot be successfully used. In countries where mail is less reliable, such as India and Mali, it is advisable not to send direct mail containing samples of products. In other countries where the mailing system is reliable, such as Saudi Arabia, mail might not constitute a traditional medium for sending samples, and a direct mail package might be perceived as suspicious. In Rwanda and Burundi, the only broadcast medium available is the radio; however, international brands are rarely advertised on this medium. To reach the mass market in these two countries, the only appropriate communication medium is the billboard. Furthermore, it is preferable that the advertisement has few words and relies on pictorials to convey the message because many target consumers are illiterate.

All this competition, including other noise, such as audience inattention, from other channels of communication and from programming could negatively affect the decoding process, such that the target consumer does not fully comprehend the communication. To reduce the impact of these communication impediments, companies can do the following:

① Hire research firms to evaluate the message in multiple international environments.

② Evaluate the effectiveness of the communication in attracting target market attention, using recall tests and other memory-based procedures.

③ Evaluate the effectiveness of the communication in obtaining consumers to purchase the product.

The company then uses this feedback in modifying or designing future communication strategies.

18.5 Other Promotional Methods 其他促销手段

除了国际广告、国际公关活动这些常用的促销手段外,还有一些非常有效的国际促销手段,在此重点讲授国际博览会和国际服务两种手段。

18.5.1 International Exhibition 国际博览会

The basic form of the exposition can be divided into two categories: one is a comprehensive exposition, no matter what kind of goods, you can participate. The second is a professional exposition, that is, a certain category of commodities is the object of exhibitors.

Data from UNESCO shows that as many as 1.64 million cultural relics have been lost from China, which have been collected by 47 museums around the world. The British Museum is the museum with the most lost cultural relics in China. It currently has 23,000 Chinese cultural relics in its collection, and about 2,000 have been on display for a long time. The collection of Chinese cultural relics in the museum encompasses the entire art category of China and spans the entire Chinese history, including carved books, calligraphy and painting, jade, bronze, pottery, and ornaments.

18.5.2 International Service 国际服务

The Boeing Company of the United States can be described as one of the most financially powerful companies in the world today. It not only wins the popularity of users from all over the world by manufacturing sophisticated aircraft, but also wins praise for its dedication and thoughtful service to customers.

Once, Alaska Airlines urgently needed a special landing device so that the aircraft could land on the muddy temporary runway for some reasons. After Boeing learned about it, it did not hesitate to send this device to Alaska Airlines, which solved the urgent difficulties for the company. This moved not only the airline, but also many passengers. On another occasion, an Air Canada aircraft malfunctioned due to icing of the exhaust pipe. Boeing immediately sent engineers to take a flight to Vancouver to perform maintenance work day and night, and finally eliminated the fault, reducing the delay time of the airline flight. This has also become a common example.

In December 1978, Alitalia's DCX passenger plane crashed in the Mediterranean, and the airline urgently needed a replacement passenger plane. Alitalia President Nordio made a special request to Boeing Chairman Wilson: "Can Boeing quickly send a Boeing 727 passenger plane?" At that time, there were many orders for this type of aircraft, and it would take at least two years to produce. However, Boeing took into account the special situation of Alitalia, made a slight adjustment on the delivery table and asked the company to arrange production more tightly. In this way, Alitalia got this type of aircraft within one month, which solved its urgent need. In order to thank Boeing for its excellent service, Alitalia decided to cancel the plan to purchase Douglas DC-O aircraft and turned to Boeing, ordering nine Boeing 747 super-large passenger aircraft at once. It can be seen that thoughtful service is an excellent channel to expand sales and win customers.

Conclusion 结语

The components of the international promotional mix are international advertising, international sales force management, international sales promotion, and public relations and publicity. The international communication process involves the sender encoding a message and sending it via a medium to the receiver, who then decodes the messages; the goal is to have the message sent be identical to the message received. In an international communications context, the process is complicated by interferences (noise) injected by cultural and language differences between the advertiser, sponsor, and the target audiences.

International advertising defined as a non-personal communication by an identified sponsor across international borders, using broadcast, print, and/or interactive media-faces many international challenges. The primary challenge is attributed to the lack of uniformity in media infrastructure, formats, and practices accepted in different markets.

Multinationals today have increased their advertising agency choices. Depending on availability of local talent and capability, companies advertising in international markets have a choice between advertising using a local agency, using an international agency, or using a local agency to advertise international agency messages.

An important decision facing international firms is whether to use a standardized message worldwide or to adapt the message to local markets. Standardization would lead to great economies of scale and cost savings; in reality, standardization may not be possible because of variations in the advertising and media infrastructures because of differences in consumer literacy, motivations, or consumer interests, and due to difference in advertising legislation. The role of self-media and e-commerce platforms in sales promotion have become increasingly prominent. Chinese multinational companies should make full use of modern technology to serve their international sales promotion.

The Chapter's Referential Questions 本章参考题

(1) What are the important features of an international media infrastructure that are likely to affect local advertising strategies?
国际媒体基础设施有哪些重要特征可能会影响当地的广告策略?

(2) Describe how the local media format, features and trends differ around the world.
谈谈世界各国媒体在广告形式、特点和发展趋势方面如何有所不同。

(3) How do multinational firms determine their budget for advertising?
跨国企业是怎样制定其广告预算的?

(4) How do you undestand that different contributions of the promotions tools towards selling a product?
你怎样理解在产品销售方面不同的促销工具产生不同的经济效益?

(5) What factors do you have to consider when making advertising decisions?
在进行广告决策时需要考虑哪些因素?

(6) List several ways in which multinational companies budgeting for their

international advertising campaigns.
列出跨国公司制定国际广告预算决策的几种方法。

(7) Discuss about China's advertising regulations and the advertising restrictions.
谈谈中国政府颁发的广告管理条例中对于商业广告的限制性规定。

(8) Talk about the principles that should be followed in international public relations activities.
谈谈国际公关活动应遵循的原则。

Further Reading 拓展阅读